KidCORDANCE

About the Writers

Best-selling author and speaker Rick Osborne has written and/or co-written several books that help children learn more about the Bible. These include the *I Want to Know About...* series, *The Quest Bible for Kids*, *The Amazing Treasure Bible Storybook*, and the *101 Questions Children Ask* series. Rick and his wife, Elaine, operate Lightwave Publishing in British Columbia, Canada, where they live with their three children. Lightwave is a recognized leader in developing quality resources that encourage, assist, and equip parents to build Christian faith in their families. For more information and exciting activities for your children, please visit the website at www.lightwavepublishing.com. Ed Strauss and Kevin Miller are staff writers at Lightwave.

Big Ideas from the Bible
and Where to Find Them

Rick Osborne

with
Ed Strauss and Kevin Miller

Zonderkidz

The Children's Group of ZondervanPublishingHouse

For Lightwave:
Managing Editor – Elaine Osborne
Text Director – K. Christie Bowler
Art Director – Terry Van Roon
Illustrator – Lillian Crump
Desktop – Andrew Jaster

Library of Congress Cataloging-in-Publication Data

Osborne, Rick.
    Kidcordance : big ideas from the Bible and where to find them /
Rick Osborne, with Ed Strauss and Kevin Miller.
      p. cm.
    ISBN 0–310–22472–1
    1. Bible—Dictionaries, Juvenile. I. Strauss, Ed, 1953–   .
II. Miller, Kevin, 1971–   .   III. Title.
BS440.075   1999
220.3—dc21

                         98–55702
                           CIP
                           AC

Zonder**kidz**

The Children's Group of ZondervanPublishingHouse

Published by Zondervan Publishing House, Grand Rapids, Michigan 49530, U.S.A.
http://www.zondervan.com

Printed in Mexico.

LIGHT wave
building Christian faith in families

A Lightwave Production
P.O. Box 160 Maple Ridge B.C., Canada V2X 7G1 http://www.lightwavepublishing.com

99 00 /DR/ 5 4

Table of Contents

What Is a Bible?

Did you know God has a book out? His book is the most well-known, unique book ever written. It's the Bible! Why did God put this best-seller together? Here are four reasons:

His Autobiography: The Bible tells us about God's character and values, who he is, and what he does, so we can begin to understand him. In the New Testament, God sent his Son, Jesus, who is the "exact likeness" of God to show us exactly what he is like!

His Plan: God wanted to tell us his plan for the world. Adam and Eve disobeyed God and wrecked their relationship with him—and everyone else's relationship with him as well. As a result, we all sin and displease God. But God had a plan to repair the relationship. The Bible tells us how God sent Jesus to deal with sin and make a way for us to be together.

A Love Letter: God loves us, and the Bible is his love letter to us. The Bible is all about God and us. God gave us his book so we can have a wonderful life and a loving relationship with him.

An Instruction Manual: Everyone wants to be happy and have a good life, but how? Well, if you want to know how to operate a VCR or put together a model car, you pull out the instruction manual. So if you want to know how to have a great life, pull out God's instruction manual—the Bible!

In the Bible, God gives us guidelines and principles to follow, and rules that tell us how to act and live for the best possible results. He tells us how to handle our money, how to honor and be close to God, how to treat others, how to have good friendships, and much more. Want a good life? Follow the instruction manual and you will! Guaranteed!

God made us to live a certain way—a way that lines up with what he's like. The way to have the best life is to follow his rules and principles. God wrote them down for us in the Bible so we'd know how to have a great life.

What Is a Concordance?

Every verse in the Bible has a *reference* that lets us know exactly where to find it. For example, the reference for *"It is more blessed to give than to receive"* is Acts 20:35. (*Acts* is the *book* it's in, 20 is the *chapter* of the book, and 35 is the *verse*.)

If you don't know a reference, think how long it would take you to find the verse! Wow! You'd have to read through the whole Bible! Or if you thought *"It is more blessed to give than to receive"* was in the gospels, you'd spend hours looking for it there but still not find it. That's why a concordance is such a help! You're probably wondering—

What is a concordance?

A concordance (kon-**kord**-ants) is a book that lists Bible words alphabetically. Under every word are references where that word is found. Beside each reference is a phrase—a few words from the verse—in which that word is used.

When would you use it?

Often you have no idea where to find something in the Bible. Where is the story of Samson? Where does it say, *"Blessed are those who show mercy"*? A concordance can help you find those stories and verses. Also, if you want a good idea of what God says about something, you can look up verses where that word is used.

How do you use it?

If all you can remember is part of a verse, pick an important word—in this case, "mercy"—and look it up in your concordance. Study the references listed under **Mercy**. Beside each reference is a phrase where that word is used. Read the phrases until you find *"Blessed are those who show mercy."* (Note: Often only the first letter of the word you're looking for is used.) The references under Mercy might look like this:

Blessed are those who show mercy	Matthew 5:7
loves us deeply. He is full of mercy	Ephesians 2:4
was because of his mercy. He saved	Titus 3:5

See how easy it is to use a concordance? Now you can look up Matthew 5:7 in your Bible and read the entire verse.

How to Use the Kid-cordance

Most concordances are an alphabetical list of words with Bible verses under them. That can be a big help. But when we put together the *Kidcordance*, we wanted to go "the extra mile" to help you understand the most important truths, characters, places, and stories in the Bible. So we put these words in the main section and wrote a short definition after each one. After the definition we have a **Key Verse**. This verse captures the main thought of that word. Extra verses below that show other important places that word is used in the Bible.

Some words—like "Jesus"—are particularly important. Topics like these are followed by a **Suggested Reading**, which lists Bible chapters where you can really dig for treasure! On top of that, these extra-important topics have a **Didjaknow?** section, which gives even more exciting facts!

In the back of the *Kidcordance* is an extra concordance with lots of other words you might need to look up. We couldn't fit them all in the main section, but we knew you'd want to check them out too!

Following that are the **Famous Bible Stories**. All the most exciting stories, from Adam and Eve to Jonah and the fish to the Lost Son—and much, much more!—can be found here.

We also have three pages of **Favorite Bible Verses**. These are some of the most important verses in the Bible. If you memorize these verses, they will strengthen you spiritually.

Oh! And as you probably noticed, the *Kidcordance* is specially designed to help you find verses in the **New International Reader's Version** (NIrV) Bible. You may not always be able to use it to help you find verses in other Bible versions, however. For example, in the NIrV Jeremiah 32:18 says, "You show your love," but in the KJV (King James Version) it reads, "Thou shewest lovingkindness." So stick to the NIrV!

How to Do a Bible Study

If you want to understand things like love, or how to pray or have great friendships, you can do a *topical study*. Here's how:

1. Get a notebook and call it your *Treasure Chest*. You'll fill it with gold and jewels you dig out of the Bible!

2. Choose a topic to study, say "love."

3. Pray. God understands his book, the Bible, better than anyone. So ask for his help.

4. Look up "love" in the *Kidcordance*. If you read the definition slowly and carefully, you will get a good understanding of what "love" is. Pause and think about the meaning of the **Key Verse**. Remember, this verse is the truth of God! It's important, and he wants you to get it deep in your heart and live it!

5. Read the **Key Verse** and the other verses we give on "love." When you look them up in your Bible, take the time to read the verses *around* them also, to see how they fit into what the writer is saying. Ask yourself questions: *Who* is loving? *How* is love shown? Then write your answers in your *Treasure Chest*.

6. Read the chapters listed under **Suggested Reading**. Under *Love*, you will find 1 Corinthians 13 listed. Read it. Think about it. Ask questions. For example, when you come to verse 5 and it says that love "does not look out for its own interests," ask yourself: "What does that mean?" Write down your thoughts.

7. The *Kidcordance* is a great Bible study tool, but we couldn't list every verse about "love" in the Bible. Go looking for other places in the Bible that talk about love. To do this, you will need more tools. Look up "love" in a Bible dictionary. Like concordances, Bible dictionaries are alphabetical and easy to use. Just look up "love," and there you are: love stuff.

8. If you're into computers you'll strike gold! There are many Bible study tools on disc or CD-ROM. If your computer has a concordance, do a "search" on "love," and just see what the computer kicks onto your screen!

9. *Act!* Now you get to live out what you've learned. Ask God for ways to put what you've learned into action and build it into your life. God is ready to help.

Aaron

Aaron was Moses' older brother. We first read about him when God called him to help Moses convince Pharaoh to set the Israelites free from slavery. God used Aaron to speak for Moses because Moses couldn't speak well, and Aaron was a good speaker. Later, God made Aaron, his sons, and their descendants the priests of Israel.

HE LOVES FROGS, AND HE JUST READ HOW AARON HELD HIS ROD OVER THE PONDS OF EGYPT AND FROGS CAME UP AND COVERED THE LAND.

EGYPT- Plague of frogs Welcome!

Key Verse

> "Aaron told them everything the Lord had said to Moses. He also did the miracles in the sight of the people." (Exodus 4:30)

What about your brother, Aaron the Levite?   Exodus 4:14
Later on, Moses and Aaron went to Pharaoh. They said ...   Exodus 5:1–6:12
They said ... "Come. Make us a god that will lead us."   Exodus 32:1–35
He must be appointed by God, just as Aaron was.   Hebrews 5:1–4

Abba

In Aramaic (the language Jesus spoke) Abba means "Daddy" or "Papa." In Jesus' time, "Abba" was what children called their father. Jesus used this word when he prayed to God in the Garden of Gethsemane. He called God "Abba," or "Daddy," to show his disciples that God loves us like a father loves his children.

Key Verse

> "You received the Holy Spirit, who makes you God's child. By the Spirit's power we call God 'Abba.' Abba means Father." (Romans 8:15)

How much more will your Father ... give good gifts to ...   Matthew 7:11
Abba means Father.   Mark 14:36
He gave them the right to become children of God.   John 1:12–13
By his power we call God "Abba."   Galatians 4:6

Abraham

Abraham lived in the city of Ur. One day God told him to move to Canaan. So Abraham left with his wife, Sarah, and their belongings. God made an agreement (a "covenant") with Abraham. He promised that Abraham would have as many descendants as there are stars. That sounded strange, because Abraham had no children, and he was 100 years old and Sarah was 90! God also promised that Abraham would become a blessing to the world. God kept his promises! Abraham had a son, Isaac, and Isaac's family grew into a nation—the Jews. And through his most important descendant, Jesus, Abraham has blessed the world!

WHAT DO YOU MEAN YOU'RE TOO OLD? ABRAHAM WAS 100 AND SARAH WAS 90 WHEN THEY HAD KIDS!

Key Verse

"You will not be called Abram anymore. Your name will be Abraham, because I have made you a father of many nations. I will give you many children. Nations will come from you. And kings will come from you." (Genesis 17:5–6)

The Lord had said to Abram, "Leave your country ..."	Genesis 12:1
The Lord accepted Abram because he believed.	Genesis 15:6
Will a son be born to a man who is 100 years old?	Genesis 17:17
Abraham lived ... 175 years. He took his last breath ...	Genesis 25:7–8
Abraham believed because he had hope.	Romans 4:18
Abraham had faith. So he offered Isaac as a sacrifice.	Hebrews 11:17

Suggested Reading

Abraham and Lot.	Genesis 13–14
God makes a covenant with Abraham.	Genesis 17:1–22
God asks Abraham to sacrifice Isaac.	Genesis 22:1–19

Didjaknow?

Unbelievers used to say that many cities and empires talked about in the Bible never really existed. The Bible said Abraham's hometown was Ur. The scoffers said that there was no such place. But in 1922, archaeologist Leonard Woolley went to Iraq and excavated the city of Ur. "God is true, even though every human being is a liar" (Romans 3:4).

Adam and Eve

Adam and Eve were the first people God created. They lived in the Garden of Eden. One day Satan tempted Eve to eat a fruit that God said was forbidden. So she and Adam ate it. Suddenly they were afraid of God because they had sinned and disobeyed him. God sent them out of the Garden. Because Adam and Eve sinned, all people are born sinful.

Key Verse

"So God created man in his own likeness. He created him in the likeness of God. He created them as male and female." (Genesis 1:27)

Then the Lord God formed a man ...   Genesis 2:7
The Lord God put the man in the Garden of Eden ...   Genesis 2:15–17
The woman saw that the fruit of the tree was good to eat.   Genesis 3:6
... Lord God drove the man out of the Garden of Eden ...   Genesis 3:23

Admit

(See Confess)

Adultery

Adultery is having a physical relationship with someone you're not married to. We should love everyone, but some relationships are more important than others. The closest relationships are between husbands and wives. When people marry, they promise to be faithful and to physically love *only each other* for the rest of their lives. Adultery breaks this promise.

Key Verse

"Do not commit adultery." (Exodus 20:14)

A man who commits adultery has no sense.   Proverbs 6:32
Do not commit adultery.... Do not even look at a woman ...   Matthew 5:27–28
Does the law allow a man to divorce his wife?   Mark 10:2–9
God will judge the person who commits adultery.   Hebrews 13:4

Advice

(See Counselor)

Altar

An altar was a table where a priest offered sacrifices to God. The Hebrew word for altar means "a place of slaughter or sacrifice." But the altars in the Old Testament were not only used for sacrifices. They were also used to remind the Israelites of their past or to call attention to major events.

Key Verse

"Suppose you are offering your gift at the altar. And you remember that your brother has something against you. Leave your gift in front of the altar. First go and make peace with your brother. Then come back and offer your gift." (Matthew 5:23–24)

Then Noah built an altar to honor the Lord.	Genesis 8:20
Build an altar out of acacia ... Cover the altar with bronze.	Exodus 27:1–2
... must sprinkle the blood against every side of the altar.	Leviticus 3:2
I saw souls under the altar.	Revelation 6:9

Amen

Amen is the word we use at the end of our prayers. It means "may it become" or "so let it be." By saying "Amen" we are saying that we trust God and we know that he has already heard and answered our prayers. We also say Amen to show we agree with someone else's prayers.

...AND PLEASE LET THE SNOW STOP SO JASON CAN GO TO SCHOOL.

OH, MAN.

THAT'S AMEN, DEAR.

Key Verse

"Give praise to the Lord forever! Amen and Amen." (Psalm 89:52)

Then all of the people said, "Amen!" ... "Praise the Lord."	1 Chronicles 16:36
... whole community said, "Amen." They praised the Lord.	Nehemiah 5:13
The four living creatures said, "Amen."	Revelation 5:13–14

Angel

Angels are spiritual beings who live in God's presence and work in his service. Angels were created sometime before the creation of the world. The Bible tells of angels bringing messages to God's people, protecting them, helping them escape impossible situations, strengthening them, feeding them, and even fighting for them. The Bible never mentions that angels have wings or halos. Nor does it say that people *become* angels when they die. Angels sometimes appear as ordinary men or as majestic beings. Angels are awesome beings that deserve respect, but they are not to be worshiped or prayed to; they are only created beings like us.

Key Verse

> **"Praise the Lord, you angels of his. Praise him, you mighty ones who carry out his orders and obey his word." (Psalm 103:20)**

... Lord will command his angels to take good care of you.	Psalm 91:11
Angels came and took care of him.	Matthew 4:11
But the angel said to her, "Do not be afraid, Mary."	Luke 1:30
I ... heard the voice of millions and millions of angels.	Revelation 5:11–12
Then I saw another mighty angel coming ... from heaven.	Revelation 10:1

Suggested Reading

Two angels warn Lot to leave Sodom.	Genesis 19:1–29
Angels announce the birth and resurrection of Jesus.	Luke 2:8–18; Matthew 28
An angel frees the apostle Peter from prison.	Acts 12:1–19

Didjaknow?

The "Angel of the Lord" was a mysterious messenger of God who appeared at many points in the Old Testament. He was sometimes described as the Lord himself (Genesis 16:7–13; Exodus 3:2–4:17; 23:20; Judges 6:11–23), but at other times as an angel sent by God. The Lord used this messenger to appear to human beings because no one could live if they saw God himself.

Angry/Anger

To be angry is to be upset by something that you think isn't right. It's okay to be angry as long as it's about the right things—and as long as it doesn't lead to sin. For example, it's okay to get angry when we see a little child being picked on by a bully, but it's not okay to be angry just because things don't go our way. It was right for Jonathan to be angry when his father wanted to kill David (1 Samuel 20:32–34). But it's unwise to get upset about little things. People who have a quick temper get into all kinds of trouble.

Key Verse

> "Scripture says, 'When you are angry, do not sin.' Do not let the sun go down while you are still angry. Don't give the devil a chance." (Ephesians 4:26–27)

Moses ... burned with anger. He threw the tablets ...	Exodus 32:19
Foolish people are easily upset.	Proverbs 12:16
Anyone who gets angry quickly shows how foolish he is.	Proverbs 14:29
How dare you turn my Father's house into a market!	John 2:16
Everyone should be quick to listen.... slow to get angry.	James 1:19
A man's anger doesn't produce the kind of life God wants.	James 1:20

Suggested Reading

Cain kills his brother when he gets angry.	Genesis 4:1–12
Esau is angry and wants to kill Jacob.	Genesis 27:41–42
Jesus is angry in the right way.	Mark 3:5; 11:15–17; John 2:12–25

Didjaknow?

What do you do if someone's mad at *you?* Proverbs 15:1 says: "A gentle answer turns anger away. But mean words stir up anger." If you answer back gently, the angry person will usually calm down. But if you talk to them the same mean way they're talking to you, they'll only get angrier. It may take a while, but Proverbs 15:18 says, "A person who is patient calms things down." It can be hard to control what we say, but if we can do that, James says we can control just about anything (James 3:2)!

Animal

Animals are mentioned many times throughout the Bible: They were created by God on the fifth day, saved on the ark by Noah, and used as sacrifices to God by the Israelites. God used "unclean" animals to plague the Egyptians. Animals are also used in the Bible to represent people. For example, Jesus is called "the Lion of the tribe of Judah."

Key Verse

"Then God said, 'Let us make man in our likeness. Let them rule over the fish in the waters and the birds of the air. Let them rule over the livestock and over the whole earth. Let them rule over all of the creatures that move along the ground.'" (Genesis 1:26)

Sacrifice a bull ... It is a sin offering to pay for their sins.	Exodus 29:36
The Lord opened the donkey's mouth...."What have I ...?"	Numbers 22:28
... you women ... are already as fat as the cows in Bashan.	Amos 4:1
Peter had a vision ... animals ... reptiles ... birds ...	Acts 10:10–12

Anoint(ing)

Anoint means "to put oil on someone (or something) to mark that person (or thing) for a special task." An important kind of anointing happened when God chose someone to do a special job, like be a king, a priest, or a prophet. In the New Testament, people were "anointed by the Spirit." God poured his Spirit on people to enable them to do his work.

Key Verse

"The Spirit of the Lord and King is on me. The Lord has anointed me to tell the good news to poor people. He has sent me to comfort those whose hearts have been broken. He has sent me to announce freedom for those who have been captured. He wants me to set prisoners free from their dark prisons." (Isaiah 61:1)

Dress Aaron ... Anoint him and set him apart.	Exodus 40:13–15
Samuel took ... olive oil. He poured it on Saul's head.	1 Samuel 10:1
The Spirit of the Lord ... has anointed me.	Luke 4:18

Antichrist

(See Beast)

Apostle

An apostle is a special messenger of God. Jesus had many disciples, and one day "he called for his disciples to come to him. He chose 12 of them and made them apostles" (Luke 6:13). He chose these 12 to learn from him, and sent them out to preach, heal diseases, and drive out demons. After Jesus' resurrection, he sent them to be his witnesses throughout the world. The word "apostle" was also used by Paul to include people who, like himself, were not included among the original disciples, but who saw Jesus after he was risen and were given a special job by him.

Key Verse

"[Jesus] appointed 12 of them and called them apostles. From that time on they would be with him. He would also send them out to preach. They would have authority to drive out demons." (Mark 3:14–15)

Here are the names of the 12 apostles.... Simon Peter ...   Matthew 10:2–4
Matthias ... was added to the 11 apostles.   Acts 1:26
The apostles did many wonders and miraculous signs.   Acts 2:43
... high priest and ∴ companions ... jealous of the apostles.   Acts 5:17
... were supposed to see the apostles ... about this question.   Acts 15:2
He ... gave some the gift to be apostles.   Ephesians 4:11

Suggested Reading

God breaks some of the apostles out of jail.   Acts 5:12–42
Paul explains how badly apostles were treated.   1 Corinthians 4:9–13
God has appointed apostles to lead the church.   1 Corinthians 12:27–31

Didjaknow?

According to tradition, almost all of the apostles were killed for preaching about Jesus. Some were beheaded, some were stoned, and others were crucified, just like Jesus. One story says that the apostle Peter asked to be crucified upside down because he did not think he was worthy to die the same way Jesus did.

Aramaic

The Old Testament was written in Hebrew, but a few parts were written in Aramaic, a language that is a lot like Hebrew. The New Testament was written in Greek, with a sprinkling of Aramaic words. Aramaic was the language of Aram (Syria). When Jesus was born, the priests still read and spoke Hebrew, but ordinary Jews most often spoke Aramaic.

Key Verse

"Artaxerxes became king of Persia. During his rule, Bishlam, Mithredath, Tabeel and their friends wrote a letter to him. It was written in the Aramaic language. And it used the Aramaic alphabet." (Ezra 4:7)

... Stone Walkway. In the Aramaic language ... Gabbatha.	John 19:13
The sign was written in the Aramaic, Latin and Greek ...	John 19:19–20
... they heard that he was speaking to them in Aramaic ...	Acts 22:2
I heard a voice speak to me in ... Aramaic ... "Saul! Saul!"	Acts 26:14

Archaeology

Archaeology is the study of things from the past. In Bible lands there are many small hills (*tells*) that used to be cities. Archaeologists dig into these *tells*. The pottery and other things they find help us understand how the people of that city lived. Thousands of biblical places that have been dug up help us understand the Bible better.

Key Verse

"King Darius gave an order. He had a search made in the official records that were stored among the treasures at Babylon. A scroll was found in a safe storeroom at Ecbatana in the land of Media." (Ezra 6:1–2)

Terah started out from Ur ... [Ur has been discovered!]	Genesis 11:31
... palace [Ahab] ... decorated with ivory. [Discovered!]	1 Kings 22:39
... sold horses ... to ... Hittite ... [Hittite empire found!]	2 Chronicles 1:17
Nineveh has more than 120,000 ... [Nineveh now dug up!]	Jonah 4:11

Ark, Noah's

The ark was a huge ship that Noah built under God's direction to save his family and the animals from the Flood. Every living thing on earth died in the Flood except those in the ark. The ark was *huge!* It was almost 100 feet longer than a football field, was higher than a three-story building, and could hold two or more of every animal!

Key Verse

> "So make yourself an ark out of cypress wood. Make rooms in it. Cover it with tar inside and out." (Genesis 6:14)

So God said ... "I am going to put an end to all people."	Genesis 6:13
Pairs of "clean" animals ... came ... entered the ark.	Genesis 7:8–9
For 40 days the flood kept coming on the earth.	Genesis 7:17
... the ark came to rest on the mountains of Ararat.	Genesis 8:4

Ark of the Covenant

The ark of the covenant was a beautiful chest that contained the Ten Commandments and other holy objects. The ark symbolized the presence of God, and when the Israelites carried it into battle they often won (Joshua 6:3–16). When the Israelites trusted in the ark rather than in God, they were beaten (1 Samuel 4:1–11). The ark disappeared when Nebuchadnezzar's armies destroyed Jerusalem in 586 B.C.

Key Verse

> "When the ark started out, Moses said, 'Lord, rise up! Let your enemies be scattered. Let them run away from you.' When the ark came to rest, Moses said, 'Lord, return. Return to the many thousands of people in Israel.'" (Numbers 10:35–36)

... a chest out of acacia wood.... Cover it ... with pure gold.	Exodus 25:10–11
The ark will go into the Jordan River ahead of you.	Joshua 3:11
... get trumpets ... carry them in front of the ark.	Joshua 6:4
The Philistines had captured the ark of God. They took it ...	1 Samuel 5:1

Armor of God

Roman soldiers had to train hard and often had a tough life. They carried weapons and wore armor of metal and leather to protect themselves in battle. God showed Paul that Christians were soldiers for Jesus. Paul also knew that Christians needed spiritual armor to protect them from attacks of the devil. He wrote about the armor of God in Ephesians 6. When we "put on all of God's armor," we will be able to go into battle for God and be safe from spiritual attack. Faith, telling the truth, and living the way God wants really do protect us!

Key Verse

"Put on all of God's armor. Then you can stand firm against the devil's evil plans." (Ephesians 6:11)

Lord, you are like a shield that keeps me safe. You help ...	Psalm 18:35
Lord ... Pick up your large shields ... Get your spear and ...	Psalm 35:1–3
Put the belt of truth ... Put the armor of godliness on ...	Ephesians 6:14
... shield of faith.... can put out all of the flaming arrows ...	Ephesians 6:16
Put on the helmet of salvation. And take the sword of the ...	Ephesians 6:17
Let us put the armor of faith and love on our chest.	1 Thessalonians 5:8

Suggested Reading

The armies of the Lord protect God's people.	2 Kings 6:8–18
A description of the armor of God.	Ephesians 6:10–18

Didjaknow?

If you always tell the truth, you are wearing the belt of truth and are safe from the effect of lying. Living a godly life is strong armor to protect you from wrong acts and their consequences. If you are always ready to tell others about Jesus, you have your shoes on and are ready to go. If you have faith, it is like a shield to protect you from the devil's lies. Knowing that you are saved is a strong helmet to protect your mind from doubting. If you answer questions and make decisions with God's Word, you are using the sword of the Spirit and can beat back false beliefs and lies about God.

Ascension, the

(See Jesus Going to Heaven)

Assyria/Assyrians

Assyria was an empire to the east of Israel, where the nations of Syria and Iraq now are. The Assyrians didn't follow God and were Israel's enemies. They were a cruel and warlike people, and went out each year to fight other nations and get money and slaves to build their great cities—especially Nineveh, their capital. The Assyrians conquered the northern kingdom of Israel in 722 B.C.

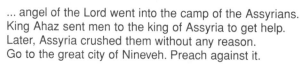

Key Verse

"Finally, the king of Assyria captured Samaria. It was in the ninth year of Hoshea. The king of Assyria took the people of Israel away from their own land. He sent them off to Assyria." (2 Kings 17:6)

... angel of the Lord went into the camp of the Assyrians. 2 Kings 19:35
King Ahaz sent men to the king of Assyria to get help. 2 Chronicles 28:16
Later, Assyria crushed them without any reason. Isaiah 52:4
Go to the great city of Nineveh. Preach against it. Jonah 1:2

Attacked and Harmed

Often people who hate Jesus "persecute" Christians. To persecute means "to attack and harm." People try to stop Christians from preaching about Jesus by arresting them, throwing them into jail, and even killing them. Christians who are killed because they believe in Jesus are called *martyrs*. It's good to "pray that we will live peaceful and quiet lives" (1 Timothy 2:2), but at some time or another, "everyone who wants to live a godly life in Christ Jesus will be treated badly" (2 Timothy 3:12). Still, God promises to help us when we are attacked and says he will repay people who persecute his children.

Key Verse

"I myself believed that I should do everything I could to oppose the name of Jesus of Nazareth.... I put many of God's people in prison. I agreed that they should die.... I hated them so much that I even went to cities in other lands to hurt them." (Acts 26:9–11)

Love your enemies. Pray for those who hurt you.	Matthew 5:44
Everyone will hate you because of me.... don't be afraid ...	Matthew 10:16–28
... the church ... began to be attacked and treated badly.	Acts 8:1–3
Herod arrested some people ... to make them suffer greatly.	Acts 12:1–2
Don't be afraid ... No one will attack you and harm you.	Acts 18:10
God ... pay back trouble to those who give you trouble.	2 Thessalonians 1:6

Suggested Reading

The disciples are persecuted.	Acts 4:1–4; 5:17–26; 6:8–15; 7:54–8:3
Paul is persecuted for witnessing.	Acts 13:49–50; 14:4–5, 19–20; 6:16–24; 17:2–10, 13; 18:12–13; 19:23–32; 21:27–36

Didjaknow?

In America, Christians aren't really persecuted because they follow Jesus. But Christians in many other countries *are* often attacked and harmed. In China and in Muslim countries, Christians even die for their faith. We should remember to pray for them! Christians in Communist Russia and eastern Europe were once greatly persecuted, but other believers prayed for them and God defeated Communism. Now the Christians live in peace.

OK MAX, CUT THE ROPE! JESUS SAID, "WHEN PEOPLE ATTACK YOU IN ONE PLACE, ESCAPE TO ANOTHER."

Baal

Baal was the chief "god" of the Canaanites. They believed that Baal controlled rain, thunder, and lightning, so if they displeased Baal, he would keep it from raining. When *God* kept it from raining and then sent fire from heaven (1 Kings 17:1; 18:24, 38), he proved that he was real and Baal was a fake and had no power at all!

Key Verse

"But I will keep 7,000 people in Israel for myself. They have not bowed down to Baal. And they have not kissed him." (1 Kings 19:18)

So Israel joined in worshiping the god Baal.	Numbers 25:3
They served Baal. They also served ... Ashtoreth.	Judges 2:13
Ahab began to serve the god Baal and worship him.	1 Kings 16:31
The god who [sends] fire down is the one and only God.	1 Kings 18:24

Babylon

Babylon may be the world's oldest city. It was founded by Nimrod (Genesis 10:10) and was located in modern-day Iraq. It was the capital of a huge empire that became Judah's enemy. The book of Jeremiah talks a lot about Babylon. The word "Babylon" is used in the book of Revelation to describe a government that mistreated God's people and that God will eventually destroy.

Key Verse

"Fallen! Babylon the Great has fallen! The city of Babylon made all the nations drink the strong wine of her terrible sins." (Revelation 14:8)

At first Nimrod's kingdom was made up of Babylon ...   Genesis 10:10
The people of Judah ... taken as prisoners to Babylonia.   1 Chronicles 9:1
Babylon was like a gold cup in my hand.   Jeremiah 51:7
He made him [Daniel] ruler over the city of Babylon ...   Daniel 2:48

Baptize

Baptism shows others that you are a Christian. It can be done a number of ways. People can be immersed in water, or have water poured or sprinkled over their heads. People get baptized because Jesus was baptized and he told us to tell people about him and baptize them. Some Christians believe that babies from Christian families should be baptized to show

that they belong to Christ. Others think that only believers in Christ should be baptized to show that Jesus is their Savior. Either way, baptism is a very important event in a Christian's life.

Key Verse

"Peter replied, 'All of you must turn away from your sins and be baptized in the name of Jesus Christ. Then your sins will be forgiven. You will receive the gift of the Holy Spirit.'" (Acts 2:38)

[Jesus] will baptize you with the Holy Spirit and with fire.	Matthew 3:11
Baptize ... in the name of the Father ... Son ... Holy Spirit.	Matthew 28:19
Anyone who believes and is baptized will be saved.	Mark 16:16
Jesus and his disciples went ... he baptized people there.	John 3:22
When you were baptized, you were buried together with ...	Colossians 2:12
He saved us by washing away our sins.	Titus 3:5

Suggested Reading

Jesus is baptized by John the Baptist.	Matthew 3:13–17
The apostle Philip baptizes an Ethiopian.	Acts 8:26–40
Believers are baptized by the Holy Spirit.	Acts 19:1–7

Didjaknow?

Have you ever been to a *big* baptism? I mean, a really, *really*, really big baptism? The apostles once had a baptism that took them hours to perform. On the day of Pentecost, about 3000 people became believers and were baptized (Acts 2:41)!

Barnabas

Barnabas was originally called Joseph, but the apostles called him Barnabas, which means Son of Help (Encouragement). Barnabas convinced the Christians in Jerusalem that Saul (the apostle Paul) had really met Jesus and become a Christian. He also helped Paul escape to Tarsus when the Jews in Jerusalem wanted to kill him. Later, Barnabas went with Paul on many of his missionary journeys.

Key Verse

"Joseph was a Levite from Cyprus. The apostles called him Barnabas. The name Barnabas means Son of Help." (Acts 4:36)

Barnabas was a good man.... full of the Holy Spirit ...	Acts 11:24
The Holy Spirit spoke. "Set apart Barnabas and Saul ..."	Acts 13:2
Paul and Barnabas went into the Jewish synagogue ...	Acts 14:1
Paul and Barnabas appointed elders ... in each church.	Acts 14:23

Beatitudes

(See The Blessings)

Beast, the

The Bible talks about someone who will be the great enemy of Christ. In the book of Revelation he is called "the Beast." Paul called him "the man of sin." Many people call him the Antichrist. The Bible says that he will rule the world a short time, and everyone will be ordered to receive his mark. When Jesus returns, he will defeat the Beast and throw him into hell.

Key Verse

"Dear children, we are living in the last days. You have heard that the great enemy of Christ is coming. But even now many enemies of Christ have already come. That's how we know that these are the last days." (1 John 2:18)

... man of sin will appear.... Jesus will overthrow him ...	2 Thessalonians 2:8
... the One who is in you is more powerful than the one ...	1 John 4:4
The dragon gave the beast his power, his throne, and ...	Revelation 13:2
... figure out what the beast's number means ... 666.	Revelation 13:18

Beauty

Beauty means "attractiveness" or "loveliness." The most important thing is to be beautiful on the inside. A person who is only beautiful on the outside is like a fine gold ring in a pig's snout—a real waste! A beautiful face or body won't last. But if you love and respect God and are kind to others, you'll have a true beauty you will never lose.

Key Verse

"Charm can fool you. Beauty fades. But a woman who has respect for the Lord should be praised." (Proverbs 31:30)

Man looks at how someone appears on the outside. But ...	1 Samuel 16:7
A beautiful woman who has no sense is like a gold ring ...	Proverbs 11:22
You thought you were so handsome that it made your ...	Ezekiel 28:17
... beauty comes from inside you.... gentle and quiet spirit.	1 Peter 3:4

Beliefs

There are many different beliefs and religions in the world. Millions of people worship idols and so-called gods. They do "righteous" deeds to try to be saved. But there is only one God, and one way to be saved: believing in God's Son, Jesus Christ.

However, even some people who claim to be Christians teach wrong things about God and Jesus. These teachings are called "false doctrine" and God says that he hates such things (Revelation 2:6). We need to read our Bibles and listen to our pastors, so we'll know which beliefs are godly and true and which are false.

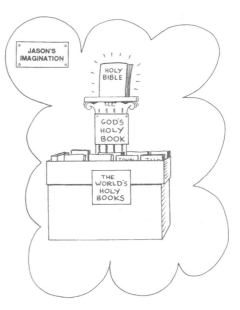

Key Verse

"There may be so-called gods either in heaven or on earth. In fact, there are many 'gods' and many 'lords.' But for us there is only one God. He is the Father.... And there is only one Lord. He is Jesus Christ." (1 Corinthians 8:5–6)

They worshiped the Lord. But ... served ... their gods.	2 Kings 17:40–41
You can't be saved by believing in anyone else ...	Acts 4:12
... offered by those who worship ... offered to demons.	1 Corinthians 10:20
Anyone who preaches a "good news" that is different ...	Galatians 1:9
Their teaching will spread like a deadly sickness ...	2 Timothy 2:17–18
You are fooling yourselves. Your beliefs are not ...	James 1:26

Suggested Reading

Beware of different "gospels."	Galatians 1:6–10
You can't be saved by keeping the Law of Moses.	Galatians 3–4
Paul warns against worshiping angels.	Colossians 2:18

Didjaknow?

Religions that don't worship God and have no faith in Jesus are false. We know that. But sometimes false prophets say they are Christian. The apostle Paul warned the pastors in Ephesus to be good shepherds of God's church. "Even men from your own people will rise up and twist the truth. They want to get the believers to follow them. So be on your guard!" (Acts 20:30–31).

Believe

To believe is to take something to be true. To believe in Jesus is to put your faith in him and trust him for your salvation. But just *knowing* that Jesus is God is not enough. Nor is just *saying* you believe Jesus is God. (James 2:19 says even the demons believe in God—and tremble!) You need to accept the truth and be forgiven! Then

SEE, THIS IS WHAT JESUS DID FOR US.

JESUS

BIBLE STORIES FOR KIDS

your true belief will show itself through your actions. In other words, if you really believe in Jesus, you will let Jesus rule your life, and your life and character will show this by changing for the better. What we believe affects who we are.

Key Verse

> "God loved the world so much that he gave his one and only Son. Anyone who believes in him will not die but will have eternal life." (John 3:16)

The Lord accepted Abram because he believed.	Genesis 15:6
The people of Nineveh believed God's warning.	Jonah 3:5
If you believe, you will receive what you ask for when ...	Matthew 21:22
Anyone who believes in him is not judged.	John 3:18
Believe in your heart that God raised him from the dead.	Romans 10:9–10
If [faith] doesn't cause us to do something, it's dead.	James 2:17

Suggested Reading

Two blind men believe in Jesus and are healed.	Matthew 9:27–31
A father's belief allows Jesus to cast out a demon.	Mark 9:14–27
A jailer and his family come to believe in Jesus.	Acts 16:16–34

Didjaknow?

If we believe and have faith in God, anything is possible. Faith is the foundation of everything that God does in our life. Jesus told his disciples that if they had faith that was as small as a mustard seed (the smallest seed they could imagine) they could tell a mountain to move, and it would obey them (Matthew 17:20)!

Bethlehem

Bethlehem is a town just a few miles south of Jerusalem in Judea. It is famous for several reasons: First, it's the town Ruth moved to when she left Moab. Second, it was the birthplace of King David. And most importantly, Jesus Christ was born there many centuries later to Mary and Joseph, who were descendants of David.

Key Verse

"Doesn't Scripture say that the Christ will come from David's family? Doesn't it say that he will come from Bethlehem, the town where David lived?" (John 7:42)

Ruth ... came with her. They arrived in Bethlehem ...	Ruth 1:22
David said, "I'm the son of Jesse from Bethlehem."	1 Samuel 17:58
Bethlehem ... out of you will come a ruler over Israel ...	Micah 5:2
Jesus was born in Bethlehem in Judea.	Matthew 2:1

Bible

(See Scripture)

Birthright

(See Oldest Son)

Blasphemy

Blasphemy (speaking evil things against God) is misusing God's name. God's name can be misused in two ways. First, by saying false things about him. Second, by using God's name as a swear word. When we misuse God's name, we deny how great he is and how much he loves us. But if we respect God's name, we'll come to know and love him more.

Key Verse

"Do not speak evil things against me." (Exodus 22:28)

Do not misuse the name of the Lord your God.	Exodus 20:7
Speaking evil things against the Holy Spirit will not be ...	Matthew 12:31
He has spoken a very evil thing against God!	Matthew 26:65
We are stoning you for saying a very evil thing.	John 10:32–33

Bless

To bless someone is to wish God's goodness upon them. We often ask God to bless others when we pray for them. In the Bible when a person blessed someone, it was a big event! They placed their hands on them and prayed out loud. Of course, praying for someone is not the only way we can bless them. We can also bless people by saying kind words to them and by being friendly with them. God blesses us by giving us life, family, friends, and possessions. His greatest blessing is forgiving our sins and making us his children. In a way, we can bless God by being thankful.

Key Verse

"Give praise to the God and Father of our Lord Jesus Christ. He has blessed us with every spiritual blessing. Those blessings come from the heavenly world. They belong to us because we belong to Christ." (Ephesians 1:3)

I'm an old man ... I'll give you my blessing before I die.	Genesis 27:2–4
Let all of those blessings rest on the head of Joseph.	Genesis 49:25–26
If you obey ... here are the blessings that will come ...	Deuteronomy 28:2
Blessed are those who always do what is fair.	Psalm 106:3
... so many blessings that you will not have ... room ...	Malachi 3:10
Pay ... back with kind words ... a blessing by doing it.	1 Peter 3:9

Suggested Reading

Isaac blesses Jacob and Esau.	Genesis 27:27–40
Israel (Jacob) blesses Joseph's sons.	Genesis 48:8–20
The blessings of God for obedience.	Deuteronomy 28:2–13

Didjaknow?

Melchizedek was the king of Jerusalem. He was also a priest of God. When Abraham was returning home after winning his battle over five kings, Melchizedek came out and *blessed* him (Genesis 14:17–20). We don't know where Melchizedek came from, we only know that he was more important than Abraham. Why? Because Hebrews 7:7 says, "Without a doubt, the more important person blesses the less important one."

Blessings, the

Jesus' talk in Matthew 5 is often called the Beatitudes. The word "Beatitude" means "blessed" or "happy and satisfied." This sermon describes the attitudes God wants us to have. Jesus said that his followers would be blessed when they were spiritually needy, merciful, honest, or rejected by others for being his disciples. The Blessings are some of Jesus' simplest but most powerful teachings.

"BLESSED ARE THOSE WHO ARE SAD. THEY WILL BE COMFORTED." BLESSED ARE THOSE WHO ARE VERY SORRY FOR BREAKING THEIR MOTHER'S FAVORITE VASE, FOR THEY SHALL BE FORGIVEN.

Key Verse

"Blessed are those who are spiritually needy. The kingdom of heaven belongs to them." (Matthew 5:3)

Blessed are those who are hungry ... for what is right.	Matthew 5:6
Blessed are those who show mercy. They will be shown ...	Matthew 5:7
Blessed are those whose hearts are pure.... will see God.	Matthew 5:8
Blessed are those who suffer for doing what is right.	Matthew 5:10

Blind(ness)

There are two types of blindness mentioned in the Bible: physical blindness, which means being unable to see physical things; and spiritual blindness, which keeps people from seeing God's truth. Jesus healed many people who were blind, both physically and spiritually. The apostle Paul went through temporary physical blindness so that Jesus could cure his spiritual blindness.

Key Verse

"The Lord gives sight to those who are blind. The Lord lifts up those who feel helpless. The Lord loves those who do what is right." (Psalm 146:8)

Do not put anything in front of blind people that will ...	Leviticus 19:14
Blind people receive sight. Disabled people walk.	Matthew 11:5–6
... Pharisees are blind guides. If a blind person leads ...	Matthew 15:14
You are blind. You have forgotten that your past sins ...	2 Peter 1:9

Blood

Blood is the liquid in our bodies that keeps us alive. In the Bible, blood often means life. But the payment for sin is death. That's why blood had to be shed to pay for sin and make things right. Animals were sacrificed to temporarily pay for people's sins. The blood of the Lamb of God, Jesus, paid for our sins forever.

Key Verse

"The life of each creature is in its blood. So I have given you the blood of animals to pay for your sin on the altar. Blood is life. That is why blood pays for your sin." (Leviticus 17:11)

The blood on your houses ... When I see the blood, I will ... Exodus 12:13
This is my blood ... poured out to forgive the sins of many. Matthew 26:28
Through his blood our sins have been forgiven. Ephesians 1:7
Without the spilling of blood, no one can be forgiven. Hebrews 9:22

Body

God gave us all amazing, complicated bodies. Just as we need every part of our body for it to function properly, we need every person in the church for it to work properly. God compares his church to a body to show how Christians should work together. God has given each

Christian special talents and abilities that can be used to help others. As Christians, we are all part of "the body of Christ."

Key Verse

"Brothers and sisters, God has shown you his mercy. So I am asking you to offer up your bodies to him while you are still alive. Your bodies are a holy sacrifice that is pleasing to God. When you offer your bodies to God, you are worshiping him." (Romans 12:1)

How you made me is amazing and wonderful. Psalm 139:14
The spirit is willing. But the body is weak. Mark 14:38
... we are many persons. But in Christ we are one body. Romans 12:5
... know that your bodies are temples of the Holy Spirit? 1 Corinthians 6:19–20

Born Again

To be "born again" means to be "born of God's Spirit." We were born once physically, but because of sin, our spirit needs to be "born" and made alive. When Adam and Eve sinned and were separated from God, their spirits died. Now, because of Jesus, our spirits can be alive again (Romans 6:11). Only the Holy Spirit can do this. As Jesus told Nicodemus, "People give birth to people. But the Spirit gives birth to spirit" (John 3:6). When we believe in Jesus, God's Spirit comes into our heart, cleanses us from our sins, and makes us a "new creation." We are "born again"!

Key Verse

> **"Jesus replied, 'What I'm about to tell you is true. No one can see God's kingdom without being born again.'" (John 3:3)**

Children of God are ... born because of what God does.	John 1:13
... the same with everyone who is born through the Spirit.	John 3:8
... buried with Christ ... we also can live a new life.	Romans 6:4
Anyone who believes in Christ is a new creation ...	2 Corinthians 5:17
You have been born again by ... the living word of God.	1 Peter 1:23
They have been born again because of what God has done.	1 John 3:9

Suggested Reading

Jesus explains being "born again" to Nicodemus.	John 3:1–18

Didjaknow?

After babies are born, they need milk to grow! That's why, once you have been "born again," you should read your Bible. First Peter 2:2 says, "Like babies that were just born, you should long for the pure milk of God's word. It will help you grow up as believers." If you don't read God's Word, you'll stay a spiritual baby. As Paul said to the Corinthians, "The words I spoke to you were like milk, not like solid food. You weren't ready for solid food yet" (1 Corinthians 3:2).

Bride

A bride is a woman who has recently been married or is just about to be married. God's relationship with Israel is compared to that of a bridegroom and bride. When the Israelites sinned, especially if they worshiped idols, their sin was compared to adultery (see

Jeremiah 3:6–8; see also *Adultery*, page 11). Christ is also called the Bridegroom, and the church is called his bride.

Key Verse

> "Let us be joyful and glad! Let us give him glory! It is time for the Lamb's wedding. His bride has made herself ready." (Revelation 19:7)

Complete this daughter's wedding week. Then we'll ...	Genesis 29:27
As a groom is happy with his bride, I will be full of joy ...	Isaiah 62:5
Husbands, love your wives. Love them just as Christ ...	Ephesians 5:25
Come, I will show you the bride, the wife of the Lamb.	Revelation 21:9

Brother

Famous brothers of the Bible include Cain and Abel, Moses and Aaron, and Jacob and Esau in the Old Testament; and Peter and Andrew, and James and John (the Sons of Thunder) in the New Testament. In the New Testament Christians are told to love each other like brothers.

Key Verse

> "Keep on loving each other as brothers and sisters." (Hebrews 13:1)

Esau became a skillful hunter.... Jacob ... stayed at home ...	Genesis 25:27
There he saw two brothers.... Simon Peter and ... Andrew.	Matthew 4:18
Who is my mother? And who are my brothers?	Matthew 12:48–50
Lord, how many times should I forgive my brother ...?	Matthew 18:21–22

Caesar

Caesar was the name of the ruler of the Roman world. He was also called the emperor or king. Rome had many emperors. When Jesus was born, Augustus was caesar. He required that a list be made of every person in the whole Roman world. After Augustus, Tiberius ruled. He was caesar during Jesus' ministry and crucifixion. Then followed Claudius, who kicked all Jews out of Rome. Then Nero was emperor. When a fire broke out in Rome, Nero blamed the Christians for starting it. This began a terrible persecution of Christians. Nero was the one who ordered Peter and Paul to be killed.

Key Verse

"Tiberius Caesar had been ruling for 15 years. Pontius Pilate was governor of Judea. Herod was the ruler of Galilee." (Luke 3:1)

... Caesar Augustus made a law. It required that a list ...	Luke 2:1
Anyone who claims to be a king is against Caesar!	John 19:12
The emperor Claudius had ordered all the Jews to leave ...	Acts 18:2
... have made an appeal to Caesar. To Caesar you will go!	Acts 25:12
Obey the king. He is the highest authority ...	1 Peter 2:13, 17

Suggested Reading

God is the one who put the Roman caesars in power.   Romans 13:1–7

Didjaknow?

In the years after Nero, the caesars claimed to be gods, and all loyal Roman citizens were ordered to burn a pinch of incense to the emperor and worship him. Christians refused to do this, so they were accused of being disloyal citizens and were persecuted.

Caiaphas

Caiaphas was the high priest who asked Pilate to crucify Jesus. Caiaphas and Annas and the other priests loved their power and authority. Caiaphas was afraid that Jesus would change things, and that they would lose power, so he said that Jesus needed to die. The mob that arrested Jesus took him to the home of Caiaphas. Caiaphas asked, "Are you the Christ? Are you the Son of the Blessed One?" When Jesus said, "I am," Caiaphas said, "You have heard him say a very evil thing against God [blasphemy]" (Mark 14:61–64). He sent Jesus to Pilate to have him crucified. Caiaphas later persecuted Peter, John, and the other Christians.

Key Verse

"One of them spoke up. His name was **Caiaphas**. He was high priest at that time. He said, 'You don't know anything at all!... It is better if one man dies for the people than if the whole nation is destroyed.'" (John 11:49–50)

Then the chief priests met ... in the palace of Caiaphas ...	Matthew 26:3
Those who had arrested Jesus took him to Caiaphas ...	Matthew 26:57
Annas and Caiaphas were high priests.	Luke 3:1–2
... Annas.... father-in-law of Caiaphas, the high priest ...	John 18:13
Then the Jews led Jesus from Caiaphas to the ... governor.	John 18:28
Annas, the high priest, was there. So were Caiaphas, John ...	Acts 4:6

Suggested Reading

Jesus' trial before Caiaphas and the Sanhedrin.	Matthew 26:57–68
Caiaphas prophesies about Jesus.	John 11:49–52
Jesus is taken to Annas's house, then Caiaphas's house.	John 18:1–28

Didjaknow?

Under the Romans, the Jews didn't have their own king, so the high priest had great power. Unfortunately, during the days of Jesus and the apostles, the priesthood was controlled by a selfish and powerful family. Annas was high priest before Caiaphas, and Annas made sure that five of his sons became high priests after him. He wanted his family to stay in control. Caiaphas had married Annas's daughter, so he was considered "family."

Cain and Abel

Adam and Eve had two sons, Cain and Abel. One day Cain, a farmer, offered some of the crops he'd grown to the Lord. Abel, a shepherd, brought a lamb to the Lord. The Lord was pleased with Abel and his offering, but not with Cain and his offering. So Cain attacked Abel and killed him. This was just the beginning of the evil things people would do because they were separated from God.

Key Verse

"Don't be like Cain. He belonged to the evil one. He murdered his brother. And why did he murder him? Because the things Cain had done were wrong. But the things his brother had done were right." (1 John 3:12)

Cain gathered ... things he had grown ... as an offering ...	Genesis 4:3
There Cain attacked his brother Abel and killed him.	Genesis 4:8
So Cain went away ... He lived in the land of Nod.	Genesis 4:16
Abel ... offered to God a better sacrifice than Cain did.	Hebrews 11:4

Camel

A camel is a large animal that stores water in a hump on its back. For thousands of years, camels have been used for traveling or to carry loads. Camels are made to survive in the desert. They can go days without water. Camels are also strong. They can travel up to 40 miles a day with a 400-pound load on their back.

JASON'S IMAGINATION

SCHOOL BUS

Key Verse

"Again I tell you, it is hard for a camel to go through the eye of a needle. But it is even harder for the rich to enter God's kingdom." (Matthew 19:24)

The servant took ten of his master's camels and left.	Genesis 24:10
[Isaac] saw camels approaching. Rebekah ... got down ...	Genesis 24:63–64
... impossible to count all of those men and their camels.	Judges 6:5
You blind guides!... you swallow a whole camel!	Matthew 23:24

Cherubim

Cherubim are a certain kind of angel mentioned in the Bible. They often have many sets of wings and more than one face. A cherub guarded the Garden of Eden after Adam and Eve were sent out. God told the Israelites to carve two cherubim for the lid of the "ark of the covenant," and both Ezekiel and the apostle John saw cherubim in their visions.

JASON'S IMAGINATION

GARDEN of EDEN

Key Verse

"Each of the cherubim had four faces. One face was the face of a cherub. The second was a man's face. The third was the face of a lion. And the fourth was an eagle's face." (Ezekiel 10:14)

God ... placed cherubim on the east side of ... Eden.   Genesis 3:24
Make two cherubim out of hammered gold ...   Exodus 25:18
I saw ... living creatures ... each of them had four faces ...   Ezekiel 1:5–9
Each of the four living creatures had six wings.   Revelation 4:6–8

Child(ren)

Children are young people like you! God loves children. Samuel was called by God when he was just a boy. Joash and Josiah became kings when they were only seven and eight years old! David and Daniel began serving God as boys, Jeremiah was called to be a prophet while still "a youth," and even Isaiah became a prophet while he was a teenager. Jesus showed God's love for children by blessing them and saying adults need to become like children to get into heaven. When we become Christians, we become God's children.

Key Verse

"[Jesus said], 'Let the little children come to me. Don't keep them away. God's kingdom belongs to people like them.'" (Mark 10:14)

Honor your father and mother.	Exodus 20:12
Train a child in the way he should go. When he is old ...	Proverbs 22:6
The boy Jesus stayed behind in Jerusalem.	Luke 2:43
He gave them the right to become children of God.	John 1:12–13

Suggested Reading

God calls Samuel when he is just a boy.	1 Samuel 3
David kills Goliath when he is just a youth.	1 Samuel 17
We must become like children to get into heaven.	Matthew 18:2–6

Didjaknow?

The prophet Isaiah spoke about a time of peace when children and wild animals—like lions, bears, snakes, and leopards—will live and play together without fear (Isaiah 11:6–8). Isaiah was describing the peace that will come when Jesus returns.

JASON'S IMAGINATION

KING JOASH, THE AMBASSADORS FROM ARAM HAVE COME TO DISCUSS TRADE NEGOTIATIONS.

Choice

Choices are when we have to decide between two or more things. We make simple choices every day: We choose what clothes to wear and what to eat for breakfast. Some of the toughest choices we have to make are deciding between right and wrong. We need to pray for God's help and find out what the Bible says about the subject.

Key Verse

> **"Choose my teaching instead of silver. Choose knowledge rather than fine gold." (Proverbs 8:10)**

Choose for yourselves right now whom you will serve ...	Joshua 24:15
How long will it take you to make up your minds?	1 Kings 18:21
You hated knowledge ... didn't choose to have respect ...	Proverbs 1:29
... she is free to marry anyone she wants to. But the one ...	1 Corinthians 7:39

Christian

Christians are people who believe in God and accept that Jesus, God's Son, died for their sins, and rose again from the dead. Christians love and obey God, and love others. Christianity isn't just a set of beliefs or religious laws. It's having a loving relationship with God. We give him our lives and try to live as he wants, and he takes care of us.

Key Verse

> "Some believers from Cyprus and Cyrene went to Antioch.... They told them the good news about the Lord Jesus.... At Antioch the believers were called Christians for the first time." (Acts 11:20, 26)

These people worship me only with their words ...	Isaiah 29:13
If you love one another ... will know you are my disciples.	John 13:35
Say ... "Jesus is Lord." Believe in your heart that God ...	Romans 10:9–10
God ... commanded us to believe in ... his Son ... to love ...	1 John 3:23

Christmas

(See Jesus' Birth)

Church

The "church" is not the building you go to on Sunday. The Bible never uses the word church to mean a building. It always means groups of believers. *People* are the church. When we become Christians, we're born into the church family. Church, like family, should be an encouraging, friendly place to be. The church has two parts—the whole church made up of all Christians, and local groups of believers who meet together. All Christians are part of the worldwide church, but we each belong to a local church too. The church's job is to teach people about God and spread the good news of Jesus.

Key Verse

> "Let us not give up meeting together. Some are in the habit of doing this. Instead, let us cheer each other up with words of hope. Let us do it all the more as you see the day coming when Christ will return." (Hebrews 10:25)

So Peter was kept in prison. But the church prayed hard ...   Acts 12:5
Do your best in using gifts that build up the church.   1 Corinthians 14:12
The church would make it known to them.   Ephesians 3:10
Husbands, love your wives ... as Christ loved the church.   Ephesians 5:25
And [Jesus] is the head of the body, which is the church.   Colossians 1:18

Suggested Reading

The church begins and grows.   Acts 2–11 (Read the whole book!)

Teaching the church; the church helping believers.   Acts 11:19–30
Members of the early church met in houses.   Colossians 4:15
Jesus wants his church to be living and active.   Revelation 3:1–3, 14–22

Didjaknow?

Church buildings come in all shapes and sizes. Throughout history, churches have been built with whatever material was available. St. Basil's Cathedral in Moscow was built of wood in the 1500s. In Mexico churches were built with adobe, a kind of red mud. In Ethiopia they were carved out of solid rock. And in Hawaii some were built from coral!

Confess

To confess is to admit that you have done wrong. It is important to ask for forgiveness and stop doing that wrong thing. Not admitting your sin, or continuing to do something even though you know it's wrong, will hurt your relationship with God and with others.

SHHHH! DON'T TELL MY DAD!

Key Verse

> **"If we admit that we have sinned, he will forgive us our sins. He will forgive every wrong thing we have done. He will make us pure." (1 John 1:9)**

I admitted my sin to you. I didn't cover up the wrong I ...   Psalm 32:5
I admit that I have done wrong. I am troubled by my sin.   Psalm 38:18
... who admits his sins and gives them up finds mercy.   Proverbs 28:13
So admit to one another that you have sinned. Pray for ...   James 5:16

Conscience

God wants us to do right, so he built a warning system in us to alert us when we are about to do something wrong. That warning system is called a conscience. Your conscience is what lets you know the difference between right and wrong. Everyone has a conscience, even those who don't know God. When you have the Holy Spirit in your heart, he makes your conscience even more sensitive. For example, your conscience will say that it's wrong to take something that's not yours. It's foolish to ignore your conscience when God is telling you something is wrong.

Key Verse

"What the law requires is written on their hearts. The way their minds judge them gives witness to that fact. Sometimes their thoughts find them guilty. At other times their thoughts find them not guilty." (Romans 2:15)

The lamp of the Lord searches a man's heart.	Proverbs 20:27
My mind tells me that what I say is true. It is guided by ...	Romans 9:1
... don't eat because of a sense of what is right and wrong.	1 Corinthians 10:28
Their sense of what is right and wrong has been burned ...	1 Timothy 4:2
Live so that you don't ... feel you've done anything wrong.	1 Peter 3:16

Suggested Reading

David's conscience won't let him kill Saul.	1 Samuel 24:1–7
Don't judge others with different opinions.	Romans 14
Respect other people's consciences.	1 Corinthians 8

Didjaknow?

When the Bible tells us clearly that something is right or wrong, our personal sense of right and wrong should agree with it. But sometimes the Bible doesn't mention certain things. For example, what if your cousin believes that watching TV is a sin? Now she's visiting for the day and you want to watch some cartoons. You know she'd be upset if you watched TV. What do you do? First Corinthians 8:1–13 tells how to handle this situation.

Content

To be content means "to be happy with what God has given you," whether it is little or much. Jesus said, "Life is not made up of how much a person has" (Luke 12:15). True life is having a relationship with God. We can be content because we know that God loves us and will take care of us. We can trust him completely.

JASON'S IMAGINATION

Key Verse

"I have learned the secret of being content no matter what happens. I am content whether I am well fed or hungry. I am content whether I have more than enough or not enough." (Philippians 4:12)

Anyone who loves wealth is never satisfied with what ...   Ecclesiastes 5:10
I have learned to be content no matter what happens ...   Philippians 4:11
If we have food and clothing, we will be happy ...   1 Timothy 6:8
Don't be controlled by ... money. Be happy with what ...   Hebrews 13:5

Cornerstone

In Bible times, the cornerstone of a building was the most important stone of all. It was a large, perfectly straight stone placed at the bottom corner of two walls. All the other stones were built on top of it, and in line with it. The Bible says that Christians are living stones that make up a spiritual building, and that Jesus is the cornerstone.

Key Verse

"You are a building that is built on the apostles and prophets. They are the foundation. Christ Jesus himself is the most important stone in the building. The whole building is held together by him." (Ephesians 2:20–21)

The stone the builders didn't accept ... most important ...   Psalm 118:22
... laying ... the most important stone for a firm foundation.   Isaiah 28:16
Jesus is "the stone you builders did not accept."   Acts 4:11
Christ is the living Stone ... the most important stone ...   1 Peter 2:4–6

Council, Church

A church council is when the leaders of the church meet to make important decisions. For example, some Jewish Christians said, "Anyone who is not a Jew must first be circumcised. Then they can become Christians." Paul and Barnabas went to Jerusalem to meet with the apostles and elders about this. The council agreed that people could become Christians without becoming Jews first.

Key Verse

"The apostles and elders met to consider this question. After they had talked it over, Peter got up and spoke to them." (Acts 15:6–7)

Peter went up to Jerusalem ... explained everything to ...	Acts 11:1–4
The apostles, the elders and the whole church decided ...	Acts 15:22
Paul sent for the elders of the church at Ephesus.	Acts 20:17–18
Paul ... went to see James. All the elders were there.	Acts 21:18

Counselor

A counselor is someone who gives you counsel or advice. Say you have a problem. Where do you go? You look for someone wise—an aunt, uncle, pastor, or teacher. They help you think through the situation and make a good choice. The Holy Spirit is our counselor. When we need wisdom, he reminds us of Bible verses and helps us make wise choices.

Key Verse

"The Friend [Counselor] is the Holy Spirit. He will teach you all things. He will remind you of everything I have said to you." (John 14:26)

Jonathan was David's uncle. He gave good advice.	1 Chronicles 27:32
I have good sense and give good advice.	Proverbs 8:14
But a wise person listens to advice.	Proverbs 12:15
I will send the Friend [Counselor] to you ... to help you ...	John 15:26

Covenant

A covenant is a serious agreement and commitment between two groups of people, or between God and people. God made several covenants with people. He promised that every nation in the world would be blessed by Abraham. Later, at Mount Sinai, God made a covenant with the people of Israel and told them to keep the Law of Moses. People kept sinning, however, so God made a new covenant: Everyone who believed in Jesus would be forgiven for their sins. This covenant was not just with the people of Israel, but with all people of the world ... and it is forever.

JASON'S IMAGINATION

YES, THIS IS SOME COVENANT! GOD PROMISES YOU MILLIONS OF DESCENDANTS, ALL THE WORLD WILL BE BLESSED BY YOU AND ... OH! IF YOU WOULD JUST SIGN HERE, PLEASE.

Key Verse

"This is my blood of the new covenant. It is poured out to forgive the sins of many." (Matthew 26:28)

I am taking an oath in my own name. I will bless you ...	Genesis 22:16
I have made a covenant with you and with Israel ...	Exodus 34:27
... his covenant to you ... is the Ten Commandments.	Deuteronomy 4:13
I will make a new covenant with the people of Israel.	Jeremiah 31:31
This cup is the new covenant in my blood.	1 Corinthians 11:25
That covenant is better than the old one ... better promises.	Hebrews 8:6

Suggested Reading

The main covenant God made with Abraham.	Genesis 17
God makes a covenant with the people of Israel.	Exodus 34
God's covenant with King David.	2 Samuel 7
Why the new covenant is better than the old.	Galatians 3–5
The difference between the old and new covenant.	Hebrews 8–9

Didjaknow?

In Numbers 18:19 God refers to his covenant with Israel as "a covenant of salt." It was a custom in the Middle East that if you ate a meal with someone, you were promising to be their friend. Because they didn't have fridges, they used salt to keep food from spoiling. The salt that preserved the food was a covenant (promise) that the friendship would also never spoil. (See Revelation 3:20.)

Covet

To covet means "to long for something that's not yours, to crave something that belongs to someone else." For example, really wanting a toy your friend has is coveting. God tells us not to envy other people or want their things, because people who covet are never satisfied, never content. God wants us to be satisfied and to find our contentment in him.

JASON'S IMAGINATION

Key Verse

"Do not long for anything that belongs to your neighbor. Do not long for your neighbor's house, wife, male or female servant, ox or donkey." (Exodus 20:17)

But in their hearts they want what belongs to others.	Ezekiel 33:31
Be on your guard against wanting to have more ... things.	Luke 12:13–15
Love for money causes all kinds of evil.... people want ...	1 Timothy 6:10
Don't be controlled by love for money. Be happy with ...	Hebrews 13:5

Creation

In the beginning, there was nothing: no sound, no light, no people—not even the universe or time or space—only God. Then God decided to make something marvelous out of nothing. God simply spoke, and everything came into being exactly as he had imagined it. God created space, the stars and the earth, rain, and trees, and vegetables (even lima beans and brussels sprouts), and lions, and kangaroos, and everything else. But he saved the best for last: When everything was ready, God created two human beings called Adam and Eve.

Key Verse

"In the beginning, God created the heavens and the earth." (Genesis 1:1)

God saw everything he had made. And it was very good.   Genesis 1:31
Don't you know who made everything?... on earth.   Isaiah 40:28
He is the God who made the world.... everything in it.   Acts 17:24–26
Ever since the world was created ... seen in what he has ...   Romans 1:20
Christ ... over all of creation. All things ... created by him.   Colossians 1:15–16
You are worthy because you created all things.   Revelation 4:11

Suggested Reading

A detailed account of the Creation.   Genesis 1–2

Didjaknow?

How old is the earth? Only God knows. Some people think it's billions of years old. Other people say it's only a few thousand years old. Whatever the age of the earth, we know one thing for sure: God created the world and everything in it.

Cross

A cross was a long beam of wood with a shorter beam *crossing* it near the top. When the Romans wanted to execute people, they crucified them, nailing their hands and feet to the cross. Those who were crucified died slowly and in great pain. Because Jesus died on a cross for our sins, the cross became a symbol of the Christian faith.

Key Verse

"So the soldiers took charge of Jesus. He had to carry his own cross. He went out to a place called The Skull.... There they nailed Jesus to the cross." (John 19:16–18)

... made fun of him ... led him away to nail him to a cross.   Matthew 27:31
They put a ... cross on his shoulders ... made him carry it ...   Luke 23:26
But we preach about Christ and his death on the cross.   1 Corinthians 1:22–23

I never want to brag about anything except the cross of ...   Galatians 6:14

Crown of Life

God has promised that if we are faithful, we'll receive a crown of life. This is not a crown like a king's crown, but a reward for winning. It's like the olive wreath that used to be given to Olympic athletes who won a race. If we "keep on running the race marked out for us" (Hebrews 12:1), we will be crowned with a wreath that won't fade away.

JASON'S IMAGINATION

WE HAVE A WHOLE NEW TEAM OF FAITHFUL SERVANTS COMING IN TOMORROW, SO WE'LL BE WORKING LATE.

CROWN OF LIFE MANUFACTURING PLANT

Key Verse

"Be faithful, even if it means you must die. Then I will give you a crown. The crown is life itself." (Revelation 2:10)

But we do it to get a crown that will last forever.   1 Corinthians 9:24–25

... doesn't receive ... crown unless he plays by the rules.   2 Timothy 2:5
After he has come through them ... will receive a crown.   James 1:12
... receive the crown of glory. It ... will never fade away.   1 Peter 5:4

Crown of Thorns

After Pilate ordered Jesus to be crucified, the Roman soldiers mocked Jesus cruelly and pretended to honor him. Since he claimed to be a king, they twisted thorns together to make a very painful crown. They placed it on his head, then fell on their knees and made fun of him. They laughed, "We honor you, king of the Jews!" (from Matthew 27:27–29).

Key Verse

"The soldiers put a purple robe on Jesus. Then they twisted thorns together to make a crown. They placed it on his head." (Mark 15:17)

The people will make fun of him and whip him.... nail ...   Matthew 20:19
... a crown. They placed it on his head. They put a stick ...   Matthew 27:29
Jesus answered, "You are right to say I am a king...."   John 18:37
The soldiers twisted thorns together to make a crown.   John 19:2

Crucify

To crucify someone is to nail him or her to a cross. It is a horrible way to die. After Pilate sentenced Jesus to death, the Romans made him carry his cross to a hill outside Jerusalem. There Jesus was nailed to a cross between two criminals. Pilate had a sign nailed to the top of Jesus' cross that said, "This is the King of the Jews." Jesus' last words were, "It is finished" (John 19:30). Then there was a great earthquake. Finally, one of the soldiers stabbed Jesus in the side with a spear, and blood and water came out, which showed that Jesus had died.

Key Verse

"The soldiers brought them to the place called The Skull. There they nailed Jesus to the cross. He hung between the two criminals." (Luke 23:33)

... nailed him to the cross, they divided up his clothes ...	Matthew 27:35
Two robbers were crucified with him. One was on his ...	Matthew 27:38
... darkness covered the whole land. It lasted three hours.	Mark 15:33
A written sign ... placed ... "This is the King of the Jews."	Luke 23:38
But they shouted, "Kill him! Kill him! Crucify him!"	John 19:15
Instead, one of the soldiers stuck his spear into Jesus' side.	John 19:34

Suggested Reading

Prophecies of Jesus' death.	Psalm 22; Isaiah 52:13–53:12
Jesus' crucifixion.	Matthew 27–28; Mark 15; Luke 23; John 19

Didjaknow?

The Romans were not the only ones to crucify criminals or enemies of the state. Many empires, including Assyria, Medo-Persia, and the Greeks, crucified people. In the Roman empire, only criminals or slaves could be crucified. No Roman citizen could be crucified. That's why the apostle Paul (who was a Roman citizen) was killed by a sword, but Peter, who was not, was crucified.

Gallery Exhibit

Curse, the

When Adam and Eve disobeyed God and ate the forbidden fruit from the tree of the knowledge of good and evil, they died spiritually. Sin entered the world, and death came with it. From that moment on, life became hard and all plants, animals, and humans began to die physically. Everyone born since then has been born sinful. This is called the Curse.

Key Verse

"But you must not eat the fruit of the tree of the knowledge of good and evil. If you do, you can be sure that you will die." (Genesis 2:17)

So I am putting a curse on the ground because of what ...	Genesis 3:16–19
... all that God created has been groaning. It is in pain ...	Romans 8:19–22
Death came because of what a man did.	1 Corinthians 15:21–22
... healing to the nations.... will no longer be any curse.	Revelation 22:2–3

Dance

In Bible times, dancing was the way the Jews celebrated happy occasions, such as a victory in battle or special holidays. For example, King David danced "with all his might" before the Lord to celebrate the return of the ark of the covenant to Jerusalem. Today, some Christians still dance for the Lord to show him how much they love him.

TODAY'S SNACK IS SUPER-GOOEY, MONSTER-CHUNK CHOCOLATE SWIRL COOKIES.

YAHOO! THANK YOU, GOD!

VACATION BIBLE CAMP

Key Verse

"David was wearing a sacred linen apron. He danced in the sight of the Lord with all his might." (2 Samuel 6:14)

They played tambourines and danced.	Exodus 15:20
A feast is celebrated every year.... join in the dancing.	Judges 21:19–21
Let them praise his name with dancing.... make music ...	Psalm 149:3
Then young women will dance and be glad.	Jeremiah 31:13

Daniel

As a young Jewish boy, Daniel was taken to Babylon. Daniel loved God and wasn't afraid to take a stand for what was right, so God blessed him greatly. God helped Daniel to learn the wisdom and science of the Babylonians, and gave him the ability to interpret dreams. Daniel also was a prophet. Because of his abilities, Nebuchadnezzar made Daniel chief of all his wise men. When the Medo-Persians conquered Babylon, Darius the Mede also made Daniel a top ruler. One time Daniel prayed to God when it was against Medo-Persian law, so he was thrown into a lions' den. But God kept Daniel safe!

Key Verse

> "The king said to Daniel, 'I'm sure your God is the greatest God of all. He is the Lord of kings. He explains mysteries. That's why you were able to explain the mystery of my dream.'" (Daniel 2:47)

Daniel decided not to make himself "unclean" by eating ...	Daniel 1:8
God gave knowledge ... Daniel could understand all ...	Daniel 1:17
The king ... made him ruler over the city of Babylon ...	Daniel 2:48
... gave the order. Daniel ... thrown into the lions' den.	Daniel 6:16
So Daniel had success while Darius was king.	Daniel 6:28
The prophet Daniel spoke about "the hated thing that ..."	Matthew 24:15

Suggested Reading

Daniel refuses to eat "unclean" food.	Daniel 1:3–16
Daniel's friends refuse to worship an idol.	Daniel 3
Daniel refuses to stop praying to God.	Daniel 6

Didjaknow?

Daniel chapter five says that Belshazzar ruled Babylon after the death of his father Nebuchadnezzar. But there was no record of Belshazzar in Babylonian tablets. The records said that Nebuchadnezzar's son, Nabonidus, was king instead. Unbelievers used to say, "See? The Bible is wrong!" Then archaeologists discovered that Nabonidus *had* been king, but couldn't take the pressure, so went off to live in an oasis in Arabia. He left his son in charge of Babylon. And his son's name? You guessed it: *Belshazzar!*

David

David was a king of Israel and an ancestor of Jesus. God called David "a man dear to his own heart." That means David cared about the things that concerned God. When David was just a boy, he killed a Philistine giant named Goliath with only a sling and a stone! Later, David became the king of Israel in place of Saul, who disobeyed God. David was followed on the throne by his

ARE YOU SURE DAVID PLAYED A HARP? MAYBE HE PLAYED A BASS GUITAR OR SOMETHING REALLY COOL?

son Solomon. God made a covenant with David to establish his kingdom forever. God fulfilled that promise through Jesus, who was born to Mary and Joseph, David's descendants. Jesus will be King forever!

Key Verse

"So Samuel got the animal horn that was filled with olive oil. He anointed David in front of his brothers. From that day on, the Spirit of the Lord came on David with power." (1 Samuel 16:13)

The Lord ... looked for a man who is dear to his heart.	1 Samuel 13:14
[David] ... went to Bethlehem to take care of ... sheep.	1 Samuel 17:15
David said ... "I'm coming against you in the name of ..."	1 Samuel 17:45
After that, Jonathan and David became close friends.	1 Samuel 18:1
Saul became very jealous of David.	1 Samuel 18:9
David was 30 years old when he became king.	2 Samuel 5:4

Suggested Reading

David kills Goliath.	1 Samuel 17
David spares Saul's life.	1 Samuel 24
God makes a covenant with David.	2 Samuel 7:8–17
David falls into sin.	2 Samuel 11:1–12:25

Didjaknow?

Slings like David used to kill Goliath were used by shepherds for protecting their flocks against wild animals. A sling was made from a small piece of leather, and small stones were used as ammunition. People twirled it around their heads, then let the stone fly at great speed. The sling is a simple weapon, but it's difficult to fire accurately. David, however, was an excellent shot. Judges 20:16 talks about 700 left-handed men who could "sling a stone at a *hair* and not miss" (italics added)!

Death

Death is the end of life. Ever since Adam and Eve sinned, pain and death have been part of life. Everything that is alive in our world eventually grows old and has to die. Plants die. Animals die. People die. But remember, this life on earth is not all there is. After we die we can live forever with God.

Key Verse

"For me, life finds all of its meaning in Christ. Death also has its benefits. Suppose I go on living in my body. Then I will be able to carry on my work. It will bear a lot of fruit. But what should I choose? I don't know. I can't decide between the two. I long to leave this world and be with Christ. That is better by far." (Philippians 1:21–23)

When you sin, the pay you get is death.	Romans 6:23
Death came ... Because of Adam, all ... die.	1 Corinthians 15:21–22
Death, where is the battle you thought you were winning?	1 Corinthians 15:55
So put to death ... your earthly nature.	Colossians 3:5

Deborah

Deborah was one of the judges. People came to her for help and wisdom. When the Canaanites attacked the Israelites, God told her to send for a man named Barak. He was afraid to fight the Canaanites by himself. Deborah went with him, but said that because Barak had been a coward, God would give credit for the victory to a woman. (That woman was Jael.)

Key Verse

"Deborah was a prophet. She was the wife of Lappidoth. She was leading Israel at that time." (Judges 4:4)

... [Deborah] served the people as their judge.	Judges 4:5
Deborah said to Barak, "Go! Today the Lord will ..."	Judges 4:14
On that day Deborah and Barak sang a song.	Judges 5:1
... until I, Deborah, came. I came as a mother in Israel.	Judges 5:7

Debt

Debt is what we owe when we borrow too much. In the Bible, when times were bad, poor people borrowed from rich people so they could live; when times were good, they repaid it. But if people borrowed more than they could repay, they fell into debt and often had to sell themselves and their families as slaves to pay it off. God wants us to pay our debts.

Key Verse

"Rich people rule over those who are poor. Borrowers are slaves to lenders." (Proverbs 22:7)

Do not charge him interest of any kind.	Leviticus 25:36
Sinful people borrow and don't pay back.	Psalm 37:21
Don't take advantage of poor people ...	Proverbs 22:22
Pay everything you owe.	Romans 13:8

Demon

Demons are angels who have "fallen," or turned away from God. They are led by Satan, who is God's enemy. Even though Satan and his demons are God's enemies, God is far more powerful than they are, because he made them. So don't be afraid. If you're a Christian, there's nothing a demon can do to hurt you.

Key Verse

"Jesus called the Twelve together. He gave them power and authority to drive out all demons and to heal sicknesses." (Luke 9:1)

[Hell] has been prepared for the devil and his angels.	Matthew 25:41
The demons shouted, "You are the Son of God!"	Luke 4:41
... the demons came out of the man ... went into the pigs.	Luke 8:33
I am absolutely sure that not even ... angels or demons ...	Romans 8:38–39

Disciple

The word disciple means "student" or "learner." If you were a young Jew in Jesus' time and wanted to study the Bible, you would choose a "rabbi" (a teacher) and become his disciple. You'd listen to and memorize his teachings. You would also watch your teacher's life and try to live like him. When your rabbi decided you were ready, he would make you a teacher. By then you would think and live just like him. Jesus used this teaching method with the men he chose to be his disciples. They lived with him and learned from him. If you follow Jesus, you're his disciple too!

Key Verse

"When morning came, he called for his disciples to come to him. He chose 12 of them and made them apostles." (Luke 6:13)

The Pharisees went out.... sent their followers to him.	Matthew 22:15–16
Then all the disciples left him and ran away.	Matthew 26:56
John's disciples told him about all these things.	Luke 7:18–19
... If you don't, you can't be my disciple.	Luke 14:33
If you obey my teaching ... you are really my disciples.	John 8:31
You are [Jesus'] disciple! ... We are disciples of Moses!	John 9:28

Suggested Reading

Jesus gathers his disciples.	Matthew 4:18–22; 9:9–13; Mark 1:14–20
Jesus' last teaching to his disciples.	John 14–16
The 12 apostles lead the early church.	Acts 6:2–7

Didjaknow?

When Jesus chose his disciples, he didn't go looking for the richest, smartest, most powerful people. Jesus had other disciples (Luke 10:1), but he chose 12 very ordinary men to be his closest followers. Before they started to follow Jesus, some of the disciples were fishermen, some were tax collectors, and some may have even once been part of a group of freedom fighters called the "zealots."

WANTED
FULL-TIME CHRISTIANS
NO PART-TIME
POSITIONS AVAILABLE

Discipline

(See Training)

Divorce

Divorce is the breakup of a marriage. God's plan is for husbands and wives to stay together until one or both of them die. But sometimes troubles arise. If these troubles get bad, sometimes the husband and wife decide to end their marriage in divorce. But this is never God's will. His plan is for the husband and wife to stay together and work things out.

Key Verse

"'I hate divorce,' says the Lord God of Israel. 'I hate it when people do anything that harms others,' says the Lord who rules over all. So guard yourself in your spirit. And don't break your promises." (Malachi 2:16)

It has been said, "Suppose a man divorces his wife."	Matthew 5:31–32
So a man must not separate what God has joined together.	Matthew 19:6
A man may divorce his wife only if she has not been ...	Matthew 19:9
I give a command ... A wife must not leave her husband.	1 Corinthians 7:10

Doubt

Doubt is when you don't believe something. There are times you should doubt. Proverbs 14:15 says, "A childish person believes anything. But a wise person thinks ..." Sometimes people tell lies and clever stories. We should doubt them too. One thing we should never doubt is God's Word. However, sometimes we do. Having doubts is not wrong, but it's what we do with them that counts. We can believe the doubts and let them set up camp in our thoughts, or we can go to God, choose to believe, and ask him to chase off the doubts like clouds on a windy day.

Key Verse

"Right away the boy's father cried out, 'I do believe! Help me overcome my unbelief!'" (Mark 9:24)

How long will they refuse to believe in me? — Numbers 14:11
You must have faith and not doubt. Then you can do ... — Matthew 21:21
You must not doubt in your heart ... believe that what ... — Mark 11:23–24
Zechariah asked the angel, "How can I be sure of this?" — Luke 1:18–20
Stay away from opposing ideas ... Some people ... — 1 Timothy 6:20–21
But when you ask, you must believe. You must not doubt. — James 1:6

Suggested Reading

Doubt stops miracles. — Matthew 13:53–58; Mark 6:1–6

Peter doubts Jesus. — Matthew 14:22–33
Thomas doubts Jesus is alive. — John 20:24–31

Didjaknow?

Peter was walking on the sea and doing fine until he saw the wind and the waves. Then he doubted and sank. Jesus asked him, "Why did you doubt me?" (Matthew 14:31). The word *doubt* here means "to stand divided." Peter's mind was divided. He believed, but he doubted too. The apostle James said, "You must not doubt. People who doubt are like waves of the sea. The wind blows and tosses them around. A man like that ... can't make up his mind" (James 1:6–8).

Dream

Often God speaks to people in their dreams about what will happen. Joseph had a dream that caused his brothers to sell him into slavery. Later, because Joseph told Pharaoh what Pharaoh's dreams meant, he was freed from prison and put in charge of Egypt. In the New Testament, God spoke to Joseph in a dream and told him that the baby his fiancée Mary would have was from God.

Key Verse

"After that, I will pour out my Spirit on all people. Your sons and daughters will prophesy. Your old men will have dreams. Your young men will have visions." (Joel 2:28)

I've heard that when you hear a dream you can explain it. — Genesis 41:15
Let the prophet who has a dream tell his dream. — Jeremiah 23:28
In the second year of Nebuchadnezzar's rule ... a dream. — Daniel 2:1
An angel of the Lord appeared to [Joseph] in a dream. — Matthew 1:20

Egypt

Egypt is a large country in North Africa, but its people can only live along the Nile River. The rest of Egypt is desert. Joseph was taken to Egypt and sold as a slave. Later, he became the most important man in Egypt, next to Pharaoh. The Israelites moved to Egypt to escape a famine, and there they grew into a nation. After Joseph died, a new pharaoh made them slaves. The people of Israel lived in Egypt 430 years. Then Moses led the Israelites out of Egypt. Many years later, Joseph and Mary fled with baby Jesus to Egypt to escape King Herod.

Key Verse

"I am the Lord your God. I brought you out of Egypt. That is the land where you were slaves." (Exodus 20:2)

Joseph had been taken down to Egypt. An Egyptian ...	Genesis 39:1
... number of those who went to Egypt with Jacob was 66.	Genesis 46:26
... Egyptians put slave drivers over the people of Israel.	Exodus 1:11
At the end of the 430 years ... [they] marched out of Egypt ...	Exodus 12:41
I brought you out of Egypt to be your God. I am the Lord.	Leviticus 22:33
Take the child and his mother and escape to Egypt.	Matthew 2:13

Suggested Reading

Joseph becomes ruler of Egypt; the Israelites move there.	Genesis 39–50
Slaves in Egypt, and the story of Moses and the Exodus.	Exodus 1–14

Didjaknow?

The pyramids in Egypt were built as tombs for the pharaohs. When Joseph arrived in Egypt, the pyramids had already been standing for hundreds of years, so the Israelites saw the same pyramids we see today. The largest pyramid, the Great Pyramid at Giza, is made up of almost 2,500,000 gigantic blocks of stone, weighing between 5,000 and 30,000 pounds each.

Elijah

Elijah was a prophet of God. He prophesied that it wouldn't rain for several years, and it didn't. Elijah challenged the prophets of Baal: He said whichever god sent down fire from heaven was the true God. The prophets of Baal prayed, but nothing happened. When Elijah prayed,

God sent down fire and devoured the sacrifice, the stones, and even the dust!

Key Verse

"Elijah was just like us. He prayed hard that it wouldn't rain. And it didn't rain on the land for three and a half years." (James 5:17)

The ravens brought him bread and meat in the morning ...	1 Kings 17:6
Elijah ... said, "If the Lord is ... God, follow him."	1 Kings 18:21
... there was only a gentle whisper. When Elijah heard it ...	1 Kings 19:12–13
Then Elijah went up to heaven in a strong wind.	2 Kings 2:11

Elisha

Elisha was the main prophet to Israel after the prophet Elijah was taken up into heaven. Through the Spirit of God, Elisha prophesied, advised and anointed kings, helped the needy, and performed many miracles. For example, he raised a young boy from the dead, and had God strike the Aramean army blind so they wouldn't attack Israel. We also know that Elisha was bald.

Key Verse

"After they had gone across, Elijah spoke to Elisha. He said, 'Tell me. What can I do for you before I'm taken away from you?' 'Please give me a double share of your spirit,' Elisha replied." (2 Kings 2:9)

Elisha ... went up to Bethel.... Some young fellows came ...	2 Kings 2:23
Elisha arrived at the house. The boy was dead.	2 Kings 4:32
He saw that Elisha was surrounded by horses and chariots.	2 Kings 6:17
Aram's army came down toward Elisha.	2 Kings 6:18

Esau

Isaac had two sons: Esau and Jacob. Esau was a tough, hairy man who loved to hunt. Because he was the oldest, Esau had the "birthright": He would inherit everything his father owned and receive a special blessing. But one day when Esau came home very hungry, he foolishly traded his birthright to Jacob for, of all things, a bowl of bean stew!

Key Verse

"See to it that no one is godless like Esau. He sold the rights to what he would receive as the oldest son. He sold them for a single meal." (Hebrews 12:16)

Red ... body covered with hair. So they named him Esau. Genesis 25:25
So Esau promised to ... He sold Jacob all of the rights ... Genesis 25:33
Esau heard his father's words.... he began crying loudly ... Genesis 27:34
Esau ran to meet Jacob. He hugged him and ... Genesis 33:4

Esther

When the Persians took over Babylonia, they freed the Jews and allowed them to return to Israel. But many Jews stayed in Persia. Among those who stayed was Esther, a young Jewish girl. Because Esther was an orphan, her older cousin Mordecai adopted her. When Esther grew up, she was so beautiful that the king married her and made her his queen.

Later, Mordecai angered an important man, Haman. Haman passed a law ordering all the Jews in the kingdom to be killed, so Mordecai begged Esther to help. Though it could have cost her life, Esther appealed to the king and saved her people.

Key Verse

"The king liked Esther more than he liked any of the other women. She pleased him more than any of the other virgins. So he put a royal crown on her head. He made her queen in Vashti's place." (Esther 2:17)

Mordecai had a cousin ... Esther. She was very beautiful.	Esther 2:7
It's possible that you became queen for a time ... like this.	Esther 4:14
... though it's against the law.... if I have to die, I'll die.	Esther 4:16
Esther said... "He's our enemy! He's this evil Haman!"	Esther 7:6
Esther made ... appeal to the king. She fell at his feet ...	Esther 8:3
So Queen Esther ... wrote a second letter.... about Purim.	Esther 9:29

Suggested Reading

Read the entire book of Esther! It's a short, exciting story.
How the Jewish Feast of Purim began.   Esther 9

Didjaknow?

Why was it was so dangerous for Esther to go see the king even though she was the queen? Because Persian law was very strict. The law said that when the king was in his inner courtyard, *no one* could go see him without being invited, or they would be killed. The only way someone could live was if the king had mercy and held out his golden rod to them (Esther 4:11).

Eternity/Eternal

We can't even imagine how long eternity is. Eternity has no beginning and no ending. It goes on forever. Sometimes we have good times that we wish would never end—such as a party or a vacation or a visit by a friend. But they do come to an end. Eternity, however, never ends. God is eternal. He always has been, and he always will be.

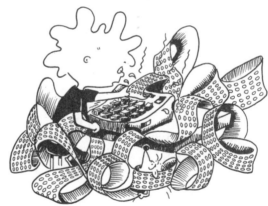

Key Verse

> **"With the Lord a day is like a thousand years. And a thousand years are like a day." (2 Peter 3:8)**

Before you created the world ... you are God.	Psalm 90:2
To you a thousand years ... like a few hours of the night.	Psalm 90:4
They will pass away. But ... Your years will never end.	Psalm 102:24–27
The eternal King will never die.... He is the only God.	1 Timothy 1:17

Evil

Evil means "bad or sinful." Evil is anything that goes against God and displeases him. This includes a selfish attitude, bad actions, and ignoring God. Ever since Adam and Eve sinned, humans have been wanting to do what is wrong. Satan also tries to get people to do evil, but we can overcome evil in ourselves by giving our lives to Jesus.

Key Verse

"Stay away from every kind of evil." (1Thessalonians 5:22)

Tree ... to tell the difference between good and evil ...   Genesis 2:9
An evil man says evil things.... from the evil ... inside him.   Matthew 12:35
Remove from your life all evil longings.   Colossians 3:5
Run away from the evil things that young people long for.   2 Timothy 2:22

Exile

(See Prisoners in Babylon)

Exodus

Exodus means "going out." The second book in the Bible is named Exodus because it tells the story of how God did miracles and used Moses to deliver the people of Israel from Egypt. Exodus describes them *going out* of the land of Egypt. The people of Israel had lived in Egypt for 430 years. At the end of that time, several million of them left Egypt together. Imagine millions of people getting ready to move with large herds of animals and everything else they owned! It was noisy and smelly and confusing. But God was in charge, and he led them out.

Key Verse

"At the end of the 430 years, to the very day, all of the Lord's people marched out of Egypt ... The Lord kept watch that night to bring them out of Egypt. So on that same night every year all of the Israelites must keep watch. They must do it to honor the Lord for all time to come." (Exodus 12:41–42)

... hurry up and leave ... If you don't ... we'll all die! — Exodus 12:33
The water flowed back ... covered ... army of Pharaoh ... — Exodus 14:28
But he brought his people out like a flock.... like sheep ... — Psalm 78:52
He ordered the Red Sea to dry up, and it did. — Psalm 106:9
Moses led them out of Egypt. He did wonders ... signs ... — Acts 7:36

Suggested Reading

The people of Israel leave the land of Egypt. — Exodus 12–14

Didjaknow?

The people of Israel had done slave labor in Egypt for 430 years, and hadn't been paid a thing for all their work. But as they left, God made sure the Egyptians paid them! The Israelites asked the Egyptians for their silver and gold, and God made the Egyptians give them whatever they asked for (Exodus 12:35–36).

Ezekiel

Ezekiel was taken to Babylon during the Exile. There God called him to be a prophet. Ezekiel is best known for the strange and wonderful things he saw. For example, he had a vision of wheels within wheels that makes you almost dizzy when you read it, and he had a vision of dry bones coming back to life. God often called Ezekiel "son of man."

Key Verse

"Son of man, I have appointed you as a prophet to warn the people of Israel. So listen to my message. Give them a warning from me." (Ezekiel 3:17)

Each one seemed to be ... a wheel inside another wheel ... — Ezekiel 1:16
... get a clay tablet.... Draw the city of Jerusalem on it. — Ezekiel 4:1–3
I saw a huge number of bones in the valley. The bones ... — Ezekiel 37:2
In visions God ... brought me to the land of Israel. — Ezekiel 40:2

Ezra

Ezra was a Jewish priest from Persia. After the Jews had returned from the Exile, 60 years after the temple was rebuilt, Ezra, a teacher of the Law, went to Jerusalem. He had official orders from the king of Persia. Ezra preached in Jerusalem, and the Jews listened to him. They repented of their disobedience and agreed to obey God's law.

JASON'S IMAGINATION

WHY DID I EVER COME TO JERUSALEM TO TEACH THE LAW?

TEACHER! WHAT IF I TRAINED PIGS TO CHEW THEIR CUD? **THEN** COULD WE EAT PORK?

TEACHER! ARE FROGS CLEAN OR UNCLEAN?

Key Verse

"Ezra was a priest and teacher. He was an educated man. He knew the Lord's commands and rules for Israel very well." (Ezra 7:11)

Ezra ... wanted to teach the Lord's rules and laws in Israel.	Ezra 7:10
Ezra, appoint judges and other court officials ... teach ...	Ezra 7:25
Many family leaders came up to Jerusalem with me ...	Ezra 8:1
Ezra was ... admitting to God that his people had sinned.	Ezra 10:1

Face

The expression on our face—whether we're happy or upset—shows others what we're feeling inside. We pout if we don't get our way, show a sad face when we're unhappy, frown when we're angry, or smile when things go well. God wants us to encourage others, not only by cheerful words, but by a cheerful face. So smile and share your joy.

Key Verse

"A happy heart makes a face look cheerful. But a sad heart produces a broken spirit." (Proverbs 15:13)

[God] said to Cain, "Why are you angry? Why ... so sad?"	Genesis 4:5–6
... looking so sad? ...You must be feeling sad ... inside.	Nehemiah 2:2
The look on their faces is a witness against them ...	Isaiah 3:9
When you go without eating, do not look gloomy ...	Matthew 6:16

Faith

Faith is believing God without needing proof. Jesus said that if you have faith as small as a mustard seed, you can move mountains. A mustard seed was the smallest seed in all Israel, yet it grew into such a large bush that it was nearly a tree. In just the same way, Jesus was saying, you can have a very small amount of faith—only the size of a mustard seed—and get results. Faith isn't a magical substance that you build up until you have enough. It's a choice. When God makes a promise, you must choose to believe it.

Key Verse

> "Faith is being sure of what we hope for. It is being certain of what we do not see." (Hebrews 11:1)

But the one who is right with God will live by faith.	Habakkuk 2:4
If you have faith as small as a mustard seed ... enough.	Matthew 17:20
He made their hearts pure because of their faith.	Acts 15:9
Without faith it isn't possible to please God.	Hebrews 11:6
In the same way, faith without good works is dead.	James 2:26
Through faith you are kept safe by God's power.	1 Peter 1:5

Suggested Reading

Example of someone who has faith in Jesus' healing.	Matthew 8:5–13
Two more people who have faith in Jesus' power.	Matthew 9:18–31
Jesus tells his disciples their faith is too small.	Matthew 17:14–21

Didjaknow?

Hebrews 11:1 says that "faith is being sure of what we hope for." The Greek word that was translated "being sure of" is *hupostasis*. A few years ago, archaeologists in Palestine dug up an old inn, and found many papers there with the word *hupostasis* on top of them. And do you know what those papers were? They were *title deeds* to property that some person owned. So what is faith? It is "the *title deed* of what we hope for." The things we have faith for are ours and we have the title deed to prove it.

JASON'S IMAGINATION

OK ANGELS, LETS MOVE, WE'VE GOT ANOTHER MOUNTAIN MOVING PRAYER REQUEST.

I THOUGHT THE MOUNTAINS WERE PRETTY GOOD WHERE THEY WERE.

Faithfulness

People who are faithful are solid and dependable, trustworthy and reliable. They can be counted on to do what they say. The Bible says that God is faithful. We can depend on his promises. When he says he'll do something, he will. We can rely on God to do what he said he would do. *We* also need to be faithful and do what we promise to do. We need to be faithful to keep our promises to others, and be faithful to God. When we live our lives the way God told us to—not just once, but day after day—that is being faithful.

Key Verse

> "Let us hold firmly to the hope we claim to have. The One who promised is faithful." (Hebrews 10:23)

God ... makes a promise, and then he keeps it.	Numbers 23:19
You have done well ... You have been faithful ...	Matthew 25:21
He serves Christ ... He faithfully works for Christ ...	Colossians 1:7
Moses was faithful in everything ... in the house of God.	Hebrews 3:2
Abraham believed that [God] ... was faithful.	Hebrews 11:11
Be faithful, even if it means you must die.... I will give ...	Revelation 2:10

Suggested Reading

Daniel's faithfulness and excellent spirit	Daniel 6:1–4
Rewards for faithful and unfaithful servants	Matthew 24:45–51
The good and faithful servants	Matthew 25:14–29

Didjaknow?

Being faithful to God means being careful to follow him closely, being diligent to obey all his commandments. It means doing what he has told us to do and not leaving any details undone or any jobs unfinished. Joseph was a faithful manager of Potiphar's house and of the prison (Genesis 39:1–6, 20–23). King David was faithful (2 Samuel 22:22–27). The men in charge of repairing God's temple were faithful (2 Kings 12:15). God is looking for faithful servants. Are you one?

Family

Your family is made up of you, your parents, your brothers, and your sisters. God wants you to have great relationships with your family. It's not always easy, but it's worth it! Through good times and bad, you love them and they love you,  and you look after each other. Christians are also called the family of God, and look after each other.

Key Verse

"Everyone should provide for his own relatives. Most of all, everyone should take care of his own family. If he doesn't, he has left the faith. He is worse than someone who doesn't believe." (1 Timothy 5:8)

Those who bring trouble on their families will receive ...	Proverbs 11:29
Let us make a special point of doing good to ... believers.	Galatians 6:10
From the Father his whole family in heaven and on earth ...	Ephesians 3:15
... someone doesn't know how to manage his own family.	1 Timothy 3:5

Family Wealth

An inheritance is a family's wealth passed down from parents to their children after the parents' death. An inheritance might be money, land, or other possessions. It's a good thing for parents to give their children physical wealth, but the best wealth is godly character. How do children inherit godliness from their parents? By following their parents' words and example.

Key Verse

"Wisdom is a good thing. It's like getting a share of the family wealth." (Ecclesiastes 7:11)

... will own this good land.... pass it on to your children ...	1 Chronicles 28:8
A good person leaves what he owns to his children and ...	Proverbs 13:22
You will receive houses and wealth from your parents.	Proverbs 19:14
... does what is right ... Blessed are his children after him.	Proverbs 20:7

Famine

Famine happens when there is a lack of food and/or water in an area. Famine was a constant threat in Bible times because rain had to come in just the right amount and at just the right time or else the crops would fail. A famous famine in the Bible was the seven-year famine in Egypt that Joseph predicted by interpreting Pharaoh's dream.

Key Verse

"[Joseph said,] 'Seven years with plenty of food are coming to the whole land of Egypt. But seven years when there won't be enough food will follow them. Then everyone will forget about all of the food Egypt had. Terrible hunger will destroy the land.'" (Genesis 41:29–30)

At that time there wasn't enough food in the land. — Genesis 12:10
... wants to keep them alive when there is no food ... — Psalm 33:18–19
He said there would not be nearly enough food ... — Acts 11:28–30
They were given power to kill people with ... hunger ... — Revelation 6:8

Fast(ing)

People fast by going without food (and sometimes water) for a certain length of time. In Bible times, people often fasted and prayed to show their dedication to God. They also fasted when they were mourning a death or some other national disaster or terrible event. Today, some Christians fast as a way to help them draw closer to God.

JASON'S DEFINITION OF A FAST:

Eating food as quickly as you can.

Key Verse

"But when you go without eating, put olive oil on your head. Wash your face. Then others will not know that you are fasting. Only your Father, who can't be seen, will know it. He will reward you. Your Father sees what is done secretly." (Matthew 6:17–18)

They didn't eat any food.... They put dust on their heads.	Nehemiah 9:1
All of the Jews were very sad. They didn't eat anything.	Esther 4:3
After 40 days and 40 nights of going without eating ...	Matthew 4:2
While they were ... fasting, the Holy Spirit spoke.	Acts 13:2–3

Father

A father is a male parent. In the Bible, God is called our "Father in heaven" (Matthew 6:9). Jesus often referred to God as his Father and told his disciples and *us* that God was *our* "Father in heaven" also (Matthew 7:11). This means that we can relate to God and have a loving, intimate relationship with him, just as we have with our earthly fathers. Fathers provide for us, love us, guide us, and teach us. God, our heavenly Father, does all these things and more! He gives us life, forgiveness, wisdom, knowledge, and everything else we need to live—both now and after we die.

Key Verse

> **"Even though you are evil, you know how to give good gifts to your children. How much more will your Father who is in heaven give good gifts to those who ask him!" (Matthew 7:11)**

Honor your father and mother.	Exodus 20:12
Listen to your father who gave you life.	Proverbs 23:22
Your Father knows what you need even before you ask ...	Matthew 6:8
This is how you should pray. "Our Father in heaven ..."	Matthew 6:9
There is only one God. He is the Father.	1 Corinthians 8:6
How great is the love the Father has given us so freely!	1 John 3:1

Suggested Reading

A father's job.	Deuteronomy 6:7–9; 11:1–21; Ephesians 6:4
Jesus prays to his Father before his arrest.	Matthew 26:36–47; Mark 14:32–43
Jesus explains his mission from his Father.	John 5:17–30
By the Spirit's power we call God "Father."	Romans 8:15–17

Didjaknow?

During Bible times, fathers in Jewish families had complete control over the lives of their children. They were totally responsible for them and provided for and looked after them, including finding them a husband or wife and giving them property. So when God becomes like our father, he becomes responsible for us and looks after every part of our lives. We trust his love to do what's best for us.

Feast

A feast is a huge meal held to celebrate a special occasion. In the Bible, the Israelites celebrated a number of feasts that were set up by God when he made his covenant with them. These feasts marked important events in Israel's history, such as harvests and their escape from Egypt. We celebrate feasts like Thanksgiving and Christmas.

Key Verse

"Three times a year you must celebrate a feast in my honor. Celebrate the Feast of Unleavened Bread. Eat bread that is made without yeast for seven days.... Celebrate the Feast of Weeks. Bring the first share of your crops from your field. Celebrate the Feast of Booths. Hold it in the fall when you gather in your crops from the field." (Exodus 23:14–16)

The Passover Feast.	Exodus 12:1–14
The Feast of Unleavened Bread.	Exodus 12:17–18
The Feast of Weeks.	Exodus 34:21–22
The Feast of Booths.	Leviticus 23:34–36

Fellowship

Fellowship means "sharing life with and having things in common with others." You can tell what a person is like by looking at who they fellowship with. So don't fellowship with bad people because you don't want to become like them or have others think you're like them. Fellowship with good people, and you'll please both God and others.

FRIENDSHIP POOL PARTY
EVERYONE WELCOME!

Key Verse

"God is faithful. He has chosen you to share life with his Son, Jesus Christ our Lord." (1 Corinthians 1:9)

They shared life together.	Acts 2:42
Bad companions make a good person bad.	1 Corinthians 15:33
I want to know Christ better.... to share in his sufferings.	Philippians 3:10
Then we share life with one another.	1 John 1:7

Fight

Fights happen when people argue about something and can't agree. God wants us to love and care for each other instead of fighting. Arguments are caused by selfishness and pride. When you can't have what you want, you argue and fight (James 4:2). Love stops fights because "it does not want what belongs to others.... It does not look out for its own interests" (1 Corinthians 13:4–5).

In the New Testament, the word "fight" also has a *good* meaning. As Christian soldiers, we are told to "fight the good fight," which means we should fight against evil and anything that stops us from obeying God.

Key Verse

"Fight the good fight along with all other believers. Take hold of eternal life. You were chosen for it when you openly told others what you believe." (1 Timothy 6:12)

That's because the Lord your God fights for you.   Joshua 23:10
Some of you argue. So aren't you following the ... world?   1 Corinthians 3:1–4
I don't fight my battles the way the people of the world ...   2 Corinthians 10:3
Our fight is not against human beings. It is against ...   Ephesians 6:12
Why do you fight and argue among yourselves?   James 4:1
But you can't have what you want. You argue and fight.   James 4:2

Suggested Reading

Proverbs talks about arguments and quarrels.   Proverbs 15:18; 16:28; 17:1, 14, 19; 20:3; 22:10; 26:17, 20–21; 28:25; 29:22; 30:33

Don't fight with others. Fight the devil.   James 4:1–7

Didjaknow?

Fights are caused by jealousy, pride, and hatred. The first fight in the Bible ended with Cain killing his brother Abel (Genesis 4:1–8). Esau hated his brother Jacob for cheating him, and wanted to kill him (Genesis 27:41). Saul was jealous of David and tried to kill him (1 Samuel 18:6–11). Jesus' disciples fought over who would be the greatest in the kingdom (Mark 9:33–34). Often we fight because we're selfish, want things our way, or want what others have. Instead we should trust God and love one another.

Fire

In the Bible, fire is often a sign of God's presence. God appeared to Moses in a burning bush. He also appeared in a pillar of fire to lead the Israelites through the wilderness. In the New Testament, fire appeared above the believers' heads when they received the Holy Spirit

(Acts 2:3–4). In the judgment, fire will burn up our bad works, leaving only the good (1 Corinthians 3:11–15).

Key Verse

> "The Lord your God is like a fire that burns everything up."
> (Deuteronomy 4:24)

The angel of the Lord appeared ... inside a burning bush.	Exodus 3:2–3
At night he led them with a pillar of fire.	Exodus 13:21
The people ... saw the glory of the Lord.... like a fire ...	Exodus 24:17
The weeds are ... burned in the fire.	Matthew 13:40–42

Fish

Fish were important in the Bible. Jesus told many stories about fish. Four of his disciples used to be fishermen on the Sea of Galilee. Jesus said that helping people believe in him was like catching fish. During the days of the early church, the fish became a symbol of Christianity because in Greek, the initials for *Jesus Christ, God's Son, Savior* spells *ichthys*, which means *fish*.

Key Verse

> "'Come. Follow me,' Jesus said. 'I will make you fishers of people.'
> At once they left their nets and followed him." (Matthew 4:19–20)

But the Lord sent a huge fish to swallow Jonah.	Jonah 1:17
The kingdom of heaven is like a net.... It caught ... fish ...	Matthew 13:47–50
... let the nets down ... caught a large number of fish.	Luke 5:3–7
They gave [Jesus] a piece of cooked fish. He ... ate it ...	Luke 24:42

Flesh

God created our flesh, our physical bodies. But because all people are sinful, the desires and habits of our flesh, or bodies, are selfish. This is why the Bible also calls our flesh our "sinful nature" and tells us to live by the Holy Spirit's power. Then we won't do what our sinful nature wants us to do (Romans 8:5). Our sinful nature makes us think only of our own needs. Of course, we have to feed and take care of ourselves, but we need to bring our bodies under God's control and think of others. Jesus said, "Love your neighbor as you love yourself" (Matthew 19:19).

Key Verse

> **"Don't live under the control of your sinful nature. If you do, you will think about what your sinful nature wants. Live under the control of the Holy Spirit." (Romans 8:5)**

Our sinful nature used to control us.... sinful longings ...	Romans 7:5–6
... duty is not to live under the control of our sinful nature.	Romans 8:12
Don't think about how to satisfy what your sinful nature ...	Romans 13:14
The Spirit does not want what ... sinful nature delights in.	Galatians 5:17
Those who belong to ... Jesus have nailed their sinful ...	Galatians 5:24

Suggested Reading

God's Spirit controls you now.	Romans 8:1–13
Don't follow your sinful nature.	Galatians 5:16–26

Didjaknow?

Paul controlled his sinful nature by disciplining his body, bringing it under control, and making it his slave. In 1 Corinthians 9:24–27 Paul compared Christians to runners in a race who have to discipline themselves, train hard, and obey the rules.

Paul said he didn't want to "break the rules and fail to win the prize." That means staying within the marked out lines of the race (Hebrews 12:1). If you take a shortcut across the lines, you may reach the finish first, but you'll be disqualified. So train hard, get your body under control, and follow God's rules.

SO WHERE'S THE FROG THIS TIME?

THAT WAS THE OLD ME. I NO LONGER GIVE IN TO MY OLD NATURE.

Flood, the

In the days of Noah, people were doing evil and violent things to each other. Things got so bad that God told Noah to build a huge ship (see *Ark*), because the greatest flood the world had ever seen was going to wipe out everything and everybody. It would show people that evil has serious consequences. The rain fell for forty days and nights, until even the highest mountains were covered with

water. Finally the water went down and the ark—with Noah's family and all the animals—landed on Mount Ararat. Then God promised that he would never again destroy the world in a flood.

Key Verse

"I am going to bring a flood on the earth. It will destroy all life under the sky. It will destroy every living creature that breathes. Everything on earth will die." (Genesis 6:17)

I created man on the earth. But I will wipe them out.	Genesis 6:7
Bring two of every living thing into the ark.	Genesis 6:19
Rain fell on the earth for 40 days and 40 nights.	Genesis 7:12
... the high mountains under the entire sky were covered.	Genesis 7:19
They knew nothing ... until the flood came ...	Matthew 24:38–39
... world's ungodly people ... He brought the flood on them.	2 Peter 2:5

Suggested Reading

Read the full story of Noah and the Flood.   Genesis 6:1–9:17

Didjaknow?

Some people think the Flood never happened. But stories of a flood similar to the one described in the Bible are found in the ancient traditions of the American Indians, of Egypt, Greece, China, India, Mexico, Britain, and other places. How could they *all* know about it separately—without ever having read the Bible—unless it really happened?

Food

You have to eat to live. So work hard, and there will be plenty to eat. God has promised to bless us with enough food. But remember: Eat to live, don't live to eat. You need to control your appetite and your desires. Eating too much of anything is called gluttony and is a sin.

Key Verse

"Jesus answered, 'It is written, "Man doesn't live only on bread. He also lives on every word that comes from the mouth of God.""' (Matthew 4:4)

... sat around pots of meat ... ate all of the food we wanted.	Exodus 16:2–4
Those who do right eat until they are full. But the ...	Proverbs 13:25
When [Jesus] came, he ate and drank as you do.	Luke 7:34
Their stomach is their god.	Philippians 3:19

Foolishness

Foolishness is the opposite of wisdom. Foolish people blurt out foolish things. They can't seem to stop talking. They act foolish too. Wise people ask advice, but foolish people think that they already know everything. They refuse to change even when they're wrong. They don't face facts. They just go on blindly and suffer the consequences. How much better to be wise!

Key Verse

"At first what he says is foolish. In the end his words are very evil. He talks too much." (Ecclesiastes 10:13–14)

... foolish ways of foolish people lead to what is foolish.	Proverbs 14:24
A man's own foolish acts destroy his life. But his heart ...	Proverbs 19:3
... being foolish. All those ... make him "unclean."	Mark 7:22–23
The wisdom of this world is foolish in God's eyes.	1 Corinthians 3:19

Forgiveness

Forgiveness means "not holding a grudge." It is telling someone that you're going to forget the bad things they've done. Through Jesus, God has forgiven us everything we ever did—or will do—wrong. We need to follow his example and forgive others. Jesus taught us to pray, "Forgive us our sins, just as we also have forgiven those who sin against us" (Matthew 6:12). That means even forgiving people who deliberately hurt us.

Key Verse

"Be kind and tender to one another. Forgive each other, just as God forgave you because of what Christ has done." (Ephesians 4:32)

Forgive people when they sin against you. If you do ...	Matthew 6:14–15
... my blood ... is poured out to forgive the sins of many.	Matthew 26:27–28
Love erases many sins by forgiving them.	1 Peter 4:8
If we admit that we have sinned, he will forgive us ...	1 John 1:9

Freedom

Freedom is not being under the control of another person or thing. Freedom means not being a slave to someone or something. It means being able to do what you love to do. After the Israelites left Egypt, they were free from Pharaoh and could serve God. When we love Jesus, God sets us free from the power of sin, so we can follow him.

Key Verse

"Christ has set us free. He wants us to enjoy freedom. So stand firm. Don't let the chains of slavery hold you again." (Galatians 5:1)

Set free those who are held by chains without any reason.	Isaiah 58:6
... you will know the truth. And the truth will set you free.	John 8:32–36
... the law of the Holy Spirit ... has set me free from the ...	Romans 8:2
The blood of Christ set you free from an empty ... life.	1 Peter 1:18

Friend

Friends are people we like being with. We enjoy doing things with friends and talking with them because they're interested in the same kinds of things as we are. Friends laugh with us when we're happy and listen to us when we're sad. True friends always stick up for us. When we're in trouble, they help us. Examples of friends in the Bible are Jonathan and David, and Paul and Barnabas. Even Jesus had a special friend, John, "the disciple Jesus loved" (John 13:23). Jesus wants us to be his friend too. If we're his friend, we enjoy following him and doing things that he likes doing.

Key Verse

"A friend loves at all times. He is there to help when trouble comes." (Proverbs 17:17)

Jonathan and David became close friends. Jonathan ...	1 Samuel 18:1
But there is a friend who sticks closer than a brother.	Proverbs 18:24
Have a ... loving heart ... you will be a friend of the king.	Proverbs 22:11
Wounds [truth that hurts] from a friend can be trusted.	Proverbs 27:6
Don't desert your friend or your father's friend.	Proverbs 27:10
I [Jesus] do not call you servants ... called you friends.	John 15:15

Suggested Reading

David and Jonathan have a very close friendship.	1 Samuel 19–20
We can be Jesus' friends by obeying and loving him.	John 15

Didjaknow?

David and Jonathan were great friends. Jonathan was the prince of Israel and of course Saul, his father, wanted Jonathan to be king one day. But Jonathan loved David so much he wanted David to be king instead. What a friend (1 Samuel 23:16–18)!

YOU SAID I COULD BRING MY BEST FRIEND. BUT... WELL... I JUST COULDN'T CHOOSE.

Fruit of the Spirit

Have you ever watched fruit grow? First there's the flower, then the bud, then the green fruit, and finally the ripe fruit. What the fruit *is* depends on the tree. The Bible says we grow fruit—character fruit! If we do only what we want, we bear bad fruit. But if we do what God wants, we bear good fruit. When we let God's Spirit work in us, he grows the fruit of the Spirit in our lives. How do we let the Spirit work in us? By reading the Bible so we learn what kind of person we should be, and by loving and obeying God.

Key Verse

"But the fruit the Holy Spirit produces is love, joy and peace. It is being patient, kind and good. It is being faithful and gentle and having control of oneself." (Galatians 5:22–23)

Those who do what is right will ... bear fruit.	Psalm 92:12–14
The fruit that godly people bear is like a tree of life.	Proverbs 11:30
Those who do what is right bear good fruit because of ...	Proverbs 12:12
A man gathers a crop from what he plants ...	Galatians 6:7–8
... do what is right ... Have faith, love and gentleness.	1 Timothy 6:11
To goodness, add ... godliness ... add kindness ... add love.	2 Peter 1:5–7

Suggested Reading

The fruit of the godly compared to that of sinners.	Psalm 1; Galatians 5:16–26

Didjaknow?

Every spring, fruit trees grow new branches called "suckers." These branches suck up a lot of the sap and energy of the tree and leave less for growing fruit. So farmers climb up on their ladders and snip off the "suckers." Then the tree uses all its sap for growing fruit. At times *we* want to do things that don't help us grow good spiritual fruit. For example, if you wanted to watch a video instead of going to church, that would be a "sucker" that needed to be snipped off. Many times God trims our lives, like the farmers, so we'll grow well.

Galilee

Galilee was the northern part of Israel; Judea was the southern part. Judea was dry, but Galilee was fertile and green, and the Sea of Galilee had many fish in it. Hundreds of years before Jesus was born, Isaiah prophesied that the Messiah would teach in Galilee. Much later, Jesus did most of his teaching there. It's also where most of his followers came from.

Key Verse

"Jesus went all over Galilee. There he taught in the synagogues. He preached the good news of God's kingdom." (Matthew 4:23)

In days to come he will honor Galilee ... a light will ...   Isaiah 9:1–2
... what the prophet Isaiah had said came true ... Galilee.   Matthew 4:13–16
... many women ... had followed Jesus from Galilee ...   Matthew 27:55
He started in Galilee and has come all the way here.   Luke 23:5

Garden of Eden

In the beginning, God created a beautiful garden in the land of Eden for Adam and Eve to live in. God put them in charge of the garden. There were two special trees there: the Tree of Life, and the Tree of the Knowledge of Good and Evil. Everything there was perfect, but after Adam and Eve sinned, they had to leave.

JASON'S IMAGINATION

Garden of Eden
no thorns or thistles grow here

Key Verse

"The Lord God had planted a garden in the east. It was in Eden. There he put the man he had formed." (Genesis 2:8)

The tree that gives life ... was in the middle of the garden.   Genesis 2:9
The Lord God put the man in the Garden of Eden.   Genesis 2:15
[They] heard the Lord God walking in the garden.... hid ...   Genesis 3:8
... Lord God drove the man out of the Garden of Eden ...   Genesis 3:23

Garden of Gethsemane

Jesus often went to the Mount of Olives with his disciples. There was a grove of olive trees there and a *gethsemane* (a stone basin for pressing oil out of olives). That's why it was called the Garden of Gethsemane. This is where Jesus was praying the night before his death, when Judas betrayed him and the disciples ran away.

Key Verse

"Then Jesus went with his disciples to a place called Gethsemane. He said to them, 'Sit here while I go over there and pray.'" (Matthew 26:36)

Jesus and his disciples went to a place called Gethsemane. Mark 14:32
Jesus went out as usual to the Mount of Olives. Luke 22:39
... grove of olive trees.... Jesus had often met ... disciples. John 18:1–2

Gentile

The Jews called everyone who was not a Jew a Gentile. The Jews knew that they were special and that God loved them in a special way, because he had made covenants with them. The Jews didn't like Gentiles and wouldn't eat with them or even enter their houses. They expected that their Messiah would only come for the people of Israel. But when Jesus came, he died for the sins of the whole world, not just the Jews. It didn't make any difference to God whether a person was a Jew or a Gentile—he wanted everybody to believe in Jesus.

Key Verse

"Is God the God of Jews only? Isn't he also the God of those who aren't Jews [Gentiles]? Yes, he is their God too." (Romans 3:29)

Do any of the worthless gods of the [Gentiles] bring rain? Jeremiah 14:22
... Jews don't have anything to do with Samaritans. John 4:9

It is against our law ... to have anything to do with ...   Acts 10:28
... good news ... for Jews ... also for those who aren't Jews.   Romans 1:16
No difference between ... Jews and those who are not.   Romans 10:12
My task was to preach to the non-Jews.   Galatians 2:7–8

Suggested Reading

How the gospel is first preached to the Gentiles.   Acts 10–11:23
Jews and Gentiles both need to be saved by grace.   Romans 3:21–24
How both Jews and Gentiles can be right with God.   Romans 10

Didjaknow?

The Jewish Christians had a hard time believing that God cared about the Gentiles. At first, they only told other Jews about Jesus. But when some believers from Cyprus and Cyrene (who were used to living among Gentiles) went to Antioch, they witnessed to them too, and a lot of people were saved (Acts 11:19–21).

Gentleness

Gentleness, a "fruit of the Spirit," means "being kind, considerate, and loving." It's a quiet inner strength that lets us serve and give to others with no worries. When we know we're loved and valued, it's easy to be gentle and serve others because we know God is taking care of us. God wants us to be gentle to everyone.

HERE'S MY WALKIE-TALKIE. I JUST PUT FRESH BATTERIES IN IT. CALL ME WHENEVER YOU NEED A FRIEND.

Key Verse

**"Let everyone know
how gentle you are.
The Lord is coming soon." (Philippians 4:5)**

A gentle answer turns anger away.   Proverbs 15:1
But the fruit the Holy Spirit produces is ... being ... gentle ...   Galatians 5:22–23
So put on tender mercy and kindness ... Be gentle ...   Colossians 3:12
... gentle ... like a mother caring for her little children.   1 Thessalonians 2:7

Gideon

Gideon was a judge who is best known for testing God. When God told him to lead his people, Gideon asked God for a sign, because he wanted to be sure he wasn't dreaming. God gave him the sign (plus one more for good measure) and then helped Gideon and his 300 men miraculously defeat an army of 32,000 soldiers!

Key Verse

"Gideon replied, 'If you are pleased with me, give me a special sign. Then I'll know that it's really you talking to me.'" (Judges 6:17)

The angel of the Lord appeared to Gideon. He said ...	Judges 6:12
Then the Spirit of the Lord came on Gideon.	Judges 6:34
Gideon separated the 300 men into three companies.	Judges 7:16
The people of Israel spoke to Gideon.... "Rule over us."	Judges 8:22

Gift, Spiritual

The Holy Spirit gives us spiritual gifts that perfectly match who God made us to be. These gifts include things like helping, teaching, words of wisdom, and healing. God wants us to do a certain job in the church, and he gives us the gifts we need to do it well. God's wonderful plan for us matches the gifts and talents he has given us.

Key Verse

"We all have gifts. They differ in keeping with the grace that God has given each of us." (Romans 12:6)

How much more will your Father ... give good gifts to ...	Matthew 7:11
You each have your own gift from God. One has ...	1 Corinthians 7:7
He also gave witness through the gifts of the Holy Spirit.	Hebrews 2:4
Every good and perfect gift is from God.	James 1:17

Giving

Giving is willingly handing over some, or all, of what we have to someone else. God asks us to give to others because he is generous, and he wants us to be like him. Jesus said a great deal about sharing with others. By giving to others, we show that we love God and others and that we trust God to provide for us. If we are generous, we never have to worry about not having enough, because everything we have is a gift from God. God will bless us with more to give as we trust and obey him with what we have.

Key Verse

"Give to the one who asks you for something. Don't turn away from the one who wants to borrow something from you." (Matthew 5:42)

The godly are always giving and lending freely.	Psalm 37:26
Anyone who gives freely will be blessed.	Proverbs 22:9
Your heart will be where your riches are.	Luke 12:34
[Jesus] said, "It is more blessed to give than to receive."	Acts 20:35
[Don't] give because you are forced to. God loves a ...	2 Corinthians 9:7
Command the rich to ... give freely.... be willing to share.	1 Timothy 6:18

Suggested Reading

Give to God and he'll give to you.	Malachi 3:10–12
Trust God to supply your needs.	Matthew 6:19–34
If you give a lot, you will receive a lot.	2 Corinthians 9:6–11

Didjaknow?

The early church used most of its offering money to care for the poor. About 155 A.D., a church leader name Justin wrote: "What is collected is deposited with the [elder], and he takes care of orphans and widows, and those who are in want ... and those who are in bonds ... and briefly, he is the protector of all those in need." In 197 A.D., another church leader, Tertullian, wrote: "These gifts are [used] to support ... poor people, to supply the wants of boys and girls destitute of means and parents, and of old persons confined to the house ... or [those] shut up in the prisons ..." We can help people by giving too.

God

God is beyond our understanding, but he has told us some things about himself in the Bible. God is the Creator of the universe, the Most High God, the beginning and the end of everything. "God is spirit" (John 4:24). That means he doesn't have a physical body like we do. He exists in three persons: Father, Son, and Holy Spirit. This is called the "Trinity." God is everywhere, he knows everything, and he can do anything. And, best of all, God is love. God loves us and wants to have a relationship with us through his Son, Jesus Christ.

JASON'S IMAGINATION

MAY GOD BE GRACIOUS TO US AND BLESS US AND MAKE HIS FACE SHINE UPON US.
PSALM 67:1 (NIV)

Key Verse

"So we know that God loves us. We depend on it. God is love. Anyone who leads a life of love shows that he is joined to God. And God is joined to him." (1 John 4:16)

Be holy, because I am holy. I am the Lord your God.	Leviticus 19:2
God judges fairly.	Psalm 7:11
I am the Lord. I do not change.	Malachi 3:6
God loved the world so much that he gave his ... Son.	John 3:16
God ... will not let you be tempted any more than ...	1 Corinthians 10:13
God is not a God of disorder. He is a God of peace.	1 Corinthians 14:33

Suggested Reading

God creates the world.	Genesis 1
God knows everything and is everywhere.	Psalm 139:1–12
The Holy Spirit is God.	Matthew 28:19
Jesus is God.	John 10:30–39

Didjaknow?

No one created God; he has always existed. We can't understand this because everything we know has a beginning and an end. Each day has a morning and a night; basketball games have an opening tip-off and a final buzzer; people are born, and they die. But God has no beginning or end. He always was and always will be.

Godly

Being godly means "to live like God, to live the kind of life God wants you to live." Godly people are loving, kind, patient, forgiving, and try to do what is right. To know how to be godly, read what God says about it in the Bible. You also need God's Spirit to give you the power to live a godly life.

Key Verse

"Instead, train yourself to be godly. Training the body has some value. But being godly has value in every way. It promises help for the life you are now living and the life to come." (1 Timothy 4:7–8)

Noah was a godly man. He was without blame ...	Genesis 6:9
You are a man of God.... Try hard to do what is ... godly.	1 Timothy 6:11
... understand the truth that leads to godly living.	Titus 1:1
God's power has given us everything ... lead a godly life.	2 Peter 1:3

Godly Sadness

Repentance is when you know you've done something wrong and are filled with godly sadness about it, you confess it, ask God to forgive you, and change so you don't do it again. When you do this, you can depend on God to forgive you and make you clean again. Jesus died so *all* our sins could be forgiven.

Key Verse

"I'm happy because your sadness led you to turn away from your sins. You became sad just as God wanted you to.... Godly sadness causes us to turn away from our sins and be saved." (2 Corinthians 7:9–10)

But anyone who admits his sins and gives them up ...	Proverbs 28:13
So turn away from your sins. Then you will live!	Ezekiel 18:32
Produce fruit that shows you have turned away from ...	Luke 3:8
If we admit that we have sinned, he will forgive us ...	1 John 1:9

Gold

Gold is a beautiful and rare metal which is considered very valuable. Because it is so soft, it is easily made into jewelry. In Old Testament times, people paid for things by weighing out a certain amount of gold. Later people invented gold coins. King Solomon was an extremely rich man. Each year, part of the taxes he received was 25 tons of gold. When he built a beautiful temple for God, he covered the inside of it with gold. The heavenly city and its streets are also made out of gold. The Bible warns us to love God more than gold.

Key Verse

"It is much better to get wisdom than gold. It is much better to choose understanding than silver." (Proverbs 16:16)

Solomon covered the inside of the main hall with ... gold.	1 Kings 6:21
Each year Solomon received 25 tons of gold.	1 Kings 10:14–15
I love your commandments more than gold.... pure gold.	Psalm 119:127
Choose knowledge rather than fine gold. Wisdom is ...	Proverbs 8:10–11
... Wise Men ... opened their treasures.... gave him gold ...	Matthew 2:11

Suggested Reading

The articles of the Tent of Meeting were made out of gold.	Exodus 25, 26, 28
Gold for the ark of the covenant, lampstands, incense altar.	Exodus 37
The articles of the temple are made out of gold.	1 Kings 6, 7
Mining for gold and other precious metals and stones.	Job 28:1–19

Didjaknow?

Jesus said, "Do not put away riches for yourselves on earth.... Instead, put away riches for yourselves in heaven" (Matthew 6:19–20). The riches of earth can't compare to the riches of heaven! The entire heavenly city is "made out of pure gold, as pure as glass," and "the main street of the city [is] made out of pure gold" (Revelation 21:18, 21). But the riches of heaven are also things like love, obedience, and good deeds.

Golgotha

The Romans made Jesus carry his cross to a hill outside the walls of Jerusalem. It was the place where they crucified criminals. The hill was called *Golgotha* in Aramaic, which means *skull*. The Romans called Golgotha Calvary—The Skull—probably because it looked a little like a skull. The garden tomb where Joseph of Arimathea buried Jesus was near Golgotha (John 19:41–42).

Key Verse

"They brought Jesus to the place called Golgotha. The word Golgotha means The Place of the Skull." (Mark 15:22)

The soldiers brought them to the place called The Skull.	Luke 23:33
... The Skull. In the Aramaic language ... called Golgotha.	John 19:17
The place where Jesus was crucified was near the city.	John 19:20
Jesus also suffered outside the city gate.	Hebrews 13:12

Goliath

Goliath was a Philistine giant who was more than nine feet tall. One day the Philistine army and the army of Israel were across from each other on two hills, ready to fight. Goliath yelled at the Israelites to send someone to fight him. No one stepped forward. Then David came. He swung his sling and killed Goliath with a stone, and the Philistines ran away.

THIS MUST BE WHAT GOLIATH ATE TO MAKE HIM SO BIG!

Key Verse

"So David won the fight against Goliath with a sling and a stone. He struck the Philistine down and killed him." (1 Samuel 17:50)

... Goliath came out ... He was more than nine feet tall.	1 Samuel 17:4
... I dare ... Israel to send a man ... to fight against me.	1 Samuel 17:10
Then David ... took his sling ... and approached Goliath.	1 Samuel 17:40
... stone hit him on the forehead ... He fell to the ground ...	1 Samuel 17:49

Goodness

God is good. It's part of his character. He's always righteous, holy, honest, fair, generous, trustworthy, kind, merciful, and loving. Because God is always good, he wants us to be good, to consistently choose right over wrong. Goodness is a "fruit of the Spirit." If we listen to God's Spirit when he tells us to do something good—and then do it!—we'll have goodness.

Key Verse

"How great your goodness is! You have stored it up for those who have respect for you." (Psalm 31:19)

I will make all of my goodness pass in front of you.	Exodus 33:19
My brothers ... I am sure that you are full of goodness.	Romans 15:14
The fruit the Holy Spirit produces is ... being ... good.	Galatians 5:22–23
Try very hard to add goodness to your faith.	2 Peter 1:5

Gospel

Gospel means "good news." The gospel is the good news that God sent his Son Jesus to take away our sins by dying on the cross and rising to life again. But gospel can also mean the story of Jesus' birth, life, death, and resurrection. There are four gospels in the Bible, written by Matthew, Mark, Luke, and John. Together, these four gospels tell only a small part of the story of Jesus—but they tell us the most important things! Each one of the four gospels was written for a different group of people to explain Jesus in a way those people could understand.

Key Verse

"I am not ashamed of the good news. It is God's power. And it will save everyone who believes. It is meant first for the Jews. It is meant also for those who aren't Jews." (Romans 1:16)

This good news ... will be preached in the whole world.	Matthew 24:14
Teach them to obey everything I have commanded you.	Matthew 28:20
The angel said ... "I bring you good news of great joy."	Luke 2:10

He has anointed me to tell the good news to poor people. Luke 4:18
Because you believed the good news, you are saved. 1 Corinthians 15:2
He came to tell everyone on earth the good news ... Revelation 14:6

Suggested Reading

Luke explains why he wrote his gospel. Luke 1:1–4
Believe the good news, and you will be saved. 1 Corinthians
15:1–4

Beware of people who preach a different gospel. Galatians 1:6–9

Didjaknow?

Matthew's gospel was written for the Jews and shows that Jesus is the Messiah, since he fulfilled the things that were foretold about the Messiah in the Old Testament. Mark's gospel is short, action-packed, and to the point. It is for anyone who doesn't know about Jesus. Luke's gospel was written for Gentiles, people who are not Jews. John's gospel is different from all the rest. It was written to convince people that Jesus is the Son of God.

Gossip

To gossip is to say things about others that are either bad, untrue, or both. Gossip hurts everyone. When we gossip, we damage people's reputations. We can also hurt the person about whom we're gossiping if they hear what we've been saying. Plus, by gossiping we damage our own reputa-

tion because we show that we are unkind and can't be trusted.

Key Verse

"With our tongues we praise our Lord and Father. With our tongues we call down curses on people. We do it even though they have been created to be like God. Praise and cursing come out of the same mouth. My brothers and sisters, it shouldn't be that way." (James 3:9–10)

Those who talk about others tell secrets. Proverbs 11:13
Anyone who talks about others comes between ... friends. Proverbs 16:28
Your tongue has the power of life and death. Those who ... Proverbs 18:21
Don't let any evil talk come out of your mouths. Ephesians 4:29

Government

A government is made up of the rulers of a country who make laws, build roads, and keep the peace. There are different kinds of governments. In a monarchy people are ruled by a king or queen. A dictatorship is when one person rules by force. In a democracy people vote to choose who will lead them. Leaders sometimes make mistakes and do wrong, but we need government.

Key Verse

"You must obey the authorities. Then you will not be punished. You must also obey them because you know it is right." (Romans 13:5)

God rules over all of the kingdoms ... He gives them to ...	Daniel 4:32
Do you owe taxes?... anything else to the government?	Romans 13:7
Pray for kings. Pray for all who are in authority.	1 Timothy 2:2
Remind God's people to obey rulers and authorities.	Titus 3:1

Grace

Grace means "a free, undeserved *gift*." Grace is doing something for someone else who doesn't deserve it. We have all sinned. We don't deserve eternal life in heaven, but Romans 6:23 says, "God gives you the *gift of eternal life* because of what Christ Jesus our Lord has done" (italics added). He is full of grace, and he will give us eternal life—and graciously meet our needs here on earth—even though he doesn't have to and we don't deserve it. Acts 20:24 says God wants us to tell others about "the good news of God's grace."

Key Verse

"The free gift of God's grace makes all of us right with him. Christ Jesus paid the price to set us free." (Romans 3:24)

But he gives grace to those who are not proud.   Proverbs 3:34
Through faith in Jesus we have received God's grace.   Romans 5:2
Those who receive ... grace ... have received God's gift ...   Romans 5:17
God loves us deeply.... God's grace has saved you.   Ephesians 2:4–5
Your salvation doesn't come from anything you do.   Ephesians 2:8
God has saved us.... because of his own purpose and grace. 2 Timothy 1:9

Suggested Reading

These two chapters give a clear picture of God's grace.   Romans 5, 11

Didjaknow?

God not only shows us grace
by giving us eternal life, but
even in *this* life he constantly
showers us with mercy and
grace. Whenever we need
help, we can come to God
through prayer. Hebrews 4:16
says, "Let us boldly approach
the throne of grace. Then we
will receive mercy. We will
find grace to help us when
we need it."

Greed

Greed is wanting more than we need or can use properly. It leads us into all
kinds of sins to get what we want. It's okay to want things, but we shouldn't
put the things we want ahead of God or other people. Instead of focusing on
getting more things for ourselves, we should focus on giving to others and
trusting God to supply all of our needs.

Key Verse

> "Watch out! Be on your guard against wanting to have more and
> more things. Life is not made up of how much a person has." (Luke
> 12:15)

Anyone who always wants more brings trouble to his ...   Proverbs 15:27
They are like dogs that love to eat. They never get enough.   Isaiah 56:11
The same is true of those who always want more and ...   Ephesians 5:5
Stop always wanting more and more.   Colossians 3:5

Greek

A Greek is a person from Greece. Greek is also the language spoken by the Greeks. Alexander the Great was from Greece, and he conquered more countries than anyone had ever done before him. In Jesus' day, even after the Romans took over, Greek was the language almost everybody understood. Paul preached the gospel to the Greeks, and the New Testament was written in Greek.

Key Verse

"Many of the Jews read the sign. The place where Jesus was crucified was near the city. The sign was written in the Aramaic, Latin and Greek languages." (John 19:20)

The woman came to Jesus ... She was a Greek, born in ...	Mark 7:25–26
"May I say something to you?" "Do you speak Greek?"	Acts 21:37
There is no Jew or Greek.... you are all one.	Galatians 3:28
In the Hebrew ... his name is Abaddon. In Greek it is ...	Revelation 9:11

Guard Your Heart

Guarding your heart means "protecting yourself from being filled up with bad things, and keeping your heart pure and safe." Many people watch garbage on TV because they like it. But junk entertainment is like junk food—it tastes good even though it's bad. God wants us to avoid junk entertainment even if it seems fun and harmless. Foolish people fill their hearts with trash, but wise people guard their hearts and fill them with wisdom and positive thoughts of God's Word. We guard our hearts by focusing on good and godly things.

Key Verse

"Above everything else, guard your heart. It is where your life comes from." (Proverbs 4:23)

Lord, may the ... thoughts of my heart be pleasing ... Psalm 19:14
I won't look at anything that is evil. Psalm 101:3–4
A good man says good ... from the good ... inside him. Matthew 12:34–35
Don't think about how to satisfy what your sinful nature ... Romans 13:14
Think about what is noble, right and pure.... excellent ... Philippians 4:8

Suggested Reading

David doesn't guard his heart and gets in big trouble. 2 Samuel 11–12

Didjaknow?

There's an old saying, "You are what you eat." Another saying is just as true: "You are what you *read*," or what you watch or listen to. If you fill your heart—your mind's memory banks—with garbage music, videos, TV shows, and comics, after a while garbage will fill your thoughts and come out of your mouth. Christians need to guard their hearts and only allow the good in.

Guilt

Guilt is the feeling we get when we know we've done something wrong, when we know we deserve punishment for breaking a rule. Feeling guilty can be good as it lets us know we've done wrong. Then we can confess and be forgiven. Everyone is born sinful and guilty. But Jesus took care of our guilt problem by dying on the cross and paying for our sins.

Key Verse

"The Lord is slow to get angry. He is very powerful. The Lord will not let guilty people go without punishing them. When he marches out, he stirs up winds and storms. Clouds are the dust kicked up by his feet." (Nahum 1:3)

It is a guilt offering. It will pay for his sin. Leviticus 5:15
God, you know ... My guilt is not hidden from you. Psalm 69:5
Can any of you prove I am guilty of sinning? John 8:46
If we admit that we have sinned, he will forgive us ... 1 John 1:9

Harvest

To harvest means "to gather crops from the fields when they are ripe." There were three important harvesttimes in Israel: the barley harvest in spring, the wheat harvest in summer, and the fruit harvest in the fall. The Jewish Harvest Feast (also called Pentecost) celebrated the wheat harvest. The Feast of Booths celebrated the fruit harvest. The Jews celebrated because they were thankful that God had provided them with good crops and food for another year. There are spiritual harvests too: Jesus said that helping people know him was like harvesting, and that Judgment Day was the final harvest.

Key Verse

"Then Jesus said to his disciples, 'The harvest is huge. But there are only a few workers. So ask the Lord of the harvest to send workers out into his harvest field.'" (Matthew 9:37–38)

Celebrate the Feast of Weeks. Bring ... share of ... crop.	Exodus 34:22
The harvest is judgment day. And the workers are angels.	Matthew 13:39
So the farmer cuts it down, because the harvest is ready.	Mark 4:26–29
Look at the fields! They are ripe for harvest right now.	John 4:35
Cut the grain.... The earth is ready to be harvested.	Revelation 14:15

Suggested Reading

Ruth, Boaz, and the barley harvest.	Ruth 1:22–3:18
The good and bad plants and the final harvest.	Matthew 13:24–30, 36–43
Two harvests: the righteous and the unrighteous.	Revelation 14:14–20

Didjaknow?

Our modern holiday and feast of Thanksgiving began when the first settlers—the Pilgrims—harvested their first crop in the New World. They held a thanksgiving feast to give thanks to the Lord for the harvest and invited some friendly Indians to the meal. The chief sent some of his warriors into the forest to hunt some turkeys, and we've been eating turkeys at Thanksgiving ever since.

Healing

To heal is to make healthy. One of the ways Jesus showed people that God loved them was by healing them. People brought all who were ill to Jesus. They brought the blind, the deaf, the paralyzed, and the crippled. Jesus healed them all. Jesus even brought people back to life who had died! God can still heal us today.

Key Verse

"Jesus went all over Galilee.... He healed every illness and sickness the people had." (Matthew 4:23)

... your skin will be healed. You will be pure and clean ...   2 Kings 5:10
He felt deep concern ... He healed their sick people.   Matthew 14:14
People brought those who were sick ... All ... were healed.   Acts 5:15–16
Are any of you sick?... The Lord will heal you.   James 5:14–15

Heart

In the Bible, our heart is our inner thoughts and feelings, not our physical heart that pumps blood. God promised, "When you look for me with all your heart, you will find me" (Jeremiah 29:13). He wants us to love and serve him from our hearts. With his Spirit in our hearts, we can do this.

Key Verse

"Love the Lord your God with all your heart and with all your soul. Love him with all your mind and with all your strength." (Mark 12:30)

You must turn to the Lord your God with all your heart ...   Deuteronomy 30:10
I will put my law in their minds.... write it on their hearts.   Jeremiah 31:33
With your heart you believe and are made right with God.   Romans 10:9–10
Christ will live in your hearts because you believe ...   Ephesians 3:17

Heaven

Heaven is the place where God and his angels live. Jesus is preparing a place in heaven for his followers. The Bible tells us that the heavenly city, called New Jerusalem, is going to come down out of heaven, to the earth, and God himself will live with us (Revelation 21:2–4). Heaven is a place of complete happiness. There's no pain or sorrow, crying or sickness, sadness or death. The best thing about heaven is that we'll be with God there. If your name is written in Jesus' Book of Life, you will be able to enter the heavenly city.

Key Verse

"There in front of me was a throne in heaven with someone sitting on it. The One who sat there shone like jewels. Around the throne was a rainbow that looked like an emerald." (Revelation 4:2–3)

... suffer ... The kingdom of heaven belongs to them.   Matthew 5:10
Jesus ... taken up into heaven. He sat down at the right ...   Mark 16:19
I am going there to prepare a place for you.   John 14:2
No eye has seen ... what God has prepared for those ...   1 Corinthians 2:9
But we have a building ... It is a house in heaven that ...   2 Corinthians 5:1
I saw the Holy City ... coming down out of heaven ...   Revelation 21:2

Suggested Reading

What it's like for Christians in heaven.   Revelation 7:9–17
A description of how marvelous heaven is.   Revelation 21–22

Didjaknow?

The kingdom of heaven is not only going to happen in the future. It's also happening right here wherever people love and obey God. We have the kingdom of heaven in our hearts now. Jesus said, "The coming of God's kingdom is not something you can see just by watching for it carefully. People will not say, 'Here it is.' Or, 'There it is.' God's kingdom is among you" (Luke 17:20–21).

Hebrew

A Hebrew is someone descended from Abraham, Isaac, and Jacob, someone who is a Jew by blood. Hebrew is also the ancient language that the Israelites spoke in the Bible, and which Israelis speak—in a different form—today. The Old Testament was written mostly in Hebrew. To us, Hebrew looks strange. It's written backwards, from right to left, and looks very different from English.

Key Verse

"I was circumcised on the eighth day. I am part of the people of Israel. I am from the tribe of Benjamin. I am a pure Hebrew." (Philippians 3:5)

Abram was a Hebrew. He was living near the large trees ...   Genesis 14:13
This is one of the Hebrew babies.   Exodus 2:5–6
Then the commander ... spoke in the Hebrew language.   2 Kings 18:28
"What people do you belong to?" ... "I'm a Hebrew."   Jonah 1:8–9

Hell

According to the Bible, hell is a very dark and very painful place. It is "the lake of fire," a place of eternal suffering, separation from God, and grim loneliness. No one will have any friends in hell. There is no love, joy, fun, laughter, or celebration in hell. Hell is separate from God and from all that is good.

Key Verse

"The lake of fire is the second death. Anyone whose name was not written in the Book of Life was thrown into the lake of fire." (Revelation 20:14–15)

Then they will go away to be punished forever.   Matthew 25:46
In hell, "The worms do not die. The fire is not put out."   Mark 9:48
Instead, he sent them to hell. He put them in dark prisons.   2 Peter 2:4
The smoke of ... suffering will rise for ever and ever.   Revelation 14:10–11

Help

The Bible says that whenever you can, you should help others. When you have God's love in your heart, you're happy to help! Even the words you speak are helpful. You should never refuse to help a brother or a sister or a friend. Don't shut your ears to requests for help, or you will also be ignored in your time of need.

Key Verse

"In everything I did, I showed you that we must work hard and help the weak." (Acts 20:35)

But there weren't enough priests ... Levites helped them.	2 Chronicles 29:34
The believers decided to provide help for the brothers ...	Acts 11:29
... he was a ... help to those who had become believers ...	Acts 18:27
She has been a great help to many people, including me.	Romans 16:2

Herod

Herod the Great was king when Jesus was born. He rebuilt the Jewish temple. Herod Antipas, his son, beheaded John the Baptist and mocked Jesus at his trial. Herod Agrippa I, a grandson of Herod the Great, killed James, the brother of John, then was eaten by worms and died. Herod Agrippa II, a great-grandson of Herod the Great, heard Paul preach the gospel.

Key Verse

"Jesus was born in Bethlehem in Judea. This happened while Herod was king of Judea." (Matthew 2:1)

Herod is going to search for the child.... to kill him.	Matthew 2:13
Herod had arrested John. He had ... put him in prison ...	Matthew 14:3
Herod was seated on his throne ... eaten by worms ...	Acts 12:21–23
Agrippa said to Paul, "You may now speak for yourself."	Acts 26:1

Holy Spirit

The Holy Spirit is God. He has qualities only God has: he's eternal—he has no beginning or end. He's omnipresent—he's present everywhere. He's equal with God. "Baptize them in the name of the Father and of the Son and of the Holy Spirit" (Matthew 28:19). He was involved in creation. The Holy Spirit came upon Mary so she'd have God's Son, Jesus. He helps people to be born into God's kingdom. He also helps us obey God and tell others about him. There's only one God, but he is three equal persons—the Father, the Son, and the Holy Spirit.

Key Verse

"But the Father will send the Friend in my name to help you. The Friend is the Holy Spirit. He will teach you all things. He will remind you of everything I have said to you." (John 14:26)

Mary ... became pregnant by the power of the Holy Spirit.	Matthew 1:18
But when the Spirit of truth comes, he will guide you ...	John 16:13
God anointed Jesus of Nazareth with the Holy Spirit ...	Acts 10:38
The Holy Spirit now controls the way we live.	Romans 8:4
The Spirit understands ... even the deep things of God.	1 Corinthians 2:10
Now the Lord is the Holy Spirit.	2 Corinthians 3:17

Suggested Reading

The Holy Spirit is involved in Creation.	Genesis 1:1–2
God fills the disciples with the Spirit.	Acts 2:1–21
How the Holy Spirit controls our lives.	Romans 8:1–17
The different gifts of the Holy Spirit.	1 Corinthians 12:1–11
How the Holy Spirit helps us live as Christians.	Galatians 5:16–25

Didjaknow?

The Holy Spirit is a "he," not an "it." The Holy Spirit is a person, and feels, thinks, and acts like a person. He even has emotions. Ephesians 4:30 says, "Do not make God's Holy Spirit sad."

Honest Lives

Another word for "honest lives" is integrity. Integrity means being pure, honest, sincere, and truthful. It means that there is no difference between your thoughts, words, and actions. If you are living an honest life, you will not say or think one thing and then do the complete opposite. You will always be truthful and sincere. God wants all Christians to be people of integrity.

Key Verse

"Those who do what is right are guided by their honest lives. But those who aren't faithful are destroyed by their trickery." (Proverbs 11:3)

Your heart must be honest. It must be without blame.	1 Kings 9:4
My God ... you are pleased when we are honest.	1 Chronicles 29:17
Anyone who lives without blame walks safely.	Proverbs 10:9
They will see the good things you do. And they will ...	Matthew 5:16

Humility

Humility is the opposite of pride. It means recognizing that all we have and can do comes from God. Jesus is the best example of humility. He showed us that being humble does not mean putting ourselves down, it means lifting others up, especially God. A humble person focuses more on God and others than on himself or herself.

Key Verse

"Don't be proud at all. Be completely gentle. Be patient. Put up with one another in love." (Ephesians 4:2)

Wisdom comes to those who are not proud.	Proverbs 11:2
Think of others as better than yourselves.	Philippians 2:3
Wise people aren't proud when they do good works.	James 3:13
Bow down to the Lord. He will lift you up.	James 4:10

Hypocrite

(See Pretender)

Idol

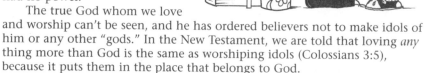

Idols are things that are more important to us than God. In the Bible, they were usually statues of false gods. People wanted to *see* who they were worshiping, so they made statues of their gods—idols of clay and wood and gold—and worshiped these. These idols had no power.

The true God whom we love and worship can't be seen, and he has ordered believers not to make idols of him or any other "gods." In the New Testament, we are told that loving *any* thing more than God is the same as worshiping idols (Colossians 3:5), because it puts them in the place that belongs to God.

Key Verse

"Do not make statues of gods that look like anything in the sky or on the earth or in the waters. Do not bow down to them or worship them. I, the Lord your God, am a jealous God." (Exodus 20:4–5)

... might say, "Let's follow other gods. Let's worship ..."	Deuteronomy 13:2
They ... followed other gods and worshiped them.	Judges 2:12
I hate those who worship worthless statues of gods.	Psalm 31:6
Those who make statues of gods will be like them.	Psalm 115:8
... a god made by human hands is ... nothing at all.	1 Corinthians 8:4
Run away from statues of gods.	1 Corinthians 10:14

Suggested Reading

The Israelites sin, building an idol of a golden calf.	Exodus 32
God punishes the Israelites for worshiping idols.	Judges 2:10–23
Anyone who worships an idol is a fool.	Isaiah 44:9–20
Paul gets into trouble with idol makers in Ephesus.	Acts 19:23–41

Didjaknow?

The nations that the ancient Israelites lived in and near worshiped many gods, or idols, and the land of Egypt was no exception. Almost everyone knows that the ancient Egyptians preserved the bodies of kings by "mummifying" them, but few people realize that the Egyptians also mummified animals they believed to represent gods. This included cats and dogs, birds, bulls, and even crocodiles!

Inheritance

(See Family Wealth)

Integrity

(See Honest Lives)

Isaac

Isaac was the son of Abraham and Sarah. He was born as a result of a promise God made to them when they were very old. Later, God tested Abraham by asking him to sacrifice Isaac. Abraham was going to obey God, but God saw his obedience and supplied a ram to sacrifice instead. Isaac married Rebekah. She gave birth to twins: Jacob and Esau.

Key Verse

"Then God said, 'I will bless Ishmael. But your wife Sarah will have a son by you. And you will name him Isaac. I will establish my covenant with him. It will be a covenant that lasts forever. It will be for Isaac and for his family after him.'" (Genesis 17:19)

Abraham was 100 years old when ... Isaac was born ...	Genesis 21:5
Sarah said, "God has given laughter [Isaac] to me."	Genesis 21:6
Take Isaac.... Give him to me ... as a burnt offering.	Genesis 22:2
Rebekah couldn't have children. So Isaac prayed ...	Genesis 25:21

Isaiah

For many years during the eighth century B.C. Isaiah was a prophet to the kingdom of Judah. His prophecies are written in Isaiah in the Old Testament. The first half of the book warns about the destruction of Judah. The second half talks about the good things that will happen after Judah is punished and they turn back to God. Most importantly, Isaiah predicted the coming of Jesus.

JASON'S IMAGINATION

AND NOW, THE MAN WHO PROPHESIED ABOUT THE COMING OF THE MESSIAH.

HOW DO YOU KNOW HE'LL BE BORN OF A VIRGIN?

WHY DO YOU SAY THE MESSIAH MUST SUFFER?

CAN YOU TELL US WHAT...

Key Verse

"Then I [Isaiah] heard the voice of the Lord. He said, 'Who will I send? Who will go for us?' I said, 'Here I am. Send me!'" (Isaiah 6:8)

Isaiah [said], "... Do you want the shadow ... forward ...?"	2 Kings 20:9
A child will be born to us.... will be called ... Mighty God.	Isaiah 9:6–7
A messenger is calling out, "In the desert prepare ..."	Isaiah 40:3
His servant [Jesus] grew up like a tender young plant.	Isaiah 53:2–12

Israel

Israel was the new name God gave to Jacob. It means "Prince of God." God promised to make Jacob (Israel) into a great nation. This is why, in the Old Testament, God's people were called "children of Israel" or "Israelites." After the Israelites conquered Canaan, the whole country was called Israel. But after King Solomon's death, the northern tribes broke away. Then only they were called Israel. David's sons only ruled over the southern kingdom of Judah. Unfortunately, the northern tribes forgot God and worshiped idols. To punish them, God allowed the Assyrians to defeat them and take them as prisoners to Assyria.

Key Verse

> **"Then the man said, 'Your name will not be Jacob anymore. Instead, it will be Israel. You have struggled with God and with men. And you have won.'" (Genesis 32:28)**

Your name is Jacob.... Your name will be Israel.	Genesis 35:10–12
The people of Israel are my servants.... out of Egypt.	Leviticus 25:42
... go into the land I ... give to the people of Israel.	Joshua 1:2
All of the elders ... anointed David as king over Israel.	2 Samuel 5:3
We don't have any share in David's ... Israel, let's go ...	1 Kings 12:16
The king of Assyria took the people of Israel away from ...	2 Kings 17:6

Suggested Reading

Israel (Jacob) wrestles with the angel of God.	Genesis 32:24–30
The Israelites are put into slavery in Egypt.	Exodus 1:8–21
The kingdom of Israel breaks away from Judah.	1 Kings 12
The kingdom of Israel is taken prisoner.	2 Kings 17

Didjaknow?

After they were taken away by Assyria, the ten tribes of Israel eventually intermarried with the people around them, and disappeared. A few of them returned to their homeland with the people of Judah. But most of them were just gone. The people of Judah were called "Jews" by the other nations. Now, 2000 years later, when the Jews returned to their homeland once again, what did they call it? Judah? No. *Israel.*

Jacob

Jacob was the son of Isaac and Rebekah. When he was young, Jacob cheated his brother Esau out of his birthright, then cheated him out of his blessing. Esau was very angry, so Jacob ran away to his uncle, Laban. On the way, Jacob had a dream of angels, and he promised to serve God. Jacob worked many years for Laban and married his daughters, Leah and Rachel. He had twelve sons and several daughters. Jacob's sons later became the tribes of Israel.

JASON'S IMAGINATION

LET'S CALL THEM RED HAIRY AND CHEATER. WHAT DO YOU THINK?

WELL, I WAS THINKING MORE ALONG THE LINES OF...

After twenty years Jacob decided to return home to see his father and Esau.

Key Verse

"Then the man said, 'Your name will not be Jacob anymore. Instead, it will be Israel. You have struggled with God and with men. And you have won.'" (Genesis 32:28)

... holding onto Esau's heel. So he was named Jacob.	Genesis 25:26
Jacob replied, "... sell me the rights that belong to you ..."	Genesis 25:31
Isn't Jacob just the right name for him? He has cheated ...	Genesis 27:36
In a dream he saw a stairway standing on the earth.	Genesis 28:12
Jacob was left alone. A man struggled with him ...	Genesis 32:24
... Jacob gave us the well.... Are you more important ...?	John 4:12

Suggested Reading

Jacob and Esau are born, Jacob cheats Esau.	Genesis 25:19–34
Jacob flees to Haran, marries, then returns home.	Genesis 27–35
Jacob's sons in Egypt to buy grain; Jacob goes.	Genesis 42–46

Didjaknow?

God performed an unusual miracle for Jacob. Jacob watched over the flocks of his father-in-law, Laban, and God blessed Jacob and increased the flocks. Instead of giving Jacob wages, Laban agreed to give him the lambs that were dark-colored or had speckles or spots. Laban kept all the white ones. Then Jacob took branches and peeled white stripes in their bark. He set these branches in the stone tubs where Laban's white sheep drank water. The sheep mated in front of the branches, and most of their lambs were born striped and spotted. As a result, Jacob ended up with most of the sheep (Genesis 30:25–43)!

James

James, the brother of Jesus, was the leader of the Christian church in Jerusalem. When certain Jews argued with Paul that Gentiles still had to obey the Law of Moses, James said that the Gentiles didn't have to keep the Jewish Law. James also wrote to Jewish believers telling them how to live well. This letter is the book of James.

Key Verse

"James, Peter and John are considered to be pillars in the church." (Galatians 2:9)

Aren't his brothers James, Joseph, Simon and Judas?	Matthew 13:55
When they finished, James spoke ... "Brothers," he said ...	Acts 15:13
Paul and the rest of us went to see James. All the elders ...	Acts 21:18
I, James, am writing this letter. I serve God and ... Jesus ...	James 1:1

Jeremiah

Jeremiah was a prophet of God when the kingdom of Judah had bad kings and people no longer obeyed God. He warned the people that if they kept sinning, the king of Babylon would attack Judah. The people didn't listen, and everything happened just as Jeremiah had warned. Jeremiah also prophesied about the new covenant that God would make with people. His prophecies are in the Bible in the book of Jeremiah.

HEAR THE WARNINGS OF THE PROPHET JEREMIAH!

SCHOOL LIBRARY Silence Please!

AS USUAL, THEY'RE NOT LISTENING.

Key Verse

"Before you were born I set you apart to serve me. I appointed you to be a prophet to the nations." (Jeremiah 1:5)

These are the words Jeremiah received from the Lord.	Jeremiah 1:1
I will hand all of the people of Judah over to ... Babylonia.	Jeremiah 20:4
And those nations will serve ... Babylonia for 70 years.	Jeremiah 25:11
I will make a new covenant with the people ...	Jeremiah 31:31

Jericho

Jericho is a city near the Jordan River, just above the Dead Sea and east of Jerusalem. Jericho was the first Canaanite city to be defeated by the Israelites. After they marched around the city for six days, the walls of Jericho came crashing down. Many centuries later, Jesus taught in Jericho. He healed blind Bartimaeus there, and met with Zacchaeus, the short tax collector.

Key Verse

"Then the Lord spoke to Joshua. He said, 'I have handed Jericho over to you. I have also handed its king and its fighting men over to you.'" (Joshua 6:2)

... priests blew the trumpets.... fighting men ... gave ... shout.	Joshua 6:20
They were leaving the city.... A blind man ... Bartimaeus.	Mark 10:46
A man was going from Jerusalem to Jericho. Robbers ...	Luke 10:30
Jesus entered Jericho ... Zacchaeus lived there.	Luke 19:1–2

Jerusalem

When David became king, he captured Jebus and renamed it "Jerusalem," which means "Possession of Peace." Jerusalem became the capital of Israel. Because Solomon built the temple of God there on Mount Zion, Jerusalem also became known as Zion. Over the centuries, Jerusalem was attacked, destroyed, and rebuilt many times! Jesus taught there and was crucified there, and Jerusalem became the center for the early church.

JASON'S IMAGINATION

HEY! THEY NEED CONSTRUCTION WORKERS IN JERUSALEM!

AGAIN?

BIBLE TIMES
JERUSALEM IN RUINS

Key Verse

"The king and his men marched to Jerusalem.... The Jebusites ... thought, 'David can't get in here.' But David captured the fort of Zion. It became known as the City of David." (2 Samuel 5:6–7)

It was the city the Lord had chosen out of all ... Israel.	1 Kings 14:21
The armies ... broke down the walls around Jerusalem.	2 Kings 25:10
Let me go to the city of Jerusalem.... I want to rebuild it.	Nehemiah 2:5
When Jesus entered Jerusalem ... whole city was stirred up.	Matthew 21:10

Jesus

Jesus is the Son of God, the "Messiah." Jesus was born to the virgin Mary, but he has always existed. He grew up just like any other person, except that he never sinned. He showed us what God is like by loving, healing, and taking care of people. The religious leaders didn't like Jesus. They paid one of Jesus' disciples to betray him. Jesus was arrested, tried, beaten, and crucified. He died on the cross to pay for our sins, and three days later he rose from the dead and appeared to his

followers. Jesus went up to heaven, and promised to return for us one day.

Key Verse

"Jesus was coming up out of the water. Just then he saw heaven being torn open. He saw the Holy Spirit coming down on him like a dove. A voice spoke to him from heaven. It said, 'You are my Son, and I love you. I am very pleased with you.'" (Mark 1:10–11)

You will ... give birth to a son. You must name him Jesus. — Luke 1:31
The Spirit led him into the desert.... devil tempted him ... — Luke 4:1–2
God loved the world so much that he gave his ... Son. — John 3:16
I am the light of the world. Those who follow me will ... — John 8:12
I and the Father are one. — John 10:30
Jesus [said], "I am the way and the truth and the life...." — John 14:6

Suggested Reading

Isaiah predicts the coming of Jesus. — Isaiah 53
Jesus predicts his own death. — Matthew 12:39–40
Jesus explains the cost of being his disciple. — Mark 8:34–38
Jesus is betrayed and arrested. — Mark 14:42–50
Jesus is put on trial. — Luke 22:63–23:25
Jesus will return again. — Acts 1:9–11

Didjaknow?

Another name for Jesus is "the Word" (John 1:1–14). This phrase explains that Jesus, even though he was God, became a human for our salvation. Words are how we communicate thoughts and ideas. Through Jesus, the Word, God made himself fully known to us (Hebrews 1:3).

Jesus' Birth

Jesus is God's Son and has always existed. But 2000 years ago, the Holy Spirit came upon Mary, a young virgin in Nazareth of Galilee who was engaged to be married to a carpenter named Joseph. She became pregnant "by the power of the Holy Spirit." Later, Mary and Joseph had to go to Bethlehem to be counted, and Jesus was born there.

Key Verse

"Today in the town of David a Savior has been born to you. He is Christ the Lord." (Luke 2:11)

The baby inside her is from the Holy Spirit.... Jesus.
After Jesus' birth, Wise Men from the east came ...
God sent the angel Gabriel to Nazareth ... to a virgin.
She gave birth to her first baby.... no room ... in the inn.

Matthew 1:20–21
Matthew 2:1–2
Luke 1:26–27
Luke 2:7

Jesus' Second Coming

Jesus' second coming is his return to earth. When Jesus went up into heaven, after rising from the dead, angels told the disciples that he would return the same way they saw him go. Jesus himself had promised that he would return on the clouds of the sky. He would come with power and great glory and send his angels with a loud trumpet call to gather us up in the clouds. We will meet the Lord in the air. Then we'll be with him forever. No one knows when Jesus will come back, not even the angels. But every day brings his return closer.

Key Verse

"'Men of Galilee,' they said, 'why do you stand here looking at the sky? Jesus has been taken away from you into heaven. But he will come back in the same way you saw him go.'" (Acts 1:11)

They will see the Son of Man coming on the clouds ...
The trumpet will sound, and the dead will be raised ...
The Lord himself will come down from heaven.

Matthew 24:3–31
1 Corinthians 15:52
1 Thessalonians 4:16

It has to do with the coming of our Lord Jesus Christ....   2 Thessalonians 2:1
The glorious brightness of Jesus' coming will destroy ...   2 Thessalonians 2:8
Look! He is coming with the clouds! Every eye will see ...   Revelation 1:7

Suggested Reading

The signs that happen just before Jesus returns.   Matthew 24
Information about Jesus' second coming.   1 Thessalonians
4:13–18; 5:1–11

What will happen before and during Jesus' coming.   2 Thessalonians 2
Living a godly life while waiting for Jesus' return.   2 Peter 3

Didjaknow?

Revelation 1:7 says, "Look! He is coming with the clouds! Every eye will see him!" A few years ago, people couldn't figure out how it would be possible for every person on earth to see Jesus at once, when he returns. But these days, our own TV satellites allow people all over the world to see the same live show at the same time. If we can do *that*, surely *God* can do a miracle to make all the world see Jesus at once!

Jesus Going to Heaven

After Jesus rose from the dead, the disciples saw him many times, and he taught them more about the kingdom of God. Finally, 40 days after his resurrection, Jesus led his disciples out of Jerusalem to the Mount of Olives. He lifted up his hands and blessed them, and while he was blessing them, he ascended—rose up—into heaven right before their eyes!

Key Verse

"When the Lord Jesus finished speaking to them, he was taken up into heaven. He sat down at the right hand of God." (Mark 16:19)

While he was blessing them ... was taken up into heaven.   Luke 24:51
... he was taken up ... a cloud hid him from their sight.   Acts 1:9
He provided the way ... Then he sat down at the right ...   Hebrews 1:3
He has gone into heaven. He is at God's right hand.   1 Peter 3:22

Job

Job was a rich man in the Bible who loved God. But suddenly he lost everything—his house, children, possessions, and health. Job couldn't understand why such terrible things had happened to him. He suffered horribly, but he never rejected God. Finally, Job realized how God is greater than anything that happens to us. God rewarded Job's faith by giving him back twice as much as he had before.

Key Verse

"Then the Lord said to Satan, 'Have you thought about my servant Job? There isn't anyone on earth like him. He is honest. He does what is right. He has respect for me and avoids evil. You tried to turn me against him. You wanted me to destroy him without any reason. But he still continues to be faithful.'" (Job 2:3)

In spite of everything, Job didn't say anything ... sinful.	Job 2:10
... Job ... called down a curse on the day he had been born.	Job 3:1
As long as I have life ... my mouth won't say evil things.	Job 27:3–4
After Job had prayed for his friends, the Lord made him ...	Job 42:10

John, the Apostle

John and his brother James were fishermen, but left their work to follow Jesus. John was one of Jesus' 12 apostles, and was called "the disciple Jesus loved." John and his brother James had quite a temper, and wanted to call down fire on a village. Jesus nicknamed them Boanerges, which means "Sons of Thunder." John became a strong leader in the early church. He and Peter preached the gospel in Samaria. Years later, John moved to Ephesus where he wrote his gospel and three short letters. After being imprisoned on the island of Patmos, John wrote the book of Revelation.

JASON'S IMAGINATION

THEN I HEARD A **LOUD** VOICE SPEAKING FROM THE TEMPLE TO THE SEVEN ANGELS...

NO WONDER JESUS CALLED HIM AND JAMES "SONS OF THUNDER"

Key Verse

"I, John, am a believer like you. I am a friend who suffers like you. As members of Jesus' royal family, we can put up with anything that happens to us. I was on the island of Patmos because I taught God's word and what Jesus said." (Revelation 1:9)

He saw James ... and his brother John.... in a boat ...   Mark 1:19–20
Jesus gave them the name Boanerges.... Sons of Thunder.   Mark 3:17
Then the disciple Jesus loved said to Simon Peter ...   John 21:7
... the disciple who gives witness ... wrote them down.   John 21:24
The leaders saw how bold Peter and John were.   Acts 4:13
James, Peter and John are considered to be pillars in ...   Galatians 2:9
... revelation ... God made it known ... to his servant John.   Revelation 1:1

Suggested Reading

Jesus calls James and John to follow him.   Matthew 4:18–22
John and James want to see a village burn up.   Luke 9:51–56
John and Peter heal a lame man and go to prison.   Acts 3–4
John and Peter preach in Samaria.   Acts 8:4–25

Didjaknow?

John did not speak very good Greek. His original language was Aramaic. He probably had help writing the gospel of John, because its Greek is good. He must have written the book of Revelation by himself, however, because it was written in quite bad Greek. Jesus told him, "Write down what you have seen." So he did. And considering that Greek wasn't his favorite subject, he did a pretty good job.

John the Baptist

John the Baptist's parents were too old to have children, but God did a miracle (Luke 1) and he was born! John was the messenger God sent to announce the coming of Jesus. He was also Jesus' cousin. People came from all over to hear John preach in the desert and to be baptized by him in the Jordan River. Jesus was baptized by John also.

Key Verse

"In those days John the Baptist came and preached in the Desert of Judea. He said, 'Turn away from your sins! The kingdom of heaven is near.'" (Matthew 3:1–2)

A messenger is calling ... "In the desert prepare the ..."   Isaiah 40:3–11
Jesus came from Galilee ... to be baptized by John.   Matthew 3:13
John wore clothes ... of camel's hair.... he ate locusts ...   Mark 1:6
I want you to give me the head of John the Baptist ...   Mark 6:25

Jonah

Jonah was a prophet in the Old Testament that God sent to Nineveh. Nineveh was Israel's enemy, so Jonah didn't want to go. He tried to run away from God but ended up getting swallowed by a huge fish. When Jonah prayed to God for help, the fish spit him out onto dry land. Then Jonah preached to Nineveh. The people believed God's warning and stopped sinning.

JASON'S IMAGINATION

SPIT IT OUT. YOU KNOW YOU'RE NOT SUPPOSE TO PUT THAT KIND OF THING IN YOUR MOUTH. YOU DON'T KNOW WHERE IT'S BEEN.

Helllllpppp!

Key Verse

"But Jonah ran away from the Lord. He headed for Tarshish. So he went down to the port of Joppa. There he found a ship that was going to Tarshish. He paid the fare and went on board.... He was running away from the Lord." (Jonah 1:3)

Then they took Jonah and threw him overboard.	Jonah 1:15
But the Lord sent a huge fish to swallow Jonah.	Jonah 1:17
The Lord gave the fish a command. And it spit Jonah up ...	Jonah 2:10
... sign ... none will be given except the sign of Jonah.	Luke 11:29

Jordan River

The Jordan River is the longest and most important river in Palestine. In the spring, when the Jordan was overflowing its banks, God parted its waters for Joshua and the Israelites to allow them to enter the Promised Land, Canaan, after they left Egypt. Thousands of years later, John baptized people in the Jordan River. Jesus' disciples baptized there also.

Key Verse

"My servant Moses is dead. Now then, I want you and all of these people to get ready to go across the Jordan River. I want all of you to go into the land I am about to give to the people of Israel." (Joshua 1:2)

... the whole Jordan River valley had plenty of water.	Genesis 13:10
As soon as the priests step into the Jordan, it will stop ...	Joshua 3:13
All of them rushed down to the Jordan River.	2 Samuel 19:17–18
Jesus came from Galilee to the Jordan ... to be baptized.	Matthew 3:13

Joseph (son of Jacob)

Joseph was the second youngest of Jacob's (Israel's) twelve sons. He was also his father's favorite. Jacob gave Joseph a special coat. This made Joseph's brothers very jealous, so they sold him as a slave into Egypt. As a slave, Joseph kept loving and obeying God, but he was falsely accused and ended up in prison anyway. Years later, God helped him explain a dream to the pharaoh, or king, of Egypt—a huge famine was coming! Pharaoh told Joseph to get Egypt ready. When Joseph's family came for food, Joseph forgave his brothers, and invited them and his father to live in Egypt.

Key Verse

"Israel loved Joseph more than any of his other sons. Joseph had been born to him when he was old. Israel made him a beautiful robe. Joseph's brothers saw that their father loved him more than any of them. So they hated Joseph. They couldn't even speak one kind word to him." (Genesis 37:3–4)

Joseph's brothers ... sold him to the Ishmaelite traders ...	Genesis 37:28
The Lord was with Joseph. He gave him great success.	Genesis 39:2
Joseph said ... "Only God knows what dreams mean."	Genesis 40:8
Pharaoh said ... "I'm putting you in charge of ... Egypt."	Genesis 41:41
Joseph recognized his brothers, but they didn't ...	Genesis 42:8
Joseph had faith. So he spoke ... about their leaving Egypt.	Hebrews 11:22

Suggested Reading

Joseph dreams he would rule over his brothers.	Genesis 37:5–11
Joseph runs from Potiphar's wife.	Genesis 39
Joseph interprets Pharaoh's dreams.	Genesis 41:14–43
Joseph reveals himself to his brothers.	Genesis 45:1–15
Joseph forgives his brothers.	Genesis 50:15–21

Didjaknow?

After Israel and his sons moved to Egypt, their descendants quickly increased in number. A later pharaoh, who didn't remember Joseph, made the Israelites into slaves and used them to build treasure cities. He ordered their newborn babies to be killed. He did this because he was afraid that the Israelites might take over the country one day. God saved the Israelites from slavery and led them out of Egypt in the Exodus.

Joseph (husband of Mary)

Joseph was thought to be Jesus' father, but God was his real father. Joseph was a carpenter. When he discovered that his fiancée, Mary, was pregnant, he planned to divorce her. But an angel told him that Mary was pregnant with the Savior, so Joseph married her. Not long afterward, they went to Joseph's hometown, Bethlehem, to register for a count of the people. That's where Jesus was born.

Key Verse

"This is how the birth of Jesus Christ came about. His mother Mary and Joseph had promised to get married. But before they started to live together, it became clear that she was going to have a baby. She became pregnant by the power of the Holy Spirit." (Matthew 1:18)

Her husband Joseph was a godly man.... he planned to ...	Matthew 1:19
The angel said, "Joseph ... don't be afraid to take Mary ..."	Matthew 1:20
When the Wise Men had left, Joseph had a dream.	Matthew 2:13–18
Joseph had a dream while he was still in Egypt.	Matthew 2:19–23

Joshua

Joshua was Moses' helper from when he was young. Shortly after they left Egypt, Moses put Joshua in charge of the Israelite army. When the Amelekites attacked them, Joshua defeated them (Exodus 17:8–15). Joshua was one of the 12 spies sent into Canaan to check out the land. Only he and Caleb told the people that, with God's help, they could conquer Canaan. After the Israelites wandered 40 years in the desert, Moses died and left Joshua in charge of the people of Israel. Joshua led the armies of Israel into Canaan and, after seven years of war, they had conquered most of the land.

Key Verse

"I lifted up my hand and promised with an oath to make this land your home. But now not all of you will enter the land. Caleb, the son of Jephunneh, will enter it. So will Joshua, the son of Nun. They are the only ones who will enter the land." (Numbers 14:30)

Joshua heard the noise of the people shouting.	Exodus 32:17
Joshua had been Moses' helper [since] he was young.	Numbers 11:28
Only two ... remained alive. One of them was Joshua ...	Numbers 14:38
Then I sent for Joshua. I spoke to him in front of all ...	Deuteronomy 31:7
On that day, Joshua ... said, "Sun, stand still ... Moon ..."	Joshua 10:12
But as for me and my family, we will serve the Lord.	Joshua 24:15

Suggested Reading

Joshua and the spies check out Canaan.	Numbers 13:1–14:33
Joshua leads the Israelites against Jericho.	Joshua 5:13–6:27

Didjaknow?

Joshua's name is a Hebrew word that means "the Lord is salvation." By his name and by his life, Joshua showed that salvation comes from God. In Greek, Joshua is pronounced *Jesus*. So you see, Jesus' name had special meaning too!

Joy

Joy is a lasting happiness. Human happiness comes and goes depending on what's happening. But joy, a deep, cheerful contentment, sticks with us no matter what. It is a "fruit of the Spirit." Being joyful doesn't mean always being happy or getting what we want. But when we remember that Jesus died to save us, and that he loves us, we can have joy.

Key Verse

"The joy of the Lord makes you strong." (Nehemiah 8:10)

Shout to the Lord with joy, everyone on earth.	Psalm 100:1
... the fruit the Holy Spirit produces is love, joy and peace.	Galatians 5:22
You welcomed our message with the joy the Holy Spirit ...	1 Thessalonians 1:6
You will face all kinds of trouble.... think of it as pure joy.	James 1:2–4

Judah, Tribe of

Judah was one of the 12 sons of Jacob. Like Jacob's other sons, his descendants became an entire tribe. By the time they left Egypt, there were 74,600 men in Judah (Numbers 1:1, 27). When they entered the land of Canaan, the tribe of Judah was given all the land between the Dead Sea and the Mediterranean Sea. King David was from Judah, and he made Jerusalem the capital of all Israel. But after the northern tribes left the kingdom, David's sons were only left with Judah to rule. Judah was now a nation, not just a tribe. Jesus, the Son of God, came from the tribe of Judah.

JASON'S IMAGINATION

OK, THE NORTHERN TRIBES ARE GONE. ALL WE HAVE LEFT IS THE TRIBE OF JUDAH. THEY'RE CALLING THEMSELVES ISRAEL SO WE CAN'T USE THAT NAME. ANY IDEAS WHAT TO CALL OURSELVES?

ISRAEL

?

Key Verse

"Instead, he [God] chose to live in the tribe of Judah. He chose Mount Zion, which he loved. There he built his holy place as secure as the heavens." (Psalm 78:68–69)

She became pregnant again. She had a son.... Judah.	Genesis 29:35
Only the tribe of Judah remained true to David's ... family.	1 Kings 12:20
Sennacherib ... captured all of the cities of Judah ...	2 Kings 18:13
... the Lord was angry.... he threw [Judah] out of his land.	2 Kings 24:20
Bethlehem, in the land of Judah ... A ruler will come out ...	Matthew 2:4–6
The Lion of the tribe of Judah [Jesus] has won the battle!	Revelation 5:5

Suggested Reading

Only Judah remains faithful to the sons of David.	1 Kings 12
Judah is taken over by the kingdom of Babylon.	2 Kings 24–25
The tribe of Judah returns to its homeland.	Ezra 2

Didjaknow?

Jacob's four oldest sons were Reuben, then Simeon, Levi, and Judah (Genesis 29:31–35). Reuben didn't get the birthright and blessing belonging to the eldest because he sinned sexually (Genesis 35:22). Simeon and Levi were next, but they didn't get the blessing because they were guilty of murder (Genesis 34:20–30). Jacob wanted Joseph and his sons to be first (Genesis 48:20–22). But Judah was actually next in line, so God gave *him* the blessing (Psalm 78:67–70).

Judas Iscariot

Judas was the disciple in charge of the disciples' money. He was also the disciple who betrayed Jesus. He believed Jesus was the Messiah—at first. But when Jesus didn't fight against the Romans, as Judas thought he should, he betrayed him to the religious leaders. The Pharisees gave Judas 30 silver coins to help them secretly arrest Jesus. After Jesus died, Judas felt so guilty that he killed himself.

Key Verse

"'The Son of Man will go just as it is written about him. But how terrible it will be for the one who hands over the Son of Man!' ... Judas was the one who was going to hand him over. He said, 'It's not I, Rabbi, is it?' Jesus answered, 'Yes. It is you.'" (Matthew 26:24–25)

One of the Twelve went to the chief priests.... Judas ...	Matthew 26:14–16
Judas ... felt deep shame and sadness for what he had ...	Matthew 27:3
So Judas went to Jesus at once.... he kissed him.	Mark 14:45
Judas bought a field with the reward he got for the evil ...	Acts 1:18–19

Judge

Judges were people God raised up to lead the Israelites. After Joshua died, the Israelites had no leader, and they turned away from God. God sent armies from other nations to punish them. Then the Israelites prayed and asked God to save them. God helped the judges defeat Israel's enemies. Famous judges include Samson, Gideon, Deborah, and Ehud. Their stories are in the book of Judges.

Key Verse

"When the Lord gave them a leader, he was with that leader. He saved the people from the power of their enemies." (Judges 2:18)

When the leader died, the people returned to ... evil ...	Judges 2:19
They cried out to the Lord.... he gave them a man to ...	Judges 3:9
[Deborah] served the people as their judge.	Judges 4:5
Israel didn't have a king. The people did anything ...	Judges 21:25

Justice

Justice means "punishing evil and rewarding righteousness." It also means not favoring anyone or taking bribes, but being fair to everyone—just as God is—judging rich and poor the same. The Old Testament prophets preached against injustice against the poor. The poor were often mistreated in court because the judges accepted money for favors, which poor people couldn't afford to buy.

Key Verse

"They must judge the people fairly. Do what is right. Treat everyone the same. Don't take money from people who want special favors. It makes those who are wise close their eyes to the truth.... Follow only what is right." (Deuteronomy 16:18–20)

Be fair to your poor people in their court cases.	Exodus 23:6
The Lord ... loves it when people do what is fair.	Psalm 11:7
How terrible ... for you who make laws that aren't fair!	Isaiah 10:1
King of the ages, your ways are true and fair.	Revelation 15:3

Kindness

Kindness is a "fruit of the Spirit." It is being pleasant, helpful, and considerate to everyone, no matter who they are or what they've done. It means being kind every day, all the time, not just when we feel like it. We should be kind to others because God showed kindness to us by saving us from our sins when we didn't know him.

Key Verse

"Think about how kind God is! Also think about how firm he is! He was hard on those who stopped following him. But he is kind to you. So you must continue to live in his kindness. If you don't, you also will be cut off." (Romans 11:22)

But I will show you my loving concern.	Isaiah 54:8
No matter what I do ... I am always kind, fair and right.	Jeremiah 9:24
The fruit the Holy Spirit produces is ... being ... kind ...	Galatians 5:22
So put on tender mercy and kindness as ... your clothes.	Colossians 3:12

King

A king is the leader of a kingdom. Kings usually inherited their position and ruled until they died or their kingdom was conquered. God was the first king of Israel, and he is "the greatest King of all" (1 Timothy 6:15). But the Israelites wanted a human king. God warned them against it, but they insisted. God chose Saul as their first king. Saul wandered away from God, so God replaced Saul with David, who was a good king. Later kings strayed from God. Jesus, a descendant of king David, is also called "the King of the Jews."

UH... JASON, NOW THAT YOU'RE OUR KING, IT'S YOUR DUTY TO WALK AT THE HEAD OF OUR ARMY AS WE GO INTO BATTLE.

WHAAAT?

Key Verse

"In spite of what Samuel said, the people refused to listen to him. 'No!' they said. 'We want a king to rule over us. Then we'll be like all of the other nations. We'll have a king to lead us. He'll go out at the head of our armies and fight our battles." (1 Samuel 8:19–20)

[God said] ... "I am the one they do not want as ... king."	1 Samuel 8:7
Here's what the king who rules over you will do.	1 Samuel 8:11
The governor asked him, "Are you the king of the Jews?"	Matthew 27:11, 29
So they ... shouted, "... Blessed is the King of Israel!"	John 12:13
... obey ... Those who now rule have been chosen by God.	Romans 13:1
The eternal King will never die.... He is the only God.	1 Timothy 1:17

Suggested Reading

The Israelites ask Samuel for a king.	1 Samuel 8
Saul is chosen as king.	1 Samuel 10:20–27
The people and king must obey God.	1 Samuel 12:12–15

Didjaknow?

In ancient Egypt the king, or "pharaoh," was worshiped as a god. In Assyria the king represented a god. Later, even Roman emperors claimed to be gods. Of course, the kings weren't gods, but they let their people believe it, because it gave them greater authority over them. Disobedience to the king was thought to be the same as disobedience to a god, and it was usually punished by death.

Kingdom (of God)

A kingdom is a region, city, or nation ruled by a king. Jesus often preached about the "kingdom of God," or the "kingdom of heaven." But it was a very different kingdom from the one people expected. His kingdom was not of this world at all. It was a spiritual kingdom. It was about loving and caring for others and obeying God.

Key Verse

"God's kingdom has nothing to do with eating or drinking. It is a matter of being right with God. It brings the peace and joy the Holy Spirit gives." (Romans 14:17)

But it is even harder for the rich to enter God's kingdom.	Matthew 19:24
God's kingdom is among you.	Luke 17:21
... who will not receive God's kingdom like a little child ...	Luke 18:15–17
No one can see God's kingdom without being born again.	John 3:3

Knowledge

Knowledge is the awareness and understanding of people, places, things, and ideas. Knowledge is not very useful by itself. We need wisdom to teach us how to use it. Respect for God is the beginning of all knowledge and wisdom. Therefore, if we want knowledge, we should ask God for it, and the wisdom to know how to use it.

Key Verse

"If you really want to gain knowledge, you must begin by having respect for the Lord. But foolish people hate wisdom and training." (Proverbs 1:7)

Apply your heart ... Listen carefully to ... knowledge.	Proverbs 23:12
How very rich are God's wisdom and knowledge!	Romans 11:33–36
Knowledge makes people proud.	1 Corinthians 8:1
... treasures of wisdom and knowledge are hidden in him.	Colossians 2:3

Lamb, Passover

A lamb is a young sheep. In the Old Testament, God told the Israelites to kill a pure lamb and put its blood on their doorposts so God's angel would pass over them and not kill their oldest child. This event was celebrated as the "Passover." In the New Testament, Jesus was the pure Passover Lamb killed for everyone. Jesus was nailed to a cross during the Passover feast, and when people put his blood on the "doors" of their hearts, God "passes over" them and forgives their sins. Jesus died so that we could live, just as the Passover lamb died so the oldest child could live.

Key Verse

> "Then Moses sent for all of the elders of Israel. He said to them, 'Go at once. Choose the animals for your families. Each family must kill a Passover lamb.'" (Exodus 12:21)

The animals you choose ... must not have any flaws.	Exodus 12:5
Each family must kill a Passover lamb.	Exodus 12:21–23
The Lamb of God! He takes away the sin of the world!	John 1:29
Christ has been offered up for us. He is our Passover lamb.	1 Corinthians 5:7
Christ ... is a perfect lamb. He doesn't have any flaws ...	1 Peter 1:19
The Lamb, who was put to death, is worthy!	Revelation 5:12

Suggested Reading

The story of the first Passover, and the reason for it.	Exodus 11–12
Lambs are used as sin offerings in the Old Testament.	Leviticus 4:32–35
Isaiah compares Jesus to a lamb.	Isaiah 53
John sees Jesus as a Lamb in heaven.	Revelation 5

Didjaknow?

The Law of Moses instructed, "Do not break any of the bones" of the Passover lamb (Exodus 12:46). Jesus was our Passover Lamb, but when he was crucified with the two thieves, the chief priests ordered the Romans to break their legs so that they'd die more quickly. The Romans did this to the thieves, but Jesus had already died, so they didn't break his legs (John 19:31–36).

Law of Moses

God wanted his people to have a relationship with him, so at Mount Sinai he gave laws to Moses that let them know who he was and how he wanted them to live. Besides the Ten Commandments, God gave them many rules about food, cleanliness, sacrifices, morals, and all areas of life. The only problem was, it was impossible for anyone to keep all the laws and never break them. Because we're sinful, Jesus had to die for our sins to save us. Now Christians are free from the Jewish law. The important thing now is to obey God's Spirit and live a godly life.

Key Verse

"Before faith in Christ came, we were held prisoners by the law. We were locked up until faith was made known.... But now faith in Christ has come. So we are no longer under the control of the law." (Galatians 3:23, 25)

I will give you the stone tablets. They contain the law ...	Exodus 24:12
I have taught ... laws, just as the Lord ... commanded me.	Deuteronomy 4:5
Moses gave us the law. Jesus Christ has given us grace ...	John 1:17
The law you received was brought by angels. But you ...	Acts 7:53
All who depend on obeying the law are under a curse.	Galatians 3:10
What was the purpose of the law? It was added ...	Galatians 3:19

Suggested Reading

God gives Moses the law on Mount Sinai.	Exodus 19–23
God gives the law, and the Israelites are to obey it.	Deuteronomy 4–6
Christians are no longer under the Law of Moses.	Galatians 3–5

Didjaknow?

God gave the Law of Moses to the Jews to show them how to live. But over the centuries, the Jews made up thousands of their own rules and traditions—called the *Mishnah*—so they would know exactly how to obey the Law. The Mishnah was passed down by word of mouth and called the Oral Law. Many Jews considered their own traditions to be more important than God's Law. But the Mishnah missed the point. Not only did many of its laws contradict the Law of Moses, but God wants us to obey him from our hearts, out of love, not from fear or just to "do everything right" so he won't be angry.

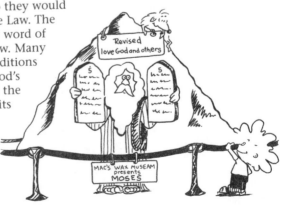

Lazarus

Lazarus was the brother of Mary and Martha, who lived in Bethany, near Jerusalem. Jesus loved Lazarus and his sisters, and often stayed at their house (Luke 10:38–39). One day Lazarus became sick and died. When Jesus arrived four days later, he raised Lazarus from the dead! After he did that, many Jews put their faith in Jesus (John 12:11).

Key Verse

"Then Jesus called in a loud voice. He said, 'Lazarus, come out!' The dead man came out. His hands and feet were wrapped with strips of linen. A cloth was around his face." (John 11:43–44)

A man named Lazarus was sick. He was from Bethany ...   John 11:1
Jesus loved Martha and her sister and Lazarus.   John 11:5
But, Lord ... Lazarus has been in the tomb for four days.   John 11:39
... came to see Lazarus. After all, Jesus had raised him ...   John 12:9

Learning

Learning is not just studying in school, but finding out life's important lessons. The Bible says to listen carefully to advice. If you listen you'll learn, gain knowledge, and grow wise. When a wise man is taught, he learns and becomes wiser. If you refuse to learn, you'll only hurt yourself. So keep an open mind. Intelligent people are always open to learn new things.

Key Verse

"Apply your heart to what you are taught. Listen carefully to words of knowledge." (Proverbs 23:12)

If you really want to gain knowledge ... begin by having ...   Proverbs 1:7–8
Let your ears listen to wisdom. Apply your heart to ...   Proverbs 2:2
Anyone who loves to be trained loves knowledge.   Proverbs 12:1
Everything that was written in the past was written to ...   Romans 15:4

Leper/Leprosy

Leprosy is a terrible skin disease that can't normally be cured. Sometimes other skin diseases are also called "leprosy" in the Old Testament. Naaman, one of the generals of the Aramean army, had leprosy. He went to see Elisha, dipped seven times in the Jordan River, and was cured (2 Kings 5:1–19). Jesus healed many people who had leprosy and other skin diseases.

Key Verse

"A man who had a skin disease [leprosy] came and got down on his knees in front of Jesus. He said, 'Lord, if you are willing to make me "clean", you can do it.' Jesus reached out his hand and touched the man. 'I am willing to do it,' he said. 'Be "clean"!' Right away the man was healed of his skin disease." (Matthew 8:2–3)

He must cry out, "Unclean! Unclean!" ... He must live ...	Leviticus 13:45–46
... making someone "clean" if he has had a skin disease.	Leviticus 14:1
Naaman was commander ... But he had a skin disease.	2 Kings 5:1
Those who have skin diseases are healed. Deaf people ...	Matthew 11:5

Life, Eternal

Life comes from God. Without God, our spirits die. That's why Jesus died for our sins: so we can be alive in our *spirits* again, and live with him in heaven. *Forever!* And life in heaven is really going to be *living!* The body you have here on earth is an imperfect, short-term body that your soul lives in. It's not made to last. But God is going to change our physical bodies and make them powerful and awesome! God will reward each of us for the good we've done, and we'll have spiritual bodies that will live forever!

JASON'S IMAGINATION

Key Verse

"Here is God's witness. He has given us eternal life. That life is found in his Son. Those who belong to the Son have life." (1 John 5:11–12)

He said, "I am the God of Abraham...." He is the God of ...	Matthew 22:32
Anyone who believes in him will ... have eternal life.	John 3:16
And those who live and believe in me will never die.	John 11:26

The body that is raised from the dead lasts forever. 1 Corinthians 15:42
We will meet the Lord in the air. And we will be with ... 1 Thessalonians
4:17
They will have the right to come to the tree of life. Revelation 22:14

Suggested Reading
The new, eternal bodies God will give us. 1 Corinthians
15:35–58
What it's like to be with Jesus in heaven. Revelation 7:9–17
What eternal life in heaven will be like. Revelation 21–22

Didjaknow?
Does eternal life only start when you get to heaven? No. Once Jesus has given you life, you have it already, right *now!* "Anyone who believes in the Son *has* eternal life" (John 3:36). John said, "I'm writing these things to you who believe in the name of the Son of God.... so you will know that you *have* eternal life" (1 John 5:13).

Lion

Long ago, lions lived in Israel. David once killed a lion with a sling to protect his sheep. Samson killed a lion with his bare hands (Judges 14:5–6). The prophet Daniel was thrown into a pit full of lions (Daniel 6:16). The devil is "like a roaring lion" (1 Peter 5:8). But Jesus is even stronger. He's the "Lion of the tribe of Judah" (Revelation 5:5).

JASON'S IMAGINATION

OK, FIFTY-TWO BLUE! SIXTEEN, FOUR! READY! DOWN! SET...

Key Verse
"Three things walk as if they were kings. Four things move as kings do. The first is a lion. It is mighty among the animals. It doesn't back away from anything." (Proverbs 30:29–30)

But David said ... "I've killed both a lion and a bear." 1 Samuel 17:34–36
... sinful people ... are like a hungry lion, waiting to attack. Psalm 17:9–12
But those who do what is right are as bold as lions. Proverbs 28:1
Lions will eat straw ... None of those animals will harm ... Isaiah 11:7–9

Long for
(See Covet)

Lord's Day

In the Bible the Sabbath, a special day of rest, was celebrated on Saturday. These days, we rest and meet with other Christians on Sunday because, after Jesus rose from the dead on Sunday "the first day of the week," Sunday became known as "the Lord's Day." In Acts, Christians met on Sunday. We follow their example and meet then to worship God.

Key Verse

"Jesus rose from the dead early on the first day of the week [Sunday]. He appeared first to Mary Magdalene." (Mark 16:9)

... evening of that first day of the week ... Jesus came in ...	John 20:19
On the first day of the week we met ... Paul spoke ...	Acts 20:7
Let us not give up meeting together.... cheer each other ...	Hebrews 10:25
The Holy Spirit took ... control of me on the Lord's Day.	Revelation 1:10

Lord's Supper

Christians celebrate the Lord's Supper, Communion, because Jesus told us to. The first Lord's Supper was when Jesus and his disciples ate their last Passover meal together the night before he died. He told us to do it to remember him and what he did when he died for us. We also eat the bread and drink from the cup to show that we belong to Jesus.

WAX MUSEUM

Key Verse

"When we give thanks for the cup at the Lord's Supper, aren't we sharing in the blood of Christ? When we break the bread, aren't we sharing in the body of Christ?" (1Corinthians 10:16)

I have ... looked forward to eating this Passover meal ...	Luke 22:15
This is my body.... Every time you eat it, do it in ...	Luke 22:19
On the night ... Jesus was handed over ... he took bread.	1 Corinthians 11:23
Anyone who eats ... must recognize the body of the Lord.	1 Corinthians 11:29

Love

Love is a strong feeling of liking and accepting a person. Loving someone also means doing what's best for the person. We show our love by what we do. The two greatest commandments in the Bible are to love God and to love other people. The apostle John wrote, "God is love" (1 John 4:8), and God loved us so much that he gave up his only Son, so that we could be saved. "Since God loved us that much, we should also love one another" (1 John 4:11). Paul wrote 1 Corinthians 13 to explain what real love is. Paul knew that only Christians with God's Holy Spirit could love in this way.

Key Verse

"'Love the Lord your God with all your heart and with all your soul. Love him with all your mind.' This is the first and most important commandment. And the second is like it. 'Love your neighbor as you love yourself.'" (Matthew 22:37–39)

... you are a God who is tender and kind.... full of love.	Psalm 86:15
I have loved you with a love that lasts forever.	Jeremiah 31:3
If you love one another, everyone will know you are ...	John 13:35
Lead a life of love, just as Christ did. He loved us.	Ephesians 5:2
How did God show his love for us? He sent his ... Son ...	1 John 4:9
Anyone who loves God must also love his brothers ...	1 John 4:21

Suggested Reading

God describes himself to Moses.	Exodus 34:5–7
What true Christian love is all about.	1 Corinthians 13
Why we must love one another.	1 John 4:7–21

Didjaknow?

How do you know if you're a Christian? You believe in Jesus and love others. First John 3:23 says, "God has commanded us to believe in the name of his Son, Jesus Christ. He has also commanded us to love one another." If you're a Christian, you'll love others. If you don't love your brother or sister whom you have seen, you can't love God whom you have not seen (1 John 4:20).

Luke

Luke was a doctor who traveled with the apostle Paul and helped preach the gospel. Luke wrote two books in the New Testament. He wrote a gospel for the Gentiles: The gospel of Luke talks about how much Jesus cares for poor people and for people nobody else likes. Luke also wrote a history of the early church called the book of Acts.

Key Verse

"Theophilus, I wrote about Jesus in my earlier book. I wrote about all he did and taught until the day he was taken up to heaven." (Acts 1:1–2)

... orderly report ... things you have been taught are true.
Our dear friend Luke, the doctor, sends greetings.
Demas has deserted me.... Only Luke is with me.
Mark, Aristarchus ... and Luke work together with me.

Luke 1:3–4
Colossians 4:14
2 Timothy 4:10–11
Philemon 24

Lying

Lying is saying something you know is not true, or making people think something that isn't true. We should always tell the truth because God always tells the truth, and because he is truth. Sometimes we lie when we do something wrong and don't want to be punished, or lie to get something we shouldn't have, or go somewhere we shouldn't go. "Little white lies" are not OK, nor is lying "once in a while." It is never right to lie. Lying goes against God. It ruins friendships and makes it hard for others to trust us. But people who tell the truth are trusted and have solid relationships.

Key Verse

"Don't lie to each other. You have gotten rid of your old way of life and its habits." (Colossians 3:9)

Keep me from cheating and telling lies.... teach me ...   Psalm 119:29
The Lord hates those whose lips tell lies. But he is ...   Proverbs 12:22
... the devil ... no truth in him.... is a liar.... father of lies.   John 8:44
... you must get rid of your lying. Speak the truth to your ...   Ephesians 4:25
God promised to give that life. And he does not lie.   Titus 1:2
He didn't ... sin. No lies ever came out of his mouth.   1 Peter 2:22

Suggested Reading

Abram gets in trouble for telling a half-truth.   Genesis 12:10–20
Jacob lies and deceives, and has to run away.   Genesis 27:1–45
Ananias and Sapphira lie, and die as a result.   Acts 5:1–10

Didjaknow?

What would you do if you were in a movie theater and a crazy person ran in and started shooting flaming arrows everywhere? You'd duck under your seat and hope someone calls the police, right? Did you know that *lying* is like that? Proverbs 26:18–19 says, "Suppose a crazy person shoots flaming arrows that can kill. A man who lies to his neighbor and says, 'I was only joking!' is just like that person." Wow! No wonder James 3:6 says, "The tongue also is a fire."

Made Fun of

Sometimes other kids may make fun of you, tease you, mock you, and call you names just because you are a Christian. They may dislike you and try to make life as miserable as possible for you because you are trying to live right. Jesus said not to try to get even when people make fun of you, but to pray for them and love them (Matthew 5:44).

HEY, BIBLE BOY!

MOCKERY RESISTANT

RIDICULE PROOF

Key Verse

"Blessed are you when people hate you, when they have nothing to do with you and say bad things about you, and when they treat your name as something evil. They do all this because you are followers of the Son of Man." (Luke 6:22)

Proud people are always making fun of me. But I don't ...   Psalm 119:51
Blessed ... when people make fun of you and hurt you ...   Matthew 5:11
They will make fun of [Jesus]. They will laugh at him ...   Luke 18:32
God ... pay back trouble to those who give you trouble.   2 Thessalonians 1:6

Magic

There is no such thing as *white* magic and *good* witches. The Bible warns God's people to have nothing to do with magic, witchcraft, astrology, or mediums, because these things are evil. When Paul was preaching the gospel, a magician called Elymas opposed him. In Ephesus, many people who had practiced magic repented and became Christians. They burned all of their books (Acts 19:19). Astrology is the belief that

the stars and planets influence life on earth. The Bible tells us not to waste time with such foolishness. A medium is someone who tries to contact the spirits of the dead. The Bible says this is absolutely forbidden!

Key Verse

> "They listen to those who practice all kinds of evil magic. But you belong to the Lord your God. He says you must not do those things." (Deuteronomy 18:14)

The Lord hates those practices.... things you must not do ...	Deuteronomy 18:9–10
Some will tell you to ... [hear from] those who have died.	Isaiah 8:19
They claim to know [the future] by watching the stars ...	Isaiah 47:13–15
A man named Simon ... had practiced evil magic there.	Acts 8:9
... evil magician ... tried to keep the governor from ...	Acts 13:8
... lake of fire ... who practice witchcraft will go there.	Revelation 21:8

Suggested Reading

God reveals mysteries, astrologers and magic can't.	Daniel 2
Simon the magician is saved, but still needs prayer.	Acts 8:4–24

Didjaknow?

When stage performers do "magic tricks," this is not evil magic. They're just doing clever tricks, and everyone knows it. The great escape artist, Harry Houdini, could escape out of all kinds of chains and locked trunks. He also did amazing "magic tricks." But he admitted it wasn't magic. He also went around exposing mediums and spiritists who pretended to contact the dead. He proved that they were fakes who deceived people to earn money.

Manna

Manna was the food that God miraculously provided for the Israelites in the wilderness during their Exodus from Egypt. Each morning the ground around the Israelite camp was white with flakes that looked like frost and tasted sweet. Manna could be baked, boiled, ground, beaten, cooked in pans, or made into cakes.

Key Verse

"The people of Israel called the bread manna. It was white like coriander seeds. It tasted like wafers that were made with honey." (Exodus 16:31)

Get two quarts of manna. Keep it for all time.	Exodus 16:32–34
The people of Israel ate manna for 40 years.	Exodus 16:35
We never see anything but this manna!	Numbers 11:6
I am the living bread that came down from heaven.	John 6:51

Mark

Mark was the cousin of Barnabas. He went on a missionary trip with Paul and Barnabas, but then left them and turned back. After that, Paul didn't want to work with him. Later, Paul forgave Mark and they worked together. Mark also worked with Peter and wrote a gospel. His gospel is full of action and often uses words like "immediately" and "as soon as."

Key Verse

"Get Mark and bring him with you. He helps me in my work for the Lord." (2 Timothy 4:11)

... Mary's house. Mary was the mother of John Mark.	Acts 12:12
Paul didn't think it was wise ... Mark had deserted them ...	Acts 15:36–39
... his greetings. So does Mark, the cousin of Barnabas.	Colossians 4:10
Mark, my son in the faith, also sends you his greetings.	1 Peter 5:13

Marriage

Marriage is the joining of a man and a woman as husband and wife. When people get married, they promise to love and be faithful to each other and to physically love only each other for the rest of their lives. This is the most important and holy promise a man and a woman can make to each other and to God.

God's plan for men and women who love each other is for them to get married and support and love each other always. Then, when they have a family, their children will be loved, secure, and well cared for.

Key Verse

"That's why a man will leave his father and mother and be joined to his wife. The two of them will become one." (Genesis 2:24)

So a man must not separate what God has joined together.	Matthew 19:6
... each man should have his own wife.... each woman ...	1 Corinthians 7:2
Husbands, love your wives.... just as Christ loved ...	Ephesians 5:25
... should honor marriage.... keep the marriage bed pure.	Hebrews 13:4

Suggested Reading

Married people should not separate.	Matthew 19:3–12
Paul gives Christians advice about marriage.	1 Corinthians 7

Didjaknow?

Most men in the Old Testament had only one wife like people today. But some men, usually kings or rich men, would marry several women at once. (Solomon had 700 wives!) A king might marry a princess from a neighboring country, for example, to make peace with that country. Other men married more than one wife because their first wives couldn't have children. No matter what the reason, God never wanted men to live this way. His plan is for a man to have one wife, and for a woman to have only one husband.

Mary

Mary was the mother of Jesus. She lived in the town of Nazareth in Galilee. While she was engaged to a man named Joseph, God sent an angel to tell her that she would become pregnant by the Holy Spirit. She would give birth to a son who would be the Messiah. Mary believed God, and she gave birth to Jesus in Bethlehem.

JASON'S IMAGINATION

OH MARY, DO I HAVE TO GO? I ENJOY BABY-SITTING JESUS SO MUCH!

I KNOW WHAT YOU MEAN.

Key Verse

"But the angel said to her, 'Do not be afraid, Mary. God is very pleased with you. You will become pregnant and give birth to a son. You must name him Jesus." (Luke 1:30–31)

"I serve the Lord," Mary answered. "May it happen ..."   Luke 1:38
Mary said, "My soul gives glory to the Lord."   Luke 1:46
But Mary kept all these things like ... treasure in her heart. Luke 2:19
Jesus' mother stood near his cross.   John 19:25

Mary Magdalene

Rabbis didn't teach women. But Jesus did! Jesus had several women followers who traveled with him. One of these women was Mary Magdalene. She stood at his cross, and later watched him be buried. After Jesus' death, Mary Magdalene and some other women came to the tomb, where Mary was the first person to see Jesus alive again! Women were important to Jesus!

Key Verse

"He [Jesus] announced the good news of God's kingdom. The Twelve were with him. So were some women who had been healed of evil spirits and sicknesses. One was Mary Magdalene. Seven demons had come out of her." (Luke 8:1–2)

Jesus rose ... He appeared first to Mary Magdalene.   Mark 16:9
Mary Magdalene.... to support Jesus ... their own money.   Luke 8:2–3
... mother stood near his cross. So did ... Mary Magdalene.   John 19:25
Mary Magdalene went to the disciples with the news.   John 20:18

Matthew

When Jesus began to preach, he chose 12 men to travel with him and to teach. One of them was Matthew, also known as Levi. He was a tax collector when Jesus chose him. He left everything and happily followed Jesus. Matthew wrote the first gospel. His gospel was written for Jews and shows that Jesus is the Messiah.

Key Verse

"As Jesus went on from there, he saw a man named Matthew. He was sitting at the tax collector's booth. 'Follow me,' Jesus told him. Matthew got up and followed him." (Matthew 9:9)

Jesus was having dinner at Matthew's house.	Matthew 9:10
... names of the 12 apostles ... Matthew the tax collector.	Matthew 10:2–3
They saw Jesus eating with "sinners" and tax collectors.	Mark 2:16
The apostles returned to Jerusalem ... Matthew ...	Acts 1:12–13

Mercy

Mercy is God's unde-served favor and blessing: He doesn't give us what we deserve. God shows mercy to us by loving us and listening to and answering our prayers, no matter who we are or what we've done. We can't earn it. Mercy can only be given freely, or it's not mercy. God is very merciful to us, and he wants us to be merciful toward others.

Key Verse

"So have mercy, just as your Father has mercy." (Luke 6:36)

Give praise to the Lord. He has heard my cry for his favor.	Psalm 28:6
We aren't asking you ... because we are godly.	Daniel 9:18
Blessed ... who show mercy. They will be shown mercy.	Matthew 5:7
... approach the throne of grace.... we will receive mercy.	Hebrews 4:16

Messiah

Messiah is the Hebrew word for anointed one or savior. The Greek word for Messiah is "Christ." During Jesus' time, the Jews were waiting for the Messiah. The Bible says the Messiah would come from the line of David, so sometimes he was called "son of David." And since David was a mighty warrior king, the Jews expected their Messiah to lead them in battle against the Romans and make the kingdom of Israel great again. But Jesus was a different Messiah from the one they expected. He came to suffer and die to save people from their sin, and to establish a heavenly kingdom, not an earthly one.

JASON'S IMAGINATION

LOOKING FOR A MESSIAH. MANDATORY QUALIFICATIONS ARE AS FOLLOWS: ★ MUST BE A GOOD FIGHTER. ★ MUST HATE ROMANS. IN ADDITION:

Key Verse

> "The woman said, 'I know that Messiah is coming.' (He is called Christ.) 'When he comes, he will explain everything to us.' Then Jesus said, 'I, the one speaking to you, am he.'" (John 4:25–26)

He suffered the things we should have suffered ...	Isaiah 53:4
... the Anointed King will be cut off. His followers will ...	Daniel 9:26
You are the Christ.... the Son of the living God.	Matthew 16:16
... Son of David!... who comes in the name of the Lord!	Matthew 21:9
... a Savior has been born to you. He is Christ the Lord.	Luke 2:11
Lord ... going to give the kingdom back to Israel now?	Acts 1:6

Suggested Reading

A description of the Messiah's suffering.	Isaiah 53
Jesus will come back as a warrior king.	Revelation 19:11–21

Didjaknow?

It was commonly believed by Jews in Jesus' day that the Messiah—the Christ—would personally kill the emperor in Rome. The Romans knew of this belief, so anyone who claimed to be the Christ would be seen as a direct threat against the emperor. It was dangerous to publicly claim to be the Christ. This is why the religious leaders told Pilate, "He [Jesus] is against paying taxes to Caesar. And he claims to be Christ, a king" (Luke 23:2).

Mind

When the Bible talks about our minds, it means our thoughts and mental attitudes. God gave us brains, and he wants us to think things through, get the facts, and be open to new ideas. Remember: We are to "love God with all our mind." That means showing we love God by what we think and what we believe.

Key Verse

"Jesus replied, '"Love the Lord your God with all your heart and with all your soul. Love him with all your mind." This is the first and most important commandment.'" (Matthew 22:37–38)

I have a brain, just like you. I'm as clever as you are. — Job 12:3
I used my mind to study everything that's done on earth. — Ecclesiastes 8:9
He has a clever mind ... He can ... solve hard problems. — Daniel 5:12
Let your way of thinking be completely changed. — Romans 12:2

Miracle

A miracle is a wonderful event that appears to disobey natural laws but shows us God's power. Only God can do real miracles. In the Bible, God worked miracles through special people like prophets and apostles. But more miracles happened when Jesus was on earth than at any other time. Jesus was able to do miracles because he was God's Son. The miracles weren't magic tricks either. They really happened! Jesus performed these miracles because he loved people and wanted to help them. He also wanted to show them he was the Messiah, the promised one from God.

Key Verse

"When Jesus came ashore, he saw a large crowd. He felt deep concern for them. He healed their sick people." (Matthew 14:14)

You are the God who does miracles.   Psalm 77:14
... to speak against ... cities where he had done ... miracles.   Matthew 11:20
They will do great signs and miracles.   Matthew 24:24
Even if you don't believe me, believe the miracles.   John 10:38

Suggested Reading

God performed many miracles for the Israelites in Old Testament times. Here are a few of them.

God turns Moses' staff into a snake.   Exodus 4:1–9
God parts the Red Sea for the Israelites.   Exodus 14
Elijah raises a boy from the dead.   1 Kings 17

Jesus also performed many miracles during his time on earth. Here are a few of them.

Jesus calms a storm.   Matthew 8:23–27
Jesus delivers people from demons.   Matthew 8:28–34;
                                                                   Mark 1:34, 39
Jesus miraculously feeds thousands.   Matthew 14:15–21;
                                                                   15:32–38

The disciples also did miracles.   Acts 3:1–10;
                                                                   5:12–16; 9:32–43

Didjaknow?

The first miracle Jesus did was to change water into wine at a wedding in Cana (John 2:1–11). In Jesus' time, wedding celebrations could last from two to seven days. Jesus arrived at the wedding when the wine had just run out. So Jesus turned more than 100 gallons of water into wine!

Miriam

Miriam was Moses' older sister. When Pharaoh gave an order that all Israelite baby boys should be thrown in the Nile River, Moses' parents put him safely inside a basket. When Pharaoh's daughter saw the basket and adopted Moses, Miriam ran and got her own mother to be Moses' nursemaid. When Miriam grew up, she became a prophetess.

Key Verse

"She [Moses' mother] got a basket.... Then she placed the child in it. She put the basket in the tall grass that grew along the bank of the Nile River. The child's sister wasn't very far away. She wanted to see what would happen to him." (Exodus 2:3–4)

... Miriam was a prophet. She took a tambourine ...   Exodus 15:20
Miriam and Aaron began to say bad things about Moses.   Numbers 12:1
Aaron, Moses and Miriam were born in ... line of Amram.   1 Chronicles 6:3
I sent Moses to lead them. Aaron and Miriam helped him.   Micah 6:4

Money

Money is used to buy things you want. What if you wanted something and there was no money? You'd have to trade something you had for what you wanted, and the store would have to want what you had. Having money makes things simple. We can do a lot of good things with money, but Jesus warned us to put our trust in God, not cash.

Key Verse

"Do not put away riches for yourselves on earth. Moths and rust can destroy them. Thieves can break in and steal them. Instead, put away riches for yourselves in heaven.... Your heart will be where your riches are." (Matthew 6:19–21)

Money that is gained in the wrong way disappears.	Proverbs 13:11
Anyone who loves money never has enough.	Ecclesiastes 5:10
Love for money causes all kinds of evil. Some people ...	1 Timothy 6:10
Don't be controlled by love for money. Be happy with ...	Hebrews 13:5

Moses

Moses was the man God chose to lead the Israelites out of Egypt, where they were slaves. Moses was born a Hebrew slave, but he ended up becoming an Egyptian prince. Forty years later he killed an Egyptian who was beating a Hebrew. He ran away into the desert where he was a shepherd for 40 more years. One day God called him to lead his people out of Egypt. So, together with his brother Aaron, Moses led his people out of Egypt and into the wilderness. There, God gave him the Ten Commandments and the rest of the law.

JASON'S IMAGINATION

Key Verse

"When the child grew older, she took him to Pharaoh's daughter. And he became her son. She named him Moses. She said, 'I pulled him out of the water.'" (Exodus 2:10)

The Lord said to Moses, "I have made you like God ..."	Exodus 7:1–2
Moses went up ... Lord called ... from the mountain.	Exodus 19:3

Moses ... burned with anger. He threw the tablets out of ...	Exodus 32:19
I finished writing the words of that law in a scroll.	Deuteronomy 31:24–26
Since then, Israel has never had a prophet like Moses.	Deuteronomy 34:10–12
... the people ... couldn't look at Moses' face ...	2 Corinthians 3:7

Suggested Reading

Moses kills an Egyptian and runs away.	Exodus 2:11–15
God appears to Moses in a burning bush.	Exodus 3:1–4:17
God sends plagues on Egypt through Moses.	Exodus 8:1–12:30
Moses parts the Red Sea.	Exodus 14
Moses sees God's glory on Mount Sinai.	Exodus 33:18–34:8
Moses disobeys God and is punished.	Numbers 20:1–13

Didjaknow?

Moses was 120 years old when he died, but he was still healthy and strong. God showed him the Promised Land, but he was not allowed to enter because he had disobeyed God. He went up on a mountain and died. No one ever found where his body was buried.

Mosaic Law

(See Law of Moses)

Most Important Stone

(See Cornerstone)

Mount of Olives

The Mount of Olives is a large hill east of Jerusalem. Jesus often went there to pray. Every Passover, tens of thousands of pilgrims from Galilee camped out on it. They cheered Jesus when he rode a donkey down the Mount into Jerusalem. After his resurrection, Jesus rose up to heaven from there. When he returns, he'll land on the Mount of Olives and split it in two!

Key Verse

"Jesus came near the place where the road goes down the Mount of Olives. There the whole crowd of disciples began to praise God with joy." (Luke 19:37)

... he will stand on the Mount of Olives.... will be split ...	Zechariah 14:4
Jesus was sitting on the Mount of Olives.... disciples ...	Matthew 24:3
Jesus went ... to the Mount of Olives. His disciples ...	Luke 22:39
... returned to Jerusalem from the Mount of Olives.	Acts 1:12

Nazareth

Joseph and Mary lived in Nazareth, a town in Galilee, north of Judea. Jesus was born in Bethlehem, then his family fled to Egypt. When they came back from Egypt, they returned to Nazareth were Jesus grew up. Nazareth means "branch" or "twig," and most Jews didn't think much of the place. Nathanael said, "Nazareth! Can anything good come from there?" (John 1:46).

Key Verse

"There he lived in a town called Nazareth. So what the prophets had said about Jesus came true. They had said, 'He will be called a Nazarene.'" (Matthew 2:23)

This is Jesus. He is the prophet from Nazareth in Galilee.   Matthew 21:11
God sent the angel Gabriel to Nazareth, a town in Galilee.   Luke 1:26
Joseph and Mary ... went to their own town of Nazareth.   Luke 2:39
Jesus went to Nazareth, where he had been brought up.   Luke 4:16

Nebuchadnezzar

Nebuchadnezzar was the king of Babylon who defeated the kingdom of Judah. At first, he only took a small group of Jews to Babylon as hostages. About ten years later the king of Judah tried to rebel, so Nebuchadnezzar completely destroyed Jerusalem and the temple, and took almost all of the rest of the Jews to Babylon. One night Nebuchadnezzar had a troubling dream, and Daniel interpreted it. Nebuchadnezzar was also the king who threw Daniel's three friends into a fiery furnace. Nebuchadnezzar became proud because of his great kingdom, so God made him live like an animal to humble him. Later, he became a believer.

DID YOU CHOOSE A MEMORY VERSE FOR TODAY?

YEAH! I'M GOING TO MEMORIZE A VERSE FROM THE BOOK OF NEBUCHADNEZZER.

Key Verse

"The Most High God was good to your father Nebuchadnezzar. He gave him authority and greatness and glory and honor. God gave him a high position. Then all of the people from every nation and language became afraid of the king." (Daniel 5:18–19)

During Jehoiakim's rule, Nebuchadnezzar marched into ... 2 Kings 24:1
... refused to remain under the control of Nebuchadnezzar. 2 Kings 24:20
In the second year of Nebuchadnezzar's rule ... a dream. Daniel 2:1
Nebuchadnezzar's anger burned against Shadrach ... Daniel 3:19
King Nebuchadnezzar ... Your royal authority has been ... Daniel 4:31
I, Nebuchadnezzar, give praise ... glory to the King ... Daniel 4:37

Suggested Reading

The Jews sinned and have to serve Nebuchadnezzar. Jeremiah 27
Nebuchadnezzar has dealings with Daniel and friends. Daniel 1–4

Didjaknow?

Nebuchadnezzar was a cruel, proud king, yet after God changed his heart and he became a believer, he became one of the writers of the Bible! What an honor! Nebuchadnezzar wrote 37 verses in Daniel 4. That's longer than the book of Philemon!

Nehemiah

Eighty years after the first Jews returned from Babylon, Jerusalem was still a city without walls. Enemies could easily overrun it. Nehemiah, a high official in the Persian court, went to Jerusalem to rebuild the walls. Some of the people around Jerusalem tried to stop them, but God helped Nehemiah and the Jews finish the wall. Read this story in the book of Nehemiah.

Knee-a
my-eye
↓
Nehemiah

Key Verse

"The people continued to build the wall. Those who carried supplies did their work with one hand. They held a weapon in the other hand. Each of the builders wore his sword at his side as he worked." (Nehemiah 4:17–18)

... wall of Jerusalem is broken down. Its gates ... burned ... Nehemiah 1:3
So we rebuilt the wall.... The people worked with all ... Nehemiah 4:6
Don't be afraid of your enemies.... Fight for your sons ... Nehemiah 4:14
So the city wall was completed ... in 52 days. Nehemiah 6:15

Nicodemus

Nicodemus was a Pharisee, one of the Jewish rulers. He knew Jesus was sent by God, so he came to talk to him secretly at night. Jesus told him, "No one can see God's kingdom without being born again" (John 3:3). Later, when the Pharisees accused Jesus, Nicodemus defended him. After Jesus died, Nicodemus and Joseph buried Jesus' body in a tomb.

Key Verse
"'How can I be born when I am old?' Nicodemus asked. 'I can't go back inside my mother! I can't be born a second time!'" (John 3:4)

... Pharisee named Nicodemus.... came to Jesus at night. — John 3:1–2
"How can this be?" Nicodemus asked. — John 3:9
Nicodemus ... spoke.... "Does our law find someone ..." — John 7:50
Nicodemus went with Joseph.... took Jesus' body. — John 19:39–40

Obey

To obey is to do as you are told. God wants us to obey his rules, like not lying or stealing, because these rules help to keep us safe. We can trust that obeying God's rules is the best thing to do because God loves us, and he wants the best for us. Children are told to obey their parents for the same reasons: because their parents care for them and know what is best. Also, learning to obey our parents and God trains us to have self-control, so that we will do well in all other areas of life.

Key Verse
"If you love me, you will obey what I command." (John 14:15)

So be faithful. Obey the commands the Lord your God ... — Deuteronomy 11:13
It is better to obey than to offer a sacrifice. — 1 Samuel 15:22–23
Children, obey your parents ... That pleases the Lord. — Colossians 3:20

Obey your leaders. Put yourselves under their authority. Hebrews 13:17
Those who obey his commands remain joined to him. 1 John 3:24

Suggested Reading

Jesus teaches how important obedience is. Matthew 7:21–28
If we love Jesus, we will obey him. John 14:15–25;
15:9–10
Don't just hear the word. Obey it, too. James 1:22–27

Didjaknow?

People in the Bible were told to do some strange things. When they obeyed, good things happened. Naaman had to dip in the Jordan River seven times to be healed (2 Kings 5). The widow of Zarephath gave her last food away and never ran out (1 Kings 17:7–16). A blind man washed his eyes in a pool and was healed (John 9:1–11).

Offering

An offering is something given to God as an act of worship or as a payment for sin. In the Old Testament, offerings were usually sacrificed to God on altars. Offerings could be anything from animals to crops to drinks. Today, we usually use the word offering to refer to the money that we offer (give) to the church.

Key Verse

"I want mercy and
not sacrifice. I want
you to recognize me
as God instead of
bringing me burnt offerings." (Hosea 6:6)

Make an altar ... Sacrifice your burnt offerings ... on it. Exodus 20:24
Tell the people of Israel to bring me an offering. Exodus 25:2
He was a sweet-smelling offering and sacrifice to God. Ephesians 5:2
... a sweet-smelling offering.... a gift that God accepts. Philippians 4:18

Oldest Son

In Bible times, the oldest son—the firstborn son—in the family received the *birthright*. These were the rights that belonged to the oldest son after his father died. A blessing was given to the oldest son, and this included a double portion of his father's land, money, and other belongings. The oldest son was also the new leader of the family.

SORRY, BUT THESE TOYS BELONG TO ME!

Key Verse

"He must recognize the full rights of the oldest son ... He must give that son a double share of everything he has. That son is the first sign of his father's strength. So the rights of the oldest son belong to him." (Deuteronomy 21:17)

Sell me the rights that belong to you as the oldest son ...	Genesis 25:30–31
Here's my older son. Put your right hand on his head.	Genesis 48:18
[Reuben's] rights as the oldest son were given to the ...	1 Chronicles 5:1
But Shimri wasn't the oldest son. His father had ...	1 Chronicles 26:10

Parable

(See Story)

Parents

God has given us parents to take care of us and raise us. They are responsible for us and teach us about God. Parents tell us to do certain things because they love us. They've learned many things we haven't and so know what is best for us. Obeying parents is one of God's top ten rules. The fifth commandment is "honor your father and mother."

Key Verse

"Honor your father and mother. Then you will live a long time in the land the Lord your God is giving you." (Exodus 20:12)

A wise child pays attention to what his father teaches ...	Proverbs 13:1
Children, obey your parents as believers in the Lord.	Ephesians 6:1
Fathers, don't make your children angry. Instead, train ...	Ephesians 6:4
Children, obey your parents ... That pleases the Lord.	Colossians 3:20

Passover

The Passover was the greatest of all Jewish Feasts. It was first celebrated in Egypt when the Jews killed a lamb and put its blood on their door frame so God's angel would not kill the oldest sons. The angel of death "passed over" every household where he saw the blood of a lamb. That's why it's called *Passover*. From then on, the Israelites celebrated Passover every year. Many years later, Jesus died at Passover as our Passover Lamb. He poured out his blood to save us. When we "put his blood" on the "doors of our hearts," God "passes over" our sins.

Key Verse

"Always remember this day. For all time to come, you and your children after you must celebrate this day as a feast [Passover] in honor of the Lord. It is a law that will last forever." (Exodus 12:14)

Eat the meat ... eat bitter plants.... bread ... without yeast.	Exodus 12:8
Blood on your houses ... I will pass over you.	Exodus 12:13
What does this holy day mean to you?... It's the Passover ...	Exodus 12:26–27
My Passover begins when the sun goes down on the ...	Leviticus 23:5
... Christ has been offered up ... He is our Passover lamb.	1 Corinthians 5:7

Suggested Reading

The story of the first Passover, and the reason for it.	Exodus 11–12
Additional rules for celebrating the Passover.	Leviticus 9:1–14
How to celebrate the Passover.	Deuteronomy 16:1–8
Jesus eats the Passover meal with his disciples.	Matthew 26:17–30

Didjaknow?

The Jews were not allowed to celebrate the Passover meal in their hometowns (Deuteronomy 16:5–6). They *had* to celebrate it in Jerusalem, where the temple was. That's why there were such huge crowds in Jerusalem every Passover (John 11:55).

Pastor

The word pastor means "shepherd." Pastors are "shepherds of God's flock"—us! Pastors have spent years studying the Bible and getting to know God. They are like spiritual coaches who coach us to live the best Christian lives we can. They train us for the life God wants and help us under-

stand what God expects. They teach us the Bible and explain the truth to us.

Key Verse

> "He gave some the gift of preaching the good news. And he gave some the gift to be pastors and teachers. He did it so that they might prepare God's people to serve. If they do, the body of Christ will be built up." (Ephesians 4:11–12)

... who preach the good news should receive their living ...	1 Corinthians 9:14
... honor. That is true ... of elders who teach and preach.	1 Timothy 5:17–18
Be shepherds of God's flock, the believers who are ...	1 Peter 5:2
Don't act as if you were a ruler ... Instead, be examples ...	1 Peter 5:3

Patience

When you have patience, you can wait for something and you don't insist on having it immediately. Patience is being calm when you face difficulties or difficult people. It's easy to be patient when we remember that everyone makes mistakes. We're all still growing and learning. God is very patient with us, and he wants us to be patient with others.

Key Verse

> "Instead, be like those who have faith and are patient. They will receive what God promised." (Hebrews 6:12)

So it's better to be patient than proud.	Ecclesiastes 7:8
The fruit the Holy Spirit produces ... is being patient ...	Galatians 5:22
We want you to be patient. Never give up.	Colossians 1:11
Be gentle and patient. Put up with each other.	Colossians 3:12–13

Paul

Paul was first called Saul. He was a Pharisee and persecuted Jesus' followers. When he was traveling to Damascus to arrest some Christians, suddenly a bright light shone from heaven! Saul had a vision of Jesus and became a Christian himself. He began to boldly preach the gospel. Saul's name was changed to Paul, and he became the apostle to the Gentiles. He went on several missionary journeys, and started churches in many cities. Later

Paul wrote letters to these churches, teaching them more about being Christians. His letters make up half of our New Testament!

Key Verse

"I am the least important of the apostles. I'm not even fit to be called an apostle.... But because of God's grace I am what I am. And his grace was not wasted on me. No, I have worked harder than all the other apostles." (1 Corinthians 15:9–10)

Saul was there. He had agreed that Stephen should die.	Acts 8:1
About midnight Paul and Silas were praying.	Acts 16:25–26
I am the apostle to the non-Jews.... the work I do ...	Romans 11:13
... every day I am concerned about all the churches.	2 Corinthians 11:28
... trusted with the task of preaching ... to the non-Jews.	Galatians 2:7–8
I was appointed to announce the good news.... an apostle ...	2 Timothy 1:11

Suggested Reading

The story of how Paul becomes a believer.	Acts 9
Paul's many adventures preaching the gospel.	Acts 13–28
Paul's rights as an apostle.	1 Corinthians 9
All the things Paul suffers for Jesus' sake.	2 Corinthians 11:22–28
Paul's relationship to Peter and the other apostles.	Galatians 2

Didjaknow?

When people in one of the Gentile churches had an important question, they would send someone from their church to visit Paul, or find someone to take him their letter. Then Paul would write a letter back to answer their questions. In those days, the only sure way to get a letter to a friend was to give it to someone who knew both you and your friend. That's the way most of the letters in the New Testament were delivered.

Peace

Peace of mind is when you know God loves you, and you don't feel bad or guilty. Peace is when you're calm, relaxed, and not worried. Peace comes from trusting God and knowing that he is in charge, and everything is working as he

designed. When you're confident that God can work out every detail and you trust that God is taking care of everything, you will have peace. Jesus is called the Prince of Peace. He bought peace between us and God with his death, and that peace spreads into our relationships.

Key Verse

"I leave my peace with you. I give my peace to you. I do not give it to you as the world does. Do not let your hearts be troubled. And do not be afraid. " (John 14:27)

Those who love your law enjoy great peace.	Psalm 119:165
I have told you these things, so that you can have peace ...	John 16:33
Then the church throughout Judea ... enjoyed ... peace.	Acts 9:31
Live in peace. And the God who gives ... peace will be ...	2 Corinthians 13:11
God's peace will watch over your hearts and your minds ...	Philippians 4:6–7
Let the peace that Christ gives rule in your hearts.	Colossians 3:15

Suggested Reading

Solomon's kingdom has a time of peace.	1 Kings 4:24–25; 5:1–5, 12
What the church is like when it's peaceful.	Acts 4:32–37

Didjaknow?

Our peace grows and spreads into our relationships. Peace inside us becomes peace between us and others. Picture this: We're all black and white and God is every color imaginable. He touches us and his color flows into us. Soon we're completely colored and the color spreads out from us into the world and people around us. That's what it's like when God, through Jesus, touches our lives with his peace. Our worries and fears calm as the color of God's peace flows into us and out to others. We paint our world with a brush of peace!

Pentecost

Pentecost was a Jewish feast day that took place seven weeks after the Passover at the end of harvest—and about 50 days after Jesus returned to heaven. Pentecost was also called the "Feast of Weeks" or the "Feast of Harvest." It is an important day to Christians because it is the day the Holy Spirit came as God promised.

Key Verse

"They saw something that looked like tongues of fire. The flames separated and settled on each of them. All of them were filled with the Holy Spirit. They began to speak in languages they had not known before. The Spirit gave them the ability to do this." (Acts 2:3–4)

Celebrate the Feast ... Bring the first share of your crops ...	Exodus 23:16
Count off seven full weeks from that day.... 50 days ...	Leviticus 23:15–16
The day of Pentecost came. The believers all gathered ...	Acts 2:1
Paul ... in a hurry to get to Jerusalem.... by ... Pentecost.	Acts 20:16

Perseverance

(See Stand Firm)

Persian

The Persians had a powerful empire in Old Testament times. With the Medes, they conquered the Babylonian empire. King Cyrus of Persia let the Jews return home to Judea to rebuild the temple. Later, a Persian king sent Ezra there to teach God's law. Then Nehemiah was sent there. He became governor of Judea. Later, a Jewish girl named Esther married Xerxes, king of Persia.

Key Verse

"Cyrus, the king of Persia, says, 'The Lord is the God of heaven. He has given me all of the kingdoms on earth. He has appointed me to build a temple for him at Jerusalem in Judah.'" (Ezra 1:2)

Ezra came up to Jerusalem ... during ... rule of Artaxerxes.	Ezra 7:1
Nehemiah.... in the 20th year that Artaxerxes was king.	Nehemiah 1:1
... Babylonia ... His kingdom ... given to Darius the Mede.	Daniel 5:30–31
... well with [Daniel] during the rule of Cyrus, the Persian.	Daniel 6:28

Peter

The apostle Peter was also known as Simon, Simon Peter, and Cephas. Before he met Jesus, Peter and his brother Andrew were fishermen. Peter loved Jesus, but he could be hotheaded and didn't always think before he acted. One minute he was hacking someone's ear off with a sword to protect Jesus. A few hours later, he denied he even knew Jesus. But Jesus forgave him, and Peter later became one of the most important leaders in the church. He preached the gospel in Judea, Samaria, Antioch, Corinth, and finally Rome, where he was martyred. He wrote the books 1 and 2 Peter in the New Testament.

Key Verse

"Simon Peter answered, 'You are the Christ. You are the Son of the living God.' Jesus replied, 'Blessed are you, Simon, son of Jonah! No mere man showed this to you. My Father in heaven showed it to you.'" (Matthew 16:16–17)

There he saw two brothers. They were Simon Peter ...	Matthew 4:18
I don't know this man you are talking about!	Mark 14:71
"Who ...?" Peter answered, "The Christ of God."	Luke 9:20
Jesus ... said, "You will be called Cephas." ... (or rock).	John 1:42
Simon Peter had a sword and pulled it out. He struck ...	John 18:10
In those days Peter stood up among the believers.	Acts 1:15

Suggested Reading

Peter's rash actions and denial of Jesus.	Matthew 26
Peter preaches, heals, and is jailed.	Acts 2–4
Peter's travels and miracles.	Acts 9:32–43; 10:1–11:18
An angel frees him from prison.	Acts 12
Paul rebukes Peter in Antioch.	Galatians 2:9–16

Didjaknow?

Paul had started the church in Corinth, Greece, but then went to pioneer a church in Ephesus, so guess who went over to teach the new Corinthian Christians? Peter! And according to 1 Corinthians 1:11–12, a lot of Corinthians loved Peter's teaching. First Corinthians 9:5 even tells us Peter's wife went with him. Peter also preached the gospel in Pontus, Galatia, Cappadocia, Asia, and Bithynia, and later wrote them a letter when he was in Rome (1 Peter 1:1).

Pharaoh

Pharaoh was the title of the kings of ancient Egypt. Abraham got in trouble with one pharaoh for pretending his wife was his sister. Another pharaoh made Joseph the ruler of all Egypt. A later pharaoh made the Israelites slaves. And God sent plagues to convince pharaoh to set his people free. The pharaohs claimed that they were gods. Funny thing though: They all died.

Key Verse

"So Pharaoh said to Joseph, 'I'm putting you in charge of the whole land of Egypt.'" (Genesis 41:41)

Sarai was taken into his palace. Pharaoh treated Abram ...   Genesis 12:15–16
Pharaoh said ... "I had a dream. No one can tell me ..."   Genesis 41:15
Pharaoh said, "Who is the Lord? Why should I obey him?"   Exodus 5:2
God says ... "I had ... reason ... making you king."   Romans 9:17

Pharisee

The Pharisees were Jewish religious leaders who were very careful to keep God's law. They were very proud of their obedience. The problem was, the Pharisees loved the Law so much that they forgot about loving God and others. The Pharisees became angry with Jesus because he told them that they weren't as wonderful as they thought they were. So they plotted to kill him.

JASON'S IMAGINATION

EXCUSE ME, I BELIEVE THIS BELONGS IN YOUR BOOK.

God's Laws

GOD'S LAWS

LOVE GOD & OTHERS

Key Verse

"How terrible it will be for you, teachers of the law and Pharisees! You pretenders! You shut the kingdom of heaven in people's faces. You yourselves do not enter. And you will not let those enter who are trying to." (Matthew 23:13–14)

... Pharisees ... plans to trap Jesus with his own words.   Matthew 22:15
But the Pharisees and the teachers ... were very angry.   Luke 6:11
Pharisee ... prayed ... "God, I thank you that I am not ..."   Luke 18:9–14
Paul ... said, "I am a Pharisee. I am the son of a Pharisee."   Acts 23:6

Philistine

The Philistines were a nation that gave the Israelites many problems during the first few centuries the Israelites lived in Canaan. Israel had a difficult time fighting them because the Philistines were better organized and had better weapons. Before David became king of Israel, he lived among the Philistines and learned their ways. As king of Israel, David used this knowledge to defeat the Philistines.

Key Verse

"Once again the people of Israel did what was evil in the sight of the Lord. So the Lord handed them over to the Philistines for 40 years." (Judges 13:1)

The people of Israel went out to fight ... the Philistines.	1 Samuel 4:1
The Philistines came near to attack Israel.	1 Samuel 7:10
A ... hero named Goliath came out of the Philistine camp.	1 Samuel 17:4
David ... won may battles over the Philistines.	2 Samuel 8:1

Plague

A plague is a display of God's power that is sent as punishment for sin and disobedience. In most cases in the Bible, plagues take the form of suffering or disease. Plagues are mentioned throughout the Bible, but the most well-known plagues are the ten that God sent to Egypt to convince Pharaoh to let the Israelites leave (Exodus 7:14–11:10; 12:29–30).

Key Verse

"Then the Lord said to Moses, 'Go to Pharaoh. Tell him, "The Lord says, 'Let my people go. Then they will be able to worship me. If you refuse to let them go, I will plague your whole country with frogs.'"'" (Exodus 8:1–2)

... meat was ... mouths ... struck them with ... plague.	Numbers 11:33
So I will strike them down with a plague.	Numbers 14:12
He will strike you with fever ... There won't be any rain.	Deuteronomy 28:22
... given power to kill people with ... hunger and sickness.	Revelation 6:8

Pleasing People

Popularity means "pleasing people, being liked and accepted by others." It's nice to be popular, but that shouldn't become your goal. Being overly concerned about what people think of you is a dangerous trap. You'll wind up doing things just to please others, rather than doing what God wants. If your "friends" are doing bad things and you want to be popular with them, you'll be tempted to go along with them. But why try to please bad kids? It just gets you in trouble. It's much better to try to please God. That will make you popular with God and with good kids!

Key Verse

"Jesus became wiser and stronger. He also became more and more pleasing to God and to people." (Luke 2:52)

When the way you live pleases the Lord ... peace with ...	Proverbs 16:7
How terrible ... when everyone says good things about you!	Luke 6:26
They loved praise from people more than praise from God.	John 12:43
Those who serve Christ ... pleasing to God.... people too.	Romans 14:18
Am I now trying to get people to think well of me?	Galatians 1:10
We aren't trying to please people. We want to please God.	1 Thessalonians 2:4

Suggested Reading

Dorcas is a popular woman in Joppa.	Acts 9:36–39
Timothy is popular in Lystra and Iconium.	Acts 16:1–2
Pleasing others to win them to Christ.	1 Corinthians 9:19–23; 10:33

Didjaknow?

You can please all of the people some of the time, and some of the people all of the time. But you can never please all of the people all of the time. So don't try. But you know, some people do so much good that *most* people like them. For example, the Pharisees couldn't say anything bad about John the Baptist, because the poor people loved him (Mark 11:29–32). And Jesus was so popular that his enemies couldn't arrest him during the Passover Feast, or the crowds would riot (Mark 14:2).

Pontius Pilate

Pontius Pilate was the Roman governor of Judah who sentenced Jesus to death. The Jews would have killed Jesus themselves, but they needed permission from the Romans to execute someone. Pilate didn't think Jesus was guilty, and he tried to release him. But when the Jews insisted that Jesus be crucified, Pilate gave in because he was afraid of them.

Key Verse

"Pilate said, 'Take him yourselves. Judge him by your own law.' 'But we don't have the right to put anyone to death,' the Jews complained." (John 18:31)

Pilate saw that he wasn't getting anywhere. Instead ...	Matthew 27:24
Pilate wanted to satisfy the crowd. So he let Barabbas ...	Mark 15:15
Pilate called together the chief priests, the rulers and ...	Luke 23:13
When Pilate heard that, he was even more afraid.	John 19:8

Popularity

(See Pleasing People)

Praise

To praise someone is to give them approval and respect. We praise God more than anyone or anything because he is *so* good, *so* wonderful, *so* powerful, *so* holy that he *deserves* more praise than anyone or anything! Even angels worship God! David wrote many psalms praising God. Psalm 150 is like a celebration where everyone shouts out how great God is!

Key Verse

"Praise him for his powerful acts. Praise him because he is greater than anything else." (Psalm 150:2)

I will thank the Lord at all times.... will always praise him.	Psalm 34:1
Praise him, all his angels.... all his angels in heaven.	Psalm 148:2
Let them praise the name of the Lord.... His glory is ...	Psalm 148:13
... never stop offering to God our praise through Jesus.	Hebrews 13:15

Prayer

Prayer is simply talking to God and having a conversation with him. It's the way we thank God and ask him to be involved in our lives. It's the way we get to know him and get closer to him. Friends talk with each other, right? Well, we're God's friends, so we talk to him. We pray. We tell God what's on our hearts—what we feel, think, want, and need. It's like having a really good conversation with someone we love and trust, no matter where we are or what we're doing. And we know God always listens to our prayers and answers them.

God's Communication station

Key Verse

"Don't worry about anything. Instead, tell God about everything. Ask and pray. Give thanks to him." (Philippians 4:6)

Please pay attention to my prayer.... Listen to my cry ...	1 Kings 8:28
When you pray, go into your room. Close the door ...	Matthew 6:6
Ask, and it will be given to you.... Everyone who asks ...	Matthew 7:7–8
... show them that they should always pray and not give up.	Luke 18:1
Never stop praying.	1 Thessalonians 5:17
The prayer of a godly person ... makes things happen.	James 5:16

Suggested Reading

David's prayer.	2 Samuel 7:18–29
Read about prayer and the Lord's Prayer.	Matthew 6:5–15
Two stories about not giving up when praying.	Luke 11:5–10; 18:1–8
The power of faith-filled prayer.	James 5:13–18

Didjaknow?

Some people pray as if God is a galactic superstore or a huge, cosmic shopping channel. They write up a shopping list and pray to have a best friend, good grades, a new jacket, their own room, etc. But the whole reason for prayer is to have a relationship with God. He wants us to know him, realize his love for us, and talk to him from our heart.

Pretender

A pretender or hypocrite is someone who says one thing and then does another. They're just pretending to be good. For example, a hypocrite preaches against stealing, and then steals something. Jesus accused the Pharisees of being pretenders. He spoke more harshly against hypocrites than anyone else. A hypocrite's actions and words don't match up. We should match our actions to our words.

Key Verse

"How terrible for you, teachers of the law and Pharisees! You pretenders! You are like tombs that are painted white. They look beautiful on the outside. But on the inside they are full of the bones of the dead. They are also full of other things that are not pure and clean." (Matthew 23:27)

You pretender! First take the piece of wood out of your ...	Matthew 7:5
... knew their evil plans. He said, "You pretenders!"	Matthew 22:18
You pretenders! You clean the outside ... inside you are ...	Matthew 23:25
Don't pretend to be something you are not.	1 Peter 2:1

Priest

In the Old Testament, a priest was a man from the tribe of Levi who served God in the temple and acted as a go-between between the people and God. The Levites were called to be priests, and Aaron was called to be the high priest. When the people of Israel sinned, they brought a lamb, goat, or bull to the temple for the priest to sacrifice and offer to God. Today, we don't need a priest to go to God for us. Jesus is our High Priest, and any time we have sinned or need help, we can go to him (Hebrews 4:15–16).

Key Verse

"Every high priest is chosen from among men. He is appointed to act for them in everything that has to do with God. He offers gifts and sacrifices for their sins." (Hebrews 5:1)

Dress Aaron in the sacred clothes.... to serve me as priest.	Exodus 40:13
Bring the men of the tribe of Levi to the priest Aaron.	Numbers 3:5
We have a high priest like that.... He serves in the ...	Hebrews 8:1–2

Day after day every priest ... offers the same sacrifices ...   Hebrews 10:11
Jesus our priest offered one sacrifice for sins for all time.   Hebrews 10:12

Suggested Reading

The many offerings priests must make.   Leviticus 1–4; 6
The high priest entering the Most Holy Room.   Leviticus 16
Zacharias, a priest in the New Testament.   Luke 1:5–25,
    57–80

Jesus, our High Priest, and his sacrifice.   Hebrews 4:14–16;
    5; 7–9

Didjaknow?

Other religions worshiped idols that had no power and gods that weren't
real. But these religions had priests too. When Elijah challenged the priests of
Baal to prove which god was real, 450 priests of Baal and 400 priests of the
goddess Asherah showed up. But their prayers were not answered (1 Kings
18:25–29). Later, Jehu tricked hundreds of the priests of Baal (2 Kings
10:18–28). Even the golden idols Jeroboam made had priests. All kinds of
worthless people could be a priest for his idols (1 Kings 12:28–32).

Prison

A prison or jail is a place to
lock up criminals.
Sometimes good people are
put in prison too, like
Joseph, Jacob's son.
Sometimes bad rulers throw
Christians in prison. The
Jewish leaders threw the
apostles in jail and Paul was
jailed several times. God
sometimes broke his people
out of prison. The Bible says
to visit those who are in
prison (Hebrews 13:3).

Key Verse

**"After Herod arrested Peter, he put him in prison. Peter was placed
under guard. He was watched by four groups of four soldiers each.
Herod planned to put Peter on public trial.... So Peter was kept in
prison." (Acts 12:4–5)**

Put [him] in prison. Don't give him anything but bread ...   2 Chronicles 18:26
I was in prison. And you came to visit me.   Matthew 25:36
Peter followed him out of the prison.... the angel was ...   Acts 12:9
He put Paul and Silas deep inside the prison.   Acts 16:24

Prisoners in Babylon

The people of Judah didn't listen to God's warnings to change their lives. They didn't repent. So Nebuchadnezzar, king of Babylon, marched against Jerusalem with his armies. He took the people of Judah far from their own land. The Jews were forced to live as prisoners in

Babylon. This was called the *Exile*. The Exile lasted 70 years. Then God brought the Jews back to their own land.

Key Verse

> "The Lord took the people of Judah and Jerusalem to Babylonia. He used Nebuchadnezzar to take them there as prisoners."
> (1 Chronicles 6:15)

Nebuchadnezzar took the rest of the people to Babylon ...   2 Chronicles 36:20
Jeremiah, sent a letter ... to Babylonia.... for the Jewish ...   Jeremiah 29:1
You will be forced to live in Babylonia for 70 years.   Jeremiah 29:10
You scattered us among the nations because we ...   Daniel 9:7

Promise

A promise is an agreement to do something for someone. God always keeps his promises. Once God decides what he's going to do and promises to do it, you can be sure he will stay true to his word. Sometimes *people* make promises, then change their mind. Or they realize they actually can't do what they promised. But God is powerful! And he doesn't change his mind! So search the Bible and find all that God has promised to do for you. You can know without a doubt that he will do all that he has promised.

Key Verse

> "God isn't a mere man. He can't lie. He isn't a human being. He can't change his mind. He speaks, and then he acts. He makes a promise, and then he keeps it." (Numbers 23:19)

The Lord is faithful and will keep all of his promises.   Psalm 145:13
... absolutely sure that God had the power to do what he ...   Romans 4:20–21
God has made a great many promises. They are all ...   2 Corinthians 1:20

The Lord has ... made a promise. He will not change ...   Hebrews 7:21
Let us hold firmly to the hope ... The One who promised ...   Hebrews 10:23
He ... given us his very great and valuable promises.   2 Peter 1:4

Suggested Reading

Several promises that God made to Abraham.	Genesis 15; 17; 18:1–15
God's promise to give a son to Hannah.	1 Samuel 1
God's promise to King David.	1 Chronicles 17:1–15
Jesus' promise to his followers.	John 14

Didjaknow?

When Abraham was 100 years old and Sarah was 90, they were too old to have children. But God promised that they would have a son. Sarah thought this was so crazy that she laughed out loud. But Abraham believed God could do it. And sure enough! God kept his promise and did a miracle. He gave them a baby, Isaac.

Promised Land

God promised Abraham that one day his descendants would own all the land of Canaan. After Moses died, Joshua led the people of Israel into Canaan, the "Promised Land." Joshua divided the land among the Israelites as their property. Forty years after Jesus died, the Romans drove the Jews out and they had no country for 2000 years. Now Israel is their homeland once again.

Key Verse

"You are now living in Canaan as an outsider. But I will give you the whole land of Canaan. You will own it forever. So will your children after you. And I will be their God." (Genesis 17:8)

Go up to the land I promised with an oath to give to ...	Exodus 33:1
You are going to enter Canaan. The land will be given ...	Numbers 34:1–2
So Joshua took the whole land ... and gave each tribe ...	Joshua 11:23
... a promise to [Abraham] ... would possess the land.	Acts 7:5

Prophecy

God called prophets to speak to people for him. A prophecy tells what will happen in the future. Only God knows the future before it happens. When a prophet said what God was going to do, that was called "giving a prophecy." The Old Testament prophets gave many prophecies about Jesus hundreds of years before his birth. And their prophecies came true!

Key Verse

"No prophecy in Scripture ever came from a prophet's own under-standing.... Instead, the Holy Spirit guided the prophets as they spoke. So prophecy comes from God." (2 Peter 1:20–21)

Asa heard that prophecy.... paid attention to the words ...	2 Chronicles 15:8
... the words the prophet Jeremiah spoke came true.	Matthew 2:17
Isaiah was right when he prophesied about you.	Matthew 15:7
Most of all, you should want the gift of prophecy.	1 Corinthians 14:1

Prophet

A prophet is a man or woman sent by God with a special message. In the Old Testament, God sent prophets to tell the people and the kings of Judah and Israel to turn back to God and obey him. The prophets also told what would happen if the people and the kings didn't obey. Prophets often began with: "This is what the Lord says."

Key Verse

"After seven days, a message came to me from the Lord. He said, 'Son of man, I have appointed you as a prophet to warn the people of Israel. So listen to my message. Give them a warning from me.'" (Ezekiel 3:16–17)

Hilkiah ... went to speak to the prophet Huldah.	2 Chronicles 34:22
The Lord ... said, "I have put my words in your mouth."	Jeremiah 1:9
How long it takes you to believe all that the prophets said!	Luke 24:25
Prophets came ... Agabus.... spoke through the Spirit.	Acts 11:27–28

Proverb

A proverb is a short statement that says in a few words something that is usually true about life. The book of Proverbs is a book of wise sayings. These proverbs were written by men who knew a lot about God from their own experience and the experiences of other people. They knew that having a truly successful life means living as God wants and as if God were watching all our actions. Most of the book of Proverbs was written by King Solomon, who had a reputation for being a wise man. Reading Proverbs will help you learn the best way to live.

NEED WISE ADVICE?

"THE PROVERBS OF JASON"

I'll think of something to say about your situation!

Key Verse

"Proverbs teach you wisdom and train you. They help you understand wise sayings. They provide you with training and help you live wisely. They lead to what is right and honest and fair." (Proverbs 1:2–3)

He spoke 3,000 proverbs. He wrote 1,005 songs.	1 Kings 4:32–33
These are the proverbs of Solomon.... the son of David ...	Proverbs 1:1
These are more proverbs of Solomon.... copied down ...	Proverbs 25:1
These sayings are the words of Agur ... He spoke them ...	Proverbs 30:1
These are the sayings of King Lemuel. His mother ...	Proverbs 31:1
What the proverbs say about them is true. "A dog ..."	2 Peter 2:22

Suggested Reading

These chapters talk about Solomon's wisdom.	1 Kings 3; 4:29–34; 10

Read the book of Proverbs in a month, one chapter a day.
Read Ecclesiastes, more wise sayings of Solomon.

Didjaknow?

Kings in the ancient world often compiled collections of their wise sayings. Kings of Egypt and Arabia were famous for their knowledge about how to deal with people. But Solomon outdid them all. He spoke 3000 proverbs. Many of those were collected and put into the book of Proverbs.

Psalms

Psalms is a book in the Bible full of worship songs called psalms. David and others used their musical skills to write psalms. They wrote worship songs that tell how great God is and that tell God we love him and want to serve him. Many psalms were used for group worship and were sung in the temple. Some psalms thank God for who he is and what he does. Others just tell God how we feel—happy or sad. Many of the psalms are not only songs, but prayers too. Some psalms were prophetic. They talked about things that would happen hundreds of years later.

WHAT'S THIS? I TOLD YOU WE WERE GOING TO READ A PSALM.

I JUST FOUND OUT THAT THE PSALMS WERE MEANT TO BE SUNG!

Key Verse

"I am David, the son of Jesse. God has given me a message. The Most High God has greatly honored me. The God of Jacob anointed me as king. I am Israel's singer of songs [psalms]." (2 Samuel 23:1)

David gave Asaph ... this psalm of thanks to the Lord.	1 Chronicles 16:7
He gave me a new song to sing. It is a hymn of praise ...	Psalm 40:3
Let the music begin.... Play sweet music on harps and ...	Psalm 81:2
Sing a new song to the Lord. Sing praise to him in the ...	Psalm 149:1
This is what is written in the second Psalm. It says ...	Acts 13:33
Speak to each other with psalms, hymns and ... songs.	Ephesians 5:19

Suggested Reading

People living God's way are blessed.	Psalm 1
Prophecies of the coming of Jesus, the Messiah.	Psalms 2; 22
The famous "Shepherd's Psalm."	Psalm 23
A psalm of protection.	Psalm 91

Didjaknow?

The psalms were written by a number of people. Psalm 90 was written by Moses. Psalms 72 and 127 were written by David's son, Solomon. Other psalms were written by Ethan, Heman, and Asaph. But more than half of the psalms were written by King David.

Queen

A queen is either the wife of a king or a female ruler of a kingdom. Two famous queens are mentioned in the Old Testament. The first is the Queen of Sheba. She came from Arabia to learn from King Solomon. She brought him many expensive gifts. The second queen is Esther. By exposing a plot of their enemies, Esther saved her people (the Jews) from being killed.

Key Verse

"The queen of Sheba heard about how famous Solomon was. She also heard about how he served and worshiped the Lord. So she came to test him with hard questions." (1 Kings 10:1)

So the queen of Sheba saw how very wise Solomon was.	1 Kings 10:4
King Solomon gave the queen of Sheba everything she ...	1 Kings 10:13
Queen Esther answered, "King Xerxes, I hope you will ..."	Esther 7:3
... in charge of all the wealth of ... the queen of Ethiopia.	Acts 8:27

Red Sea

The Red Sea is a narrow body of water that runs between Egypt and the Arabian peninsula. This is the sea that God miraculously parted for the Israelites when they were fleeing from Pharaoh's army during the Exodus. Some scholars think that the Israelites actually crossed the "sea of reeds," a shallow, marshy body of water located several miles north of the Red Sea.

Key Verse

"Then Moses reached his hand out over the Red Sea. All that night the Lord pushed the sea back with a strong east wind. He turned the sea into dry land. The waters were parted. The people of Israel went through the sea on dry ground. There was a wall of water on their right side and on their left." (Exodus 14:21–22)

So God led the people toward the Red Sea ...	Exodus 13:18
... thrown Pharaoh's chariots and army into the Red Sea.	Exodus 15:4
But the Red Sea swallowed up their enemies.	Psalm 78:53
The people had faith. So they passed through the Red Sea.	Hebrews 11:29

Religion, False

(See Beliefs)

Religion, True

(See Christian)

Repentance

(See Godly Sadness)

Rest

Rest is a break from work or activity. When we trust God to take care of us, we're able to rest from the work of looking after ourselves and trying to please him. God created the world in six days, then rested on the seventh. This

... AND PLEASE BE WITH MOM AND DAD AND LIL...

day became the Sabbath (which means rest). It represented Jesus, who would one day come and provide spiritual rest for everyone who believes in him.

Key Verse

"God's promise of enjoying his rest still stands. So be careful that none of you fails to receive it." (Hebrews 4:1)

Tomorrow will be a day of rest.... a holy Sabbath day.	Exodus 16:23
The Lord replied, "I will go with you.... give you rest."	Exodus 33:14
I find my rest in God alone. He is the One who saves me.	Psalm 62:1
Come to me ... you who are tired ... I will give you rest.	Matthew 11:28

Resurrection

Resurrection means "being raised from the dead back to life." After Jesus died on the cross for our sins, he lay in a tomb for three days. Then, early Sunday morning, God raised Jesus from the dead! This showed that God was stronger than death. He defeated it. After his resurrection, Jesus appeared to his disciples. He had a real body, and they not only saw him but touched him. Yet he could pass through locked doors (John 20:19)! When Jesus returns to earth, every believer who has ever died will be resurrected and given a new body that will live forever in heaven.

Key Verse

"Christ died for our sins, just as Scripture said he would. He was buried. He was raised from the dead on the third day ... He appeared to Peter. Then he appeared to the Twelve. After that, he appeared to more than 500 believers at the same time." (1 Corinthians 15:3–6)

He is not here! He has risen, just as he said he would! — Matthew 28:6
He taught ... He must be killed ... three days rise again. — Mark 8:31
Jesus rose from the dead ... He appeared first to ... — Mark 16:9
Jesus said to her, "I am the resurrection and the life." — John 11:25
... change our earthly bodies.... like his glorious body. — Philippians 3:21
Many who believe ... died already. They will rise first. — 1 Thessalonians 4:16

Suggested Reading

Elijah raises a widow's son from the dead. — 1 Kings 17
Jesus raises Lazarus from the dead. — John 11:1–45
Jesus resurrected from the dead to live *forever!* — Matthew 28; Luke 24; John 20

Peter raises Tabitha from the dead. — Acts 9:36–43
What are resurrected bodies like? — 1 Corinthians 15:35–57

Didjaknow?

Jesus' resurrection was real. Put these facts together: The Romans reported Jesus was dead. People did not recover from crucifixion. Jesus was buried in a cave with one exit, blocked by a stone that took several men to move. Roman soldiers put an official seal on the tomb and guarded it. Falling asleep on the job meant death for them! But a couple days later, the tomb was empty, the huge stone had been moved away, and more than 500 people said Jesus appeared to them alive! What happened? Jesus really *did* rise from the dead!

Revelation

A revelation is when God reveals or shows something to his people by his Spirit. In the Bible, God revealed things in visions or dreams, or gave people special knowledge. When God hid things, they were a mystery. When he revealed them, they were a revelation. The New Testament ends with a spectacular vision of the future. This book is called Revelation.

Key Verse

"It is written, 'No eye has seen, no ear has heard, no mind has known what God has prepared for those who love him.' But God has shown it to us through his Spirit." (1 Corinthians 2:9–10)

... God ... can explain mysteries.... he has shown you ... — Daniel 2:28
No one taught it to me.... I received it from Jesus Christ. — Galatians 1:12
I'm talking about the mystery God showed me. — Ephesians 3:3
This is the revelation that God gave to Jesus Christ. — Revelation 1:1

Reward

A reward is a gift that someone receives for accomplishing something. After we die, God will reward each of us according to what we've done in our lives. But God doesn't just reward us after we die. We receive the results of our actions here on earth as well.

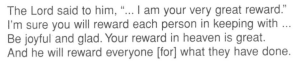

Key Verse

"You know that the Lord will give you a reward. He will give to each of you in keeping with the good you do. It doesn't matter whether you are slaves or free." (Ephesians 6:8)

The Lord said to him, "... I am your very great reward."	Genesis 15:1
I'm sure you will reward each person in keeping with ...	Psalm 62:12
Be joyful and glad. Your reward in heaven is great.	Matthew 5:12
And he will reward everyone [for] what they have done.	Matthew 16:27

Righteousness

(See Right with God)

Right with God

Righteousness means "being made right with God." Sin makes us "wrong" with God. When we put our faith and trust in Jesus, God forgives us and makes us clean and right again. God wants us to live the right way, but we aren't made righteous because of anything we do. It's a free gift from God made possible by Jesus' death on the cross.

Key Verse

"We believe in the God who raised Jesus our Lord from the dead. So God will accept our faith and make us right with himself. Jesus was handed over to die for our sins. He was raised to life in order to make us right with God." (Romans 4:24–25)

But doing what is right saves you from death.	Proverbs 11:4
The good news shows how God makes people right ...	Romans 1:17
If people trust ... Their faith makes them right with God.	Romans 4:5
... Abraham ... his faith made him right with God.	Romans 4:22

Roman

During New Testament days, the Roman empire ruled the world. Before Jesus was born, the Romans conquered the Jews and set up Herod as king of Judea. Whenever the Romans conquered an area, they made the people pay taxes. The Jews hated the Romans. But the Romans had tough soldiers in Judea to keep the peace. They

built excellent roads between major cities, making travel easy. They also made Greek the common language throughout their empire. Since everyone spoke the same language, it was a perfect time for spreading the gospel. Paul wrote the book of Romans to Christians in the capital city.

Key Verse

"In those days, Caesar Augustus made a law. It required that a list be made of everyone in the whole Roman world." (Luke 2:1)

[Roman] soldiers asked him, "... what should we do?"	Luke 3:14
The Romans will come. They will take away our temple ...	John 11:48
When the [Roman] soldiers crucified Jesus, they took ...	John 19:23
I told them that this is not the way Romans do things.	Acts 25:16
Paul ... handed over to a Roman commander ...	Acts 27:1
I am sending this letter to all of you in Rome who are ...	Romans 1:7

Suggested Reading

The great faith of a Roman commander.	Matthew 8:5–13; Luke 7:1–10
Cornelius, a Roman commander, is saved.	Acts 10
Roman governor of Cyprus becomes a Christian.	Acts 13:4–12
Paul's exciting adventures with the Romans.	Acts 21:17–36; 22:1–23:35

Didjaknow?

The Romans were harsh rulers, but if you were a Roman citizen, you had many rights. Roman law was strict—a Roman citizen could not be beaten and sent to prison without a trial. That's why, after the rulers in Philippi beat Paul and Silas and imprisoned them, they were afraid when they found out Paul and Silas were Roman citizens (Acts 16:16–39). Many years later, Paul's Roman citizenship kept him from being whipped in Jerusalem (Acts 22:22–29).

Rule

Rules are guidelines that show us the right way to do things. God has given us rules for living. He knows the best way to live. He made these rules to keep us safe and to give us great lives. If we want to please God and have a good life, we should learn his rules and live by them.

Key Verse

"Make sure you obey all of the rules I'm giving you. Then things will always go well with you and your children after you. That's because you will be doing what is good and right in the eyes of the Lord your God." (Deuteronomy 12:28)

I tell them about God's rules and laws.	Exodus 18:16
You have given me rules that I must obey completely.	Psalm 119:4
But ... hearts are far ... teach nothing but human rules.	Matthew 15:8–9
... doesn't receive ... crown unless he plays by the rules.	2 Timothy 2:5

Ruth

During a famine in the time of the judges, an Israelite family moved to Moab. Later, the man and his sons died and his wife, Naomi, returned to Israel. Ruth, her Moabite daughter-in-law, went with her. Ruth decided to follow God like Naomi did. Naomi's relative, Boaz, cared for her and Naomi. Boaz married Ruth, and their great-grandson was King David.

Key Verse

"But Ruth replied, 'Don't try to make me leave you and go back. Where you go I'll go. Where you stay I'll stay. Your people will be my people. Your God will be my God.'" (Ruth 1:16)

So Naomi returned ... Ruth, her daughter-in-law ... came ...	Ruth 1:22
Naomi had a relative ... Boaz.... a very important man.	Ruth 2:1
All of the people ... know that you are a noble woman.	Ruth 3:11
So Boaz got married to Ruth.... And she had a son.	Ruth 4:13

Sabbath

Sabbath means "rest." God made the world in six days and rested on the seventh. That's why the seventh day was called the Sabbath. Honoring the Sabbath is one of the Ten Commandments. God didn't have to tell Adam and Eve to keep the Sabbath: by trusting him they were already resting. But when they rebelled against God, their rest ended, so later God had to teach people to rest again. The Sabbath day also represented Jesus. God knew from the beginning that he'd send Jesus so we could rest from the hard work of looking after ourselves and trying to please him. Jesus is our rest.

I DON'T THINK YOU SHOULD COOK ON THE SABBATH. SO CAN WE JUST EAT CHIPS AND CHEESE DOODLES FOR LUNCH?

Key Verse

"Remember to keep the Sabbath day holy." (Exodus 20:8)

Tomorrow will be a day of rest.... a holy Sabbath day.	Exodus 16:23
I blessed the Sabbath day and made it holy.	Exodus 20:11
The Law allows us to do good on the Sabbath day.	Matthew 12:12
The Sabbath day was made for man. Man was not made ...	Mark 2:27
The Son of Man is Lord of the Sabbath day.	Luke 6:5

Suggested Reading

The disciples "break" the Sabbath.	Matthew 12:1–8; Mark 2:23–28; Luke 6:1–5
Jesus heals on the Sabbath.	Mark 3:1–6; Luke 6:6–11; John 5:1–16

Didjaknow?

The Law said the Jews weren't supposed to work on the Sabbath. So the Pharisees made laws to explain what the word "work" meant. For instance, they said it was okay to spit on a rock on the Sabbath, but it was not all right to spit on soft ground. Why? Because your spit might move the dirt—and that was work! Also, they said that walking too far on the Sabbath was work. The maximum distance you could walk was called "a Sabbath day's walk," and was less than one mile (see Acts 1:12).

Sacrifice

To sacrifice means to offer the life of something to God to gain forgiveness. The Jews sacrificed animals such as lambs, bulls, calves, goats, and doves. But the blood of their sacrifice covered their sin only for a short time. So a permanent sacrifice was needed. Jesus was the final sacrifice to pay for all sins for all time.

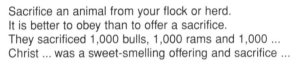

Key Verse

"Jesus our priest offered one sacrifice for sins for all time.... By that one sacrifice he has made perfect forever those who are being made holy." (Hebrews 10:12, 14)

Sacrifice an animal from your flock or herd.	Deuteronomy 16:2
It is better to obey than to offer a sacrifice.	1 Samuel 15:22
They sacrificed 1,000 bulls, 1,000 rams and 1,000 ...	1 Chronicles 29:21
Christ ... was a sweet-smelling offering and sacrifice ...	Ephesians 5:2

Sadducee

The Sadducees were a Jewish religious group. Unlike the Pharisees, the Sadducees didn't worry about keeping God's Law too exactly, and they mixed Greek ideas with the Jewish faith. For example, they didn't believe that people rise from the dead. The Sadducees often clashed with Jesus, who called them hypocrites. They were afraid that if people listened to Jesus, they wouldn't listen to them. So they plotted to kill him.

Key Verse

"The high priest and all his companions were Sadducees. They were very jealous of the apostles." (Acts 5:17)

The ... Sadducees came to put Jesus to the test.	Matthew 16:1
He was warning them against what ... Sadducees taught.	Matthew 16:12
... Sadducees do not believe ... people rise from the dead.	Luke 20:27
The Pharisees and the Sadducees started to argue.	Acts 23:7

Salvation

Salvation is a rescue or deliverance. In the New Testament we are saved from sin and its penalties. Jesus, God's Son, came to earth and died on the cross to pay the penalty for our sins. You can become a Christian by asking Jesus to take over your life. Just admit that you have done wrong things and need forgiveness, then apologize to Jesus for your sins and ask him to forgive you. That's how easy it is to receive salvation and become God's child. Then read the Bible, do what it says, and get to know God more.

Key Verse

"God didn't choose us to receive his anger. He chose us to receive salvation because of what our Lord Jesus Christ has done."
(1 Thessalonians 5:9)

He has saved me. He is my God. I will praise him.	Exodus 15:2
Everyone who calls out to me will be saved.	Joel 2:32
But anyone who stands firm to the end will be saved.	Matthew 10:22
Anyone who believes in him will ... have eternal life.	John 3:16
I'm like a gate. Anyone who enters through me ... saved.	John 10:9
Put on the helmet of salvation.	Ephesians 6:17

Suggested Reading

It's not easy for the rich to be saved.	Matthew 19:16–26; Mark 10:17–31
God shows his love by Jesus' death.	Romans 5:8–21
Jesus is the foundation of our salvation.	1 Corinthians 3:10–15

Didjaknow?

To orthodox Jews, the word "salvation" does not mean personal salvation. When they think of salvation, they think of *national* salvation: the entire nation of Israel being saved and delivered from their enemies. Even Jesus' disciples, after his resurrection, asked him, "Are you going to give the kingdom back to Israel now?" (Acts 1:6). But eternal salvation of souls is far more important than temporary deliverance from enemies.

Samaritan

The Samaritans were descendants of mixed marriages between Israelites and people the Assyrians imported into the northern kingdom. These people became known as Samaritans because they lived in Samaria, a region between Judea and Galilee. The Jews didn't like the Samaritans, partly because Samaritans thought that the place to worship God was on Mount Gerizim, not in Jerusalem, as the Jews believed.

Key Verse

"You Samaritans worship what you do not know. We worship what we do know. Salvation comes from the Jews." (John 4:22)

... brought people from Babylon.... settled ... Samaria.	2 Kings 17:24
A Samaritan came to the place where the man was ...	Luke 10:25–37
He threw himself at Jesus' feet ... man was a Samaritan.	Luke 17:16
... Jews don't have anything to do with Samaritans.	John 4:9

Samson

Samson was one of the judges. God told Samson's mother that her son must never cut his hair. Samson grew up to be very strong. But he was tricked into telling a Philistine woman the secret of his strength. So the Philistines cut his hair and captured him. Later, Samson prayed for strength, then pushed against the pillars and collapsed an entire Philistine temple.

Key Verse

"You will become pregnant. You will have a son. He must not use a razor on his head. He must not cut his hair. That is because the boy will be a Nazirite. He will be set apart to God from the day he is born." (Judges 13:5)

A young lion came roaring ... He tore the lion apart ...	Judges 14:5–6
Samson said, "By using ... jawbone I've struck down ..."	Judges 15:16
Samson led Israel for 20 years. In those days the ...	Judges 15:20
Samson said, "Let me die together with the Philistines!"	Judges 16:30

Samuel

Samuel became Israel's leader in the time period after the judges. He was different from the other judges, who had mostly been military leaders: Samuel was also a prophet. Under Samuel's leadership, the Israelites decided that they wanted to follow God. Samuel led them in victory over the Philistines. When Samuel was old, he wanted to make his sons judges over Israel. But Samuel's sons were more interested in taking bribes than obeying God. The elders of Israel demanded a king. So God used Samuel to anoint Saul as their king. Later, Samuel also anointed Israel's second king, David.

Key Verse

"The Lord came and stood there. He called out, just as he had done the other times. He said, 'Samuel! Samuel!' Then Samuel replied, 'Speak. I'm listening.'" (1 Samuel 3:10)

The Lord ... made everything Samuel said come true.	1 Samuel 3:19–20
Samuel continued to lead Israel all the days of his life.	1 Samuel 7:15
In spite of what Samuel said ... people refused to listen ...	1 Samuel 8:19
Then Samuel took ... oil. He poured it on Saul's head ...	1 Samuel 10:1
So Samuel ... anointed David in front of his brothers.	1 Samuel 16:13
Samuel and all the prophets after him spoke about this.	Acts 3:24

Suggested Reading

The Lord calls Samuel.	1 Samuel 3
The people ask for a king.	1 Samuel 8
Samuel and the witch at Endor.	1 Samuel 28

Didjaknow?

Before Samuel was born, his mother, Hannah, had not been able to have children. The Israelites thought that if a woman could not have children, God was punishing her. Hannah cried out to God to give her a son. She promised that if he did, she would give the son back to God. Hannah soon became pregnant with Samuel, and she did give him to God.

Sanhedrin

The Sanhedrin was the high council in charge of everyday life in Israel in Jesus' time, and was the final authority on religious matters. The 71 members of the Sanhedrin were chief priests, Pharisees, and Sadducees. They had their own police force and could arrest people. The high priest was the "president" of the Sanhedrin and a Sadducee. The Sanhedrin condemned Jesus to death.

CALIFORNIA

I'VE FOUND SAN DIEGO AND SAN FRANCISCO, BUT NO SAN HEDRIN.

San Francisco

San Diego

Key Verse

"The chief priests and the whole Sanhedrin were looking for something to use against Jesus. They wanted to put him to death. But they did not find any proof." (Mark 14:55)

The chief priests and the elders of the people had sent ...	Matthew 26:47
The chief priests and the teachers ... made fun of him.	Mark 15:31–32
... arrested Stephen and brought him to the Sanhedrin.	Acts 6:12
... members of the Sanhedrin were throwing stones ...	Acts 7:59

Sarah

Sarah was the wife of Abraham. She was also his half sister and was very beautiful. When she was nearly 70, she was still so beautiful that Pharaoh wanted to marry her. When she and Abraham arrived in Canaan, her name was *Sarai*. God changed her name to Sarah, which means *Princess*. He gave her a miracle baby, Isaac, when she was too old to have children.

Key Verse

"As for Sarai your wife, do not call her Sarai anymore. Her name will be Sarah. I will give her my blessing.... I will bless her so that she will be the mother of nations. Kings of nations will come from her." (Genesis 17:15–16)

... to ... Sarai.... "I know what a beautiful woman you are."	Genesis 12:11
Abraham ... laughed ... "Will Sarah have a child at ... 90?"	Genesis 17:17
The Lord was gracious ... Sarah became pregnant.	Genesis 21:1–2
The holy women ... hope in God.... Sarah was like that.	1 Peter 3:5–6

Satan

Satan is God's enemy. He is also called the Devil, Lucifer, the Serpent, and the Dragon. Satan is not as powerful as God. He is only an angel created by God. When Satan was created, he was good, but he rebelled against God and was kicked out of heaven. The Bible says Satan pretends to be an "angel of light" (2 Corinthians 11:14). He tries to make bad look good and tempts people to sin. He tricked Eve in the garden of Eden, but when he tempted Jesus, Jesus refused to give in. Satan's power was broken by Jesus' death and resurrection.

JASON'S IMAGINATION

I'M NOT SORRY, GOD!!
I'LL NEVER BE SORRY
(But I don't want you to punish me)
SO THERE!

HELL

Key Verse

"The God who gives peace will soon crush Satan under your feet." (Romans 16:20)

The woman said, "The serpent tricked me. That's why ..."	Genesis 3:13
Jesus said ... "Get away from me, Satan! It is written ..."	Matthew 4:10
I saw Satan fall like lightning from heaven.	Luke 10:18
Then Satan entered Judas, who was called Iscariot.	Luke 22:3
The devil was a murderer.... He is the father of lies.	John 8:44
The devil ... was thrown into the lake of burning ...	Revelation 20:10

Suggested Reading

The devil tempts Adam and Eve and is cursed.	Genesis 3
Satan persecutes Job.	Job 1–2
Satan symbolized by the king of Babylonia.	Isaiah 14:12–15
Satan symbolized by the king of Tyre.	Ezekiel 28:11–17
Satan is completely defeated.	Revelation 17–18; 20:7–10

Didjaknow?

Satan's power was broken when Jesus died for our sins. Colossians 2:15 says, "He took away the weapons of the powers and authorities.... He won the battle over them by dying on the cross." We still need to be on guard against the devil because "your enemy the devil is like a roaring lion. He prowls around looking for someone to chew up" (1 Peter 5:8), but by the power of Jesus' name, we have authority over him.

Saul

Saul was the first king of Israel. Saul certainly looked like a king; he was tall and good-looking. At first, Saul was very humble. With God's help, Saul became a good king and the people loved him. Later, however, he seriously disobeyed God several times, so God replaced him with King David. Because of that, Saul tried to kill David.

Key Verse

> "Kish had a son named Saul. Saul was a handsome young man. There wasn't anyone like him among the people of Israel. He was a head taller than any of them." (1 Samuel 9:2)

Then Samuel took ... oil. He poured it on Saul's head.	1 Samuel 10:1
As Saul turned to leave Samuel, God changed Saul's heart.	1 Samuel 10:9
The Lord has torn the kingdom ... away from you today.	1 Samuel 15:28
Saul ... remained David's enemy as long as he was king.	1 Samuel 18:29

Savior

A savior is someone who delivers others from evil or danger. In the Bible, the judges were referred to as saviors because they delivered the Israelites from danger. God is the greatest Savior of all! His Son, Jesus Christ, is *"The Savior"* because he delivers us from our sins and sets us free to be God's children. In fact, *Jesus* means *savior*.

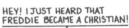

HEY! I JUST HEARD THAT FREDDIE BECAME A CHRISTIAN!

GOOD SAVE, JESUS!

Key Verse

> "It has now been made known through the coming of our Savior, Christ Jesus. He has destroyed death. Because of the good news, he has brought life out into the light. That life never dies." (2 Timothy 1:10)

They cried out to the Lord.... gave them a man to save ...	Judges 3:9, 15
Today in the town of David a Savior has been born ...	Luke 2:11
Jesus is Prince and Savior.... turn Israel ... from ... sins ...	Acts 5:31
It pleases God our Savior. He wants everyone to be saved.	1 Timothy 2:3–4

Scribe

(See Teacher of the Law)

Scripture

Scripture is God's Word. God often told the prophets to write his words in a book (scroll). The Law was called the Books of the Law. Since *Bible* is the Greek word for *book*, the Scriptures are called the Bible. The Bible is a collection of 66 books in one. It's called *The* Book because it's so important. It is an instruction manual: It tells us what's right and what's wrong. The Bible also tells us who God is and what he is like. Finally, the Bible tells us how much God loves us and how he made a way for us to have a relationship with him.

Key Verse

"God has breathed life into all of Scripture. It is useful for teaching us what is true. It is useful for correcting our mistakes. It is useful for making our lives whole again. It is useful for training us to do what is right." (2 Timothy 3:16)

... keep his life pure? By living in keeping with your word.	Psalm 119:9
Your word is like a lamp that shows me the way. It is ...	Psalm 119:105
... lives on every word that comes from the mouth of God.	Matthew 4:4
... the Holy Scriptures ... teach you how to be saved ...	2 Timothy 3:15
Suppose you listen to the word but don't do what it says.	James 1:23
No prophecy in Scripture ... came from a prophet's own ...	2 Peter 1:20

Suggested Reading

King Josiah finds the Book of God's Law.	2 Chronicles 34
Ezra reads God's Word to the people for days.	Nehemiah 8:1–9:3

Didjaknow?

The words in our Bible are accurate! It is the best-preserved ancient book in the world. For example, we have over 5000 ancient, handwritten copies or parts of copies of the New Testament, some made only 50 to 100 years after the original. The next best-kept ancient document, in terms of how many copies we have and how soon after the original they were made, is a story called *The Iliad* by a Greek writer named Homer. There are only 643 known copies of *The Iliad*, and the oldest was made 500 years after the original.

Scroll

In Bible times, they had scrolls, not books. Before paper was invented, writing was done on dried animal skin, called "parchment," or on "papyrus," made from leaves of the papyrus plant. The pieces of parchment or papyrus were then glued or sewn together to form one long strip that was rolled up from both ends. This was called a scroll.

Key Verse

"Get a scroll. Write on it all of the words I have spoken to you. Write down what I have said about Israel, Judah and all of the other nations. Write what I have said to you from the time of King Josiah until now." (Jeremiah 36:2)

I finished writing the words of that law in a scroll.	Deuteronomy 31:24
I've found the Scroll of the Law in the Lord's temple.	2 Kings 22:8
... stars ... vanish. The sky will be rolled up like a scroll.	Isaiah 34:4
The scroll of the prophet Isaiah ... He unrolled it ...	Luke 4:17

Second Coming

(See Jesus' Second Coming)

Secret

A secret is something you know that you don't tell anyone. Most of the time it's all right to have secrets. Sometimes keeping a secret is important because it's best not to give out information to just anyone. God tells us to do some things in secret—like pray or give money away—and not boast about it. It's enough that God knows.

Key Verse

"Those who talk about others tell secrets. But those who can be trusted keep things to themselves." (Proverbs 11:13)

If you talk about a matter with your neighbor, don't tell ...	Proverbs 25:9
Your giving will be done secretly.... [God] sees what ...	Matthew 6:3–4
Jesus ... gave the man a strong warning. "Don't tell ..."	Mark 1:43–45
Don't tell anyone you have reported this to me.	Acts 23:22

Sense of Right and Wrong

(See Conscience)

Servant

A slave receives no wages, but a servant is paid and rewarded for his work. In the Bible, hired workers were paid at the end of every day. Christians are servants of the Lord, and we should serve God and each other in love. If we serve God faithfully, "the Lord will give each of us a reward for our work" (1 Corinthians 3:8). It's an honor to be God's servant. Moses and David were both called "the servant of God." Jesus was also called God's servant. He lived to please his Father and to do the work God sent him to do. He even served people!

Key Verse

"Instead, anyone who wants to be important among you must be your servant.... Be like the Son of Man. He did not come to be served. Instead, he came to serve others." (Matthew 20:26, 28)

Don't take advantage of any hired worker ... Give them ...	Deuteronomy 24:14–15
I say to my servant, "Do this," and he does it.	Matthew 8:9
Here is my servant.... I am very pleased with him.	Matthew 12:18
The master will ... serve them.... good for those servants ...	Luke 12:37–38
You have done well, my good servant!... I will put you ...	Luke 19:17
He took on the very nature of a servant.... as a man.	Philippians 2:7–8

Suggested Reading

Jesus, the Suffering Servant.	Isaiah 53
We should do everything God asks us to.	Luke 17:7–10

Didjaknow?

Sometimes we think that only pastors and missionaries and "great men and women" are "serving the Lord." This isn't true. We are *all* servants of God. In Paul's day, some Christians were *slaves*. They belonged to another person and had to work all day doing what that person said. Could even a *slave* be a servant of God? Yes! Paul said, "Slaves, obey your earthly masters ... Do it out of respect for the Lord.... *You are serving the Lord Christ*" (Colossians 3:22–24, italics added).

Sheep

Sheep need to be cared for and led. They need a shepherd. God watches over his people like a shepherd. "You are the sheep belonging to my flock. You are my people" (Ezekiel 34:31). As Jesus' followers, we are his sheep. He cares for us. Jesus said, "My sheep listen to my voice.... and they follow me" (John 10:27).

JASON'S IMAGINATION

The Lost Sheep of the House of Israel.

Key Verse

"He is our God. We are the sheep belonging to his flock. We are the people he takes good care of." (Psalm 95:7)

We are your people. We are your very own sheep. Psalm 79:13
He made us ... We are the sheep belonging to ... Psalm 100:3
All of us are like sheep. We have wandered away from ... Isaiah 53:6
You were like sheep who were wandering away. 1 Peter 2:25

Shepherd

Shepherds are people who look after sheep. When Moses fled Egypt, he went to Midian where he was a shepherd for 40 years. Before he became king of Israel, David was a shepherd, taking care of his father's sheep. For thousands of years, shepherds have cared for sheep in Israel. Shepherds were not very respected, yet they were the first people to hear the wonderful news about the birth of the Messiah, Jesus. The Bible says that God is our shepherd, and we are his sheep. Jesus said that he was "the good shepherd" who looks after us, leads us, and feeds us.

JASON, NOW REMEMBER THIS IS JUST A PLAY.

SCRIPT

Key Verse

"The Lord is my shepherd. He gives me everything I need." (Psalm 23:1)

He brought him [David] ... to be the shepherd of ...	Psalm 78:70–71
He takes care of his flock like a shepherd. He gathers ...	Isaiah 40:11
Suppose a man owns 100 sheep and one of them ...	Matthew 18:12–14
They were like sheep without a shepherd. So he began ...	Mark 6:34
I am the good shepherd. The good shepherd gives his ...	John 10:11
Our Lord Jesus is the great Shepherd of the sheep.	Hebrews 13:20

Suggested Reading

The Shepherd Psalm.	Psalm 23
God is a Shepherd who rescues his sheep.	Ezekiel 34
Jesus is the Good Shepherd.	John 10:1–21, 26–29

Didjaknow?

Jesus said that a shepherd's sheep "follow him because they know his voice" (John 10:4). When two or more flocks mix together, the best way for shepherds to find all their sheep is to call them. The sheep recognize their own shepherd's voice and come to him.

Ship

The countries beside the Mediterranean Sea used large ships for trade and war. Solomon built ships that sailed to Ophir (1 Kings 9:26–28). Usually, however, the Jews had few ships, just small fishing boats on the Sea of Galilee. The Roman Empire had many ships to carry cargo and passengers. Paul once sailed on a ship carrying grain from Alexandria to Italy (Acts 27:6).

Key Verse

"And how about ships? They are very big. They are driven along by strong winds. But they are steered by a very small rudder. It makes them go where the captain wants to go." (James 3:4)

But Jonah ... found a ship that was going to Tarshish.	Jonah 1:3
Jesus got into a boat.... Suddenly a terrible storm came ...	Matthew 8:23–24
The ship was caught by the storm. We could not keep ...	Acts 27:15
... have destroyed their faith.... like a ship that has sunk.	1 Timothy 1:19

Sickness

We live in an imperfect world full of germs. Because of that, we get sick sometimes. God protects us from many sicknesses when we stay clean and pray. When we do get sick, God is able to heal us. Jesus healed many sick people. Doctors can help too. The gospel of Luke was written by a doctor who traveled with Paul.

Key Verse

"Jesus went all over Galilee.... He preached the good news of God's kingdom. He healed every illness and sickness the people had." (Matthew 4:23)

I am ... God.... I will take away sickness from among you.	Exodus 23:25
He gave them authority to ... heal every ... sickness.	Matthew 10:1
I [Paul] left Trophimus sick in Miletus.	2 Timothy 4:20
Are any of you sick? Then send for the elders of the ...	James 5:14–15

Silas

After Paul and Barnabas had a disagreement, Paul chose Silas as his helper. They traveled from city to city, preaching the gospel. In Philippi, Paul and Silas were beaten and thrown in jail. When they got out, they continued preaching the gospel. Paul and Silas traveled back to Antioch, then went on another missionary journey. After Paul died, Silas worked with Peter.

Key Verse

"Barnabas took Mark and sailed for Cyprus. But Paul chose Silas. The believers asked the Lord to give his grace to Paul and Silas as they went." (Acts 15:39–40)

Judas and Silas were prophets. They said many things to ...	Acts 15:32
The judges ordered that Paul and Silas be ... beaten.	Acts 16:22
About midnight Paul and Silas were praying.	Acts 16:25
I consider Silas to be a faithful brother. With his help I ...	1 Peter 5:12

Sin

To sin means to "miss the mark" and do something God has said not to do. We all sin. A sin can be a thought, word, or act. The first sin was when Adam and Eve doubted God's word, disobeyed him, and went their own way. Sin separates us from God, who is holy. The penalty for sin is death. But Jesus came to earth and died on the cross to pay the penalty for our sin, so we wouldn't have to. If we believe in Jesus, God will forgive us for our sin. And when God's Spirit lives in our heart, he will help us not to sin.

Key Verse

"When you sin, the pay you get is death. But God gives you the gift of eternal life because of what Christ Jesus our Lord has done." (Romans 6:23)

If you don't do what is right, sin is waiting ... to grab ...	Genesis 4:7
Sacrifice a bull ... It is a sin offering to pay for their sins.	Exodus 29:36
Blessed is the man whose sin the Lord never counts ...	Psalm 32:2
Everyone has sinned. No one measures up to God's glory.	Romans 3:23
When sin has grown up, it gives birth to death.	James 1:15
He didn't commit any sin. No lies ever came out of his ...	1 Peter 2:22

Suggested Reading

If your right eye causes you to sin.	Matthew 5:29–30
Everyone who sins is a slave to sin.	John 8:34–36
Struggling with sin.	Romans 7:7–25; 8:1–13

Didjaknow?

In the Old Testament, God had the Israelites use a "scapegoat" to take away their sins. Aaron confessed the sins of the Israelites over a live goat. The goat was then sent into the wilderness on the Day of Atonement (Leviticus 16:8, 10, 26). The person who released the goat had to wash his clothes and bathe afterward (Leviticus 16:26). This ritual symbolized the complete removal of guilt from the Israelites. Today the word scapegoat is a slang term for someone who takes all the blame.

Sinai

Sinai, also called Horeb, is a mountain in the Sinai Peninsula. When Moses was a shepherd in the desert near Sinai, the angel of the Lord appeared to him from inside a burning bush. After the Israelites left Egypt, God led them to Mount Sinai. There God put on a spectacular display of power with lightning, fire, and an earthquake. He spoke to them there and gave Moses the Law and the Ten Commandments.

Key Verse

"Exactly three months after the people of Israel left Egypt, they came to the Desert of Sinai.... They camped there in the desert in front of the mountain." (Exodus 19:1–2)

Smoke covered Mount Sinai, because the Lord came ...	Exodus 19:18
The Lord finished speaking to Moses on Mount Sinai.	Exodus 31:18
[Elijah] arrived at Horeb [Sinai].... the mountain of God.	1 Kings 19:8
One covenant comes from Mount Sinai.... in Arabia.	Galatians 4:24–25

Sinful Nature

(See Flesh)

Skill and Ability

Talents are natural skills and abilities that God has given us and that we are born with. They perfectly match who we are and what God wants us to do. Skills and talents include such things as the ability to sing, solve mathematical problems, or draw. Our talents should be trained and developed so we can use them to their fullest potential for God and others. Daniel and his friends were chosen because they had "the ability to understand  new things quickly and easily" (Daniel 1:4). God gave them wisdom as they studied in Babylon and at the end of three years "they understood all kinds of writings and subjects" (Daniel 1:17).

Key Verse

"The Lord has chosen Bezalel, the son of Uri. Uri is the son of Hur. Bezalel is from the tribe of Judah. The Lord has filled him with the Spirit of God. He has filled him with skill, ability and knowledge in all kinds of crafts." (Exodus 35:30–31)

The Lord has filled them with skill to do all kinds of work.   Exodus 35:35
... someone ... skilled at working with gold ... able to ...   2 Chronicles 2:7
The Levites were skilled in playing musical instruments.   2 Chronicles 34:12
Do you see a man who does good work? He will serve ...   Proverbs 22:29
He has a clever mind ... He can ... solve hard problems.   Daniel 5:12
How did this man learn so much without studying?   John 7:15

Suggested Reading

The extremely talented, skilled Huram.   1 Kings 7:13–50
Daniel's natural abilities and training.   Daniel 1

Didjaknow?

Sometimes someone comes along who seems to have hundreds of talents. Look at Bezalel for example: God "filled him with skill, ability and knowledge in all kinds of crafts. He can make beautiful patterns in gold, silver and bronze. He can cut and set stones. He can work with wood. In fact, he can work in all *kinds* of arts and crafts. *And* the Lord has given both him and Oholiab the ability to teach others.... They carve things ... They sew skillfully ... They use thread ... They have the skill ..." (Exodus 35:30–35, italics added). You get the picture. Many or few, *everyone* has talents to use and enjoy.

Slave

SO! YOU DON'T HAVE THE $2 THAT I LENT YOU? HMMMM M... IN THE BIBLE, PEOPLE WHO COULDN'T PAY THEIR DEBTS SOLD THEMSELVES AS SLAVES!

I'LL DO ANYTHING! JUST PLEASE DON'T MAKE ME CLEAN YOUR ROOM!

A slave is a person who is owned by someone else. Slaves have no freedom and few rights. During Bible times, prisoners of war were often made into slaves. People who couldn't pay their debts were also made into slaves. God treats everyone the same, whether they're slaves or free people (Galatians 3:28). Spiritually, we were all born "slaves to sin," and Christ died to set us free.

Key Verse

"Christ has set us free. He wants us to enjoy freedom. So stand firm. Don't let the chains of slavery hold you again." (Galatians 5:1)

Egyptians put slave drivers over the people of Israel.   Exodus 1:11
I've been like a slave who longs for the evening ...   Job 7:2
Anyone who wants to be first must be the slave of everyone.   Mark 10:44
Everyone who sins is a slave of sin.   John 8:34

Snake

God created all animals, including snakes. The devil disguised himself as a snake (serpent) when he deceived Eve in the Garden of Eden. Ever since then, people have thought of snakes as evil. But there were other snakes in the Bible. Moses' staff turned into a snake, and when the Israelites

looked at a bronze snake on a pole, they were healed.

Key Verse

"A baby will play near a hole where cobras live. A young child will put his hand into a nest where poisonous snakes live. None of those animals will harm or destroy anything or anyone on my holy mountain of Zion." (Isaiah 11:8–9)

The serpent was more clever than any of the ... animals ...   Genesis 3:1
So Moses threw it on the ground. It turned into a snake.   Exodus 4:3
The Lord said ... "Make a snake. Put it up on a pole."   Numbers 21:8
Moses lifted up the snake ... [Jesus] must be lifted up also.   John 3:14

Solomon

Solomon was the king of Israel after his father, David. One day God told Solomon that he would give him whatever he asked for. Solomon did not ask for money, power, or a long life, as many people would have. He asked for wisdom. God was so pleased with Solomon's request that he gave him tremendous wisdom—as well as wealth, power, and a long life. Solomon built the temple in Jerusalem. He also wrote parts of Psalms and Proverbs, and he wrote Ecclesiastes and Song of Songs. Sadly, when Solomon was old, he started worshiping the gods that his many wives worshiped.

Key Verse

"God made Solomon very wise. His understanding couldn't even be measured. It was like the sand on the seashore. People can't measure that either." (1 Kings 4:29)

Solomon sat on the throne of his father David.... king ...	1 Kings 2:12
The Lord appeared to Solomon at Gibeon. He spoke ...	1 Kings 3:5
... He said, "Cut the living child in two. Give half ..."	1 Kings 3:24–25
So Solomon built the temple and finished it.	1 Kings 6:14
People from the whole world wanted to meet Solomon ...	1 Kings 10:24
... Solomon's wisdom.... one ... more important ... is here.	Luke 11:31

Suggested Reading

God makes Solomon very wise.	1 Kings 4:29–34
Solomon builds the temple.	1 Kings 6
Solomon is visited by the Queen of Sheba.	1 Kings 10:1–13
Solomon's riches.	1 Kings 10:14–29
Solomon's wives turn him away from God.	1 Kings 11:1–13

Didjaknow?

Solomon was extremely rich. Each year he received 25 tons of gold. Today that would almost be enough money to buy a $10 pizza for every man, woman, and child in Alaska, Arizona, Colorado, Idaho, Montana, Nebraska, Nevada, New Mexico, North Dakota, Oregon, South Dakota, Utah, Washington, and Wyoming— with enough money left over for a big tip for the totally exhausted delivery person.

Spirit

Like angels, people are spiritual beings. Our spirit is the real us, and it will live forever. It lives inside our physical body. Because of sin, without God our spirits are dead. But Jesus and his Holy Spirit have made us alive again. When our physical body dies, our spirit will go to live with God in heaven.

Key Verse

"The Spirit himself joins with our spirits. Together they give witness that we are God's children." (Romans 8:16)

His spirit became very sad, and he was troubled.	John 11:33
Who can know the thoughts of another ...? Only a ...	1 Corinthians 2:11
His spirit will be saved on the day the Lord returns.	1 Corinthians 5:5
The body without the spirit is dead.	James 2:26

Stand Firm

Perseverance, or standing firm in your faith, means "having the endurance to keep going, even when everything seems to be pulling you the other way." It is finishing what you're doing no matter what life throws at you. When we stand firm for what we believe, our character grows and we become stronger. And what gives us the strength to stand firm? What helps us stay true to God when we're tempted? Keeping our eyes on Jesus and remembering our reward in heaven. That makes it worth it all!

Key Verse

"My dear brothers and sisters, stand firm. Don't let anything move you....
Because you belong to the Lord, you know that your work is not worthless." (1 Corinthians 15:58)

We know that our suffering gives us the strength to go on.	Romans 5:3–5
We don't give up.... Our troubles ... last only for a short ...	2 Corinthians 4:16–17
Let us not become tired of doing good.... don't give up.	Galatians 6:9
So think about [Jesus]. Then you won't ... lose hope.	Hebrews 12:2–3
... all kinds of trouble.... produce in you the strength ...	James 1:2–3
You must stand firm. The Lord will soon come back.	James 5:8

Suggested Reading

Stand firm, stay faithful when tempted.	Hebrews 10:19–39

Didjaknow?

No matter what storm hits the Rock of Gibraltar, it doesn't move. It stands firm. It can't be moved. It's still there when the storm ends. People who are strong and stand up to the storms of life are called rocks. Jesus said a wise person who obeys his sayings is like someone who builds their house on a rock. That house can survive all the rain and floods and storms of life, and still stand firm (Matthew 7:24–25). God is the strongest, most reliable rock of all. "How great he is! *He* is the Rock" (Deuteronomy 32:3–4, italics added)!

Star

Stars are mentioned many times in the Bible. In the Old Testament, God promised Abraham that he would have as many descendants as there are stars. In the New Testament, God announced the birth of Jesus with a bright star in the east. This star was noticed by the wise men who came to worship Jesus. The Bible mentions many stars and star groups by name.

Key Verse

"They asked, 'Where is the child who has been born to be king of the Jews? When we were in the east, we saw his star. Now we have come to worship him.'" (Matthew 2:2)

I will make your children after you as many as the stars ...	Genesis 22:17
He made the Big Dipper and Orion.... southern stars.	Job 9:9
Pleiades ... Orion ... Can you lead out the ... Little Dipper?	Job 38:31–32
I think about the heavens.... stars that you have set in ...	Psalm 8:3–4

Stealing

"Do not steal" is one of God's commandments (Exodus 20:15). It is also against man's law. When you steal, it shows that you're not trusting God to supply your needs. It proves that you think your needs are more important than other people's needs. And since no one trusts a thief, it shows you value things more than good relationships with other people.

Key Verse

"Those who have been stealing must never steal again. Instead, they must work. They must do something useful with their own hands. Then they will have something to give to people in need." (Ephesians 4:28)

A thief must pay for what he has stolen.... he must ...	Exodus 22:3
Do not put away riches ... Thieves can break in ... steal ...	Matthew 6:19
You know what the commandments say.... Do not steal.	Luke 18:20
You preach against stealing. But you steal!	Romans 2:21

Stephen

Stephen was a follower of Jesus and one of the leaders of the early church. He was a powerful preacher who performed many miracles. The Jewish leaders didn't like what Stephen was doing, so they dragged him out of the city and stoned him. Stephen was the first Christian to be killed for his faith. As he died, he had a vision of Jesus in heaven.

Key Verse

"While the members of the Sanhedrin were throwing stones at Stephen, he prayed. 'Lord Jesus, receive my spirit,' he said. Then he fell on his knees. He cried out, 'Lord! Don't hold this sin against them!' When he had said this, he died." (Acts 7:59–60)

Stephen was full of God's grace and power. He did ...	Acts 6:8
... Stephen.... his face was like the face of an angel.	Acts 6:15
He looked up ... saw Jesus standing at God's right hand.	Acts 7:55
Saul was there. He had agreed that Stephen should die.	Acts 8:1

Story

JASON, COME HELP ME WEED.

BUT MOM, JESUS SAID IN HIS PARABLE OF THE WEEDS, THAT YOU *SHOULDN'T* PULL THE WEEDS OUT. YOU SHOULD LET THEM GROW TOGETHER WITH THE GOOD PLANTS UNTIL HARVEST.

Jesus told a lot of stories to help people understand what he was teaching. These stories are called "parables." The parables Jesus told were lessons about God that taught people how to live. Jesus also taught that, when we understand something about God or how he wants us to live, we're responsible to do it. Everything Jesus taught is still true today.

Jesus was not the only one who told stories. Several men and women in the Old Testament told parables and stories. Sometimes when it was dangerous to tell the truth openly, people told stories to get their message across.

Key Verse

"Jesus spoke all these things to the crowd by using stories. He did not say anything to them without telling a story." (Matthew 13:34)

Nathan ... said, "Two men lived in the same town. One ..."	2 Samuel 12:1–9
Jehoash ... said, "A thorn bush ... sent a message to a ..."	2 Kings 14:9
[The Wise and Foolish Builders] He builds his house ...	Matthew 7:24–27
[The Story of the Farmer] ... other seed fell on good soil.	Matthew 13:1–23

[The Story of the Lost Sheep] Suppose a man owns 100 ...   Matthew 18:10–14
[The Story of the Lost Son] ... a man who had two sons.   Luke 15:11–32

Suggested Reading

A woman from Tekoa tells a story.   2 Samuel 14:1–16
Jesus tells six different stories.   Matthew 13
Jesus tells six more stories.   Matthew 21:28–45;
                                                            22:1–14; 25:1–46

Didjaknow?

Often people talked in parables because it was dangerous to tell the truth
plainly. One day a man named Abimelech killed all of Gideon's sons. Only
the youngest son, Jotham, escaped. Later, when a crowd met at Shechem to
crown Abimelech king, Jotham stood on top of a hill and shouted so the
people below could hear him. He told them a funny story about how the trees
decided to make a thornbush their king. Everyone listened to his story.
Suddenly Jotham told them that the story was about *them!* Before they could
grab him, Jotham ran down the other side of the hill and was gone (Judges 9).

Synagogue

JASON'S IMAGINATION

After their temple in Jerusalem was
destroyed by the Babylonians, the Jews
built the synagogues to replace it. Every
town had its own synagogue where
people got together to read from the
Scriptures and pray. Synagogues were
also schools where Jewish children
learned to read and write. In New
Testament times, synagogues were
everywhere, and Paul often visited
them to tell the Jews about Jesus.

Key Verse

"These laws of Moses have been
preached in every city from the earliest times. They are read out
loud in the synagogues every Sabbath day." (Acts 15:21)

Jesus went all over Galilee.... taught in the synagogues.   Matthew 4:23
Then a man named Jarius came. He was a synagogue ruler. Mark 5:22–24
On the Sabbath day [Jesus] went into the synagogue ...   Luke 4:16
They preached God's word in the Jewish synagogues.   Acts 13:5

Tabernacle

(See Tent of Meeting)

Talent

(See Skill and Ability)

Tax Collector

Tax collectors were men who collected taxes from the Jews for the Romans. They were hated by their fellow Jews because they gathered more than they should have and then pocketed the extra amount. Jesus, however, accepted and loved tax collectors. He even chose one, Matthew, as one of his disciples. And Zacchaeus, a tax collector from Jericho, also became a follower of Jesus.

Key Verse

"As Jesus went on from there, he saw a man named Matthew. He was sitting at the tax collector's booth. 'Follow me,' Jesus told him. Matthew got up and followed him." (Matthew 9:9)

... dinner at Matthew's house.... tax collectors ... came.	Matthew 9:10–13
Tax collectors also came to be baptized.	Luke 3:12–13
Two men went up to the temple ... One ... a tax collector.	Luke 18:10
Zacchaeus ... was a chief tax collector and was very rich.	Luke 19:2–10

Teacher of the Law

Teachers of the Law wrote and made copies of the Law. They knew the Scriptures were God's words, so they treated them with great respect. They wrote out the Scriptures so often that they memorized large chunks of them. And because they knew the Law so well, they taught people what it meant. Many of them were against Jesus, but many also believed in him.

Key Verse

"'The teachers of the law and the Pharisees sit in Moses' seat,' he said. 'So you must obey them. Do everything they tell you. But don't do what they do. They don't practice what they preach.'" (Matthew 23:2–3)

... to bring out the Scroll ... Ezra was a teacher of the law.	Nehemiah 8:1
... a teacher of the law ... said, "Teacher I will follow ..."	Matthew 8:19
Every teacher of the law who has been taught about the ...	Matthew 13:52
How terrible it will be for you, teachers of the law ...	Matthew 23:13–14

Temple

Solomon built a beautiful temple, or house, for God in Jerusalem. This temple was where the Israelites worshiped God and brought sacrifices for almost 500 years. When the people of Judah sinned, God allowed the Babylonians to burn the temple down. The Jews later rebuilt it, but the new temple wasn't nearly as beautiful as Solomon's temple. Several hundred years later, King Herod tried to make the Jews like him by building the temple as beautiful as he could. This was the temple Jesus went to. Only a few years after the building was complete, it was destroyed again by the Romans.

Key Verse

"David asked if he could build a house for the God of Jacob. Instead, it was Solomon who built it for him. But the Most High God does not live in houses made by human hands." (Acts 7:46–48)

So this temple I've built certainly can't hold you!	1 Kings 8:27
... finished building the temple.... God ... commanded ...	Ezra 6:14
Jesus' disciples were talking about the temple.... how ...	Luke 21:5–6
... when you will not worship the Father ... in Jerusalem.	John 4:20–24
Don't you know that you yourselves are God's temple?	1 Corinthians 3:16
I didn't see a temple in the city.... the Lamb and ... God ...	Revelation 21:22

Suggested Reading

How Solomon builds and dedicates the temple.	1 Kings 5–8
The preparations David makes to build the temple.	1 Chronicles 22
The building of the second temple, after the Exile.	Ezra 3–6

Didjaknow?

King Herod had been rebuilding and decorating the temple for years before Jesus was born. When Jesus was thirty, around A.D. 26, the temple had been worked on for 46 years (John 2:20). The temple was—*finally!*—finished 38 years later in A.D. 64. Only six years later, in A.D. 70, the Romans destroyed it, knocking every stone to the ground.

Temptation

A temptation is a desire to do something wrong. It's not a sin to be tempted, but it is a sin to give in to temptation. When Jesus taught his disciples to pray, he told them to ask God to protect them from temptation. Jesus was tempted by Satan in the desert, and he was tempted in all the ways we are, but he never sinned.

Key Verse

"You are tempted in the same way all other human beings are. God is faithful. He will not let you be tempted any more than you can take. But when you are tempted, God will give you a way out so that you can stand up under it." (1 Corinthians 10:13)

... led Jesus into the desert. There the devil tempted him.   Matthew 4:1
I was afraid that Satan might have tempted you in some ...   1 Thessalonians 3:5
[He] has been tempted in every way, just as we are.   Hebrews 4:15
But your own evil longings tempt you. They lead you ...   James 1:14

Ten Commandments

The Ten Commandments are God's guidelines for living. God gave them to Moses on Mount Sinai. They were part of a covenant God made with the Israelites in which they agreed to be his people, and he agreed to be their God. Although God gave the Ten Commandments to the Israelites more than 3000 years ago, they are still important today. The Ten Commandments show who God is and how we should act toward him and each other. They cover things like how to worship God, how to treat other people's property, and how to treat our parents.

Key Verse

"Moses was there with the Lord for 40 days and 40 nights. He didn't eat any food or drink any water. The Lord wrote on the tablets the words of the covenant. Those words are the Ten Commandments." (Exodus 34:28)

The Lord ... gave him the two tablets ... made out of stone.   Exodus 31:18
Words were written on both sides of the tablet, front ...   Exodus 32:15

Moses ... threw the tablets out of his hands. — Exodus 32:19
Moses came down from Mount Sinai. He had the two ... — Exodus 34:29–30
The words on them were written by the finger of God. — Deuteronomy 9:10
These and other commandments ... included in one rule. — Romans 13:9

Suggested Reading

The Ten Commandments. — Exodus 20:1–17;
Deuteronomy
5:5–22

The Israelites turn away from God. — Exodus 32
God carves a second set of tablets. — Exodus 34:1–5

Didjaknow?

The Ten Commandments are in a special order. One to three tell us to love and honor God in our hearts and with our actions and words. Obeying them makes obeying the others possible. Number four links the first three, about loving God, to the last six, about loving people. Five shows us God's plan for how we learn to obey God and love people. Six tells us to love people from our hearts and respect life. Seven tells  us how to keep our most important relationships safe. Eight and nine tell us to love people with our actions and words. And ten tells us to keep our inner thoughts and attitudes right, which is the key to obeying all the rest.

Tenth

Another word for tenth is "tithe." In Old Testament times, God commanded the Israelites to give a tithe of all they produced to the priests and to the poor. Their giving showed that they trusted God to supply their needs, and showed that they were thankful for his care. Many Christians use the word "tithe" to describe giving a portion of their income back to God.

Key Verse

"A tenth of everything the land produces belongs to me. That includes grain from the soil and fruit from the trees. It is holy. It is set apart for me." (Leviticus 27:30)

Be sure to set apart a tenth of everything your fields ... — Deuteronomy 14:22
The year for giving the tenth to people who have ... needs. — Deuteronomy 26:12
The people ... began to give freely.... a tenth of everything. — 2 Chronicles 31:5–6
Bring the entire tenth to the storerooms in my temple. — Malachi 3:8–10

Tent of Meeting

The Tent of Meeting was where the Israelites worshiped God before Solomon built the temple in Jerusalem. It was built in the desert and had two rooms. The larger room was called the Holy Place, and the priests went in and out of it every day. The smaller room was called the Most Holy Place, where the ark of the covenant was.

Key Verse

"Then the Lord said to Moses, 'Set up the holy tent, the Tent of Meeting. Set it up on the first day of the first month.'" (Exodus 40:1–2)

Have them make a sacred tent for me. I will live among ...	Exodus 25:8
Make the holy tent ... like the pattern I will show you.	Exodus 25:9
Then the cloud covered the Tent of Meeting. The glory ...	Exodus 40:34–38
... I am ... in a palace ... the ark of God remains in a tent.	2 Samuel 7:2

Testament

Testament is another word for "covenant." The new covenant (forgiveness of sins) went into effect when Jesus died on the cross. The second half of our Bible is called the New Testament because—in the original language—Matthew 26:28 says, "This is my blood of the *new testament*" (italics added). Testament also means "a will." Jesus made a will, and after he died, we received the inheritance: forgiveness and eternal life!

Key Verse

"That's why Christ is the go-between of a new covenant.... He died to set them free from the sins they committed under the first covenant. What happens in the case of a will?... A will is in effect only when somebody has died." (Hebrews 9:15–17)

I will make a new covenant with the people of Israel.	Jeremiah 31:31
[Jesus] said, "This cup is the new covenant in my blood."	Luke 22:20
He has given us the power to serve under a new covenant.	2 Corinthians 3:6
Jesus makes the promise of a better covenant certain.	Hebrews 7:22

Test

God tests us to help us grow strong and to make us more like Jesus. Sometimes God allows us to get in a difficult situation where we have to make a hard choice, so we can see what's in our hearts. Or he lets us do without something that we think we need to teach us to "give thanks no matter what happens" (1 Thessalonians 5:18). Sometimes God waits to answer our prayers to teach us to keep loving and trusting him. We may be tempted to stop trusting, but if we keep believing, eventually the answer comes, and our faith grows.

Key Verse

"Blessed is the man who keeps on going when times are hard. After he has come through them, he will receive a crown. The crown is life itself. God has promised it to those who love him." (James 1:12)

There the Lord ... put them to the test.   Exodus 15:25
He wanted to put you to the test and know what was in ...   Deuteronomy 8:2–3
The Lord left some nations ... to put ... Israel to the test.   Judges 3:1–4
Fire tests silver. Heat tests gold.... the Lord tests our hearts. Proverbs 17:3
The Pharisees and Sadducees ... put Jesus to the test.   Matthew 16:1
We want to please God. He puts our hearts to the test.   1 Thessalonians 2:4

Suggested Reading

God tests Abraham on Mount Moriah.   Genesis 22:1–18

Didjaknow?

If there were never any tests in school, your teachers would have a hard time knowing which students were actually learning something and which were not. But after you take a test, it's pretty clear how much you know. God gives us "tests" for the same reason. But he's not just interested in how many facts and figures we can remember on test day— and then forget. God

knows our hearts. But he wants *us* to know what's in our hearts too. That's why he *keeps* on testing us.

Thankfulness

Thankfulness is when we show appreciation to God and others for what they do for us. God is so wonderful and loving that we have plenty of reasons to thank him every day. He gives us our life, our health, our friends, our family, salvation, wisdom, guidance, money, food, clothing—he gives us everything! We should be very thankful to him. If we have a thankful heart toward God, we'll *also* be thankful to people for the things they do for us. When we thank someone for what they do, it makes that person feel loved and appreciated.

Key Verse

> "Give thanks to the Lord, because he is good. His faithful love continues forever." (1 Chronicles 16:34)

Give thanks as you enter the gates of his temple.	Psalm 100:4
Give thanks to the Lord, because he is good.	Psalm 107:1
They knew God. But they ... didn't thank him.	Romans 1:21
But let us give thanks to God! He wins the battle for us ...	1 Corinthians 15:57
... you were appointed to live in peace. And be thankful.	Colossians 3:15
Give thanks no matter what ... God wants you to thank ...	1 Thessalonians 5:18

Suggested Reading

Give thanks and praise to the Lord.	1 Chronicles 16:7–13, 29–36
Ten lepers are healed. Only one thanks Jesus.	Luke 17:11–19

Didjaknow?

Thankfulness benefits us too! Ever been around people who complain a lot? They're rarely grateful and don't seem to know what "thank you" means. If you watch them you'll notice that they're miserable most of the time. Being thankful and looking for good things to be thankful for helps us to appreciate the positive things people and God do for us. It helps us to be happy and content.

AND THANK YOU, GOD, FOR DANCING FEET AND THE FOOD WE'RE ABOUT TO EAT!

Throne

A throne is the great seat that kings sit on. A throne represents a king's power and authority. King David sat on the throne of Israel. So did his son, Solomon. God promised that David would always have a son on his throne after him. This was fulfilled in his descendant, Jesus. God sits on a throne in heaven, and Jesus sits at his right hand.

YOU MAY APPROACH THE THRONE.

Key Verse

"Then he made a large throne. It was decorated with ivory. It was covered with fine gold. The throne had six steps.... A statue of a lion stood on each side of the throne. Twelve lions stood on the six steps.... Nothing like that throne had ever been made for any other kingdom." (1 Kings 10:18–20)

You will always have a man on the throne of Israel.	1 Kings 9:5
He sat down at the right hand of the throne of the King ...	Hebrews 8:1
... who overcome the right to sit with me on my throne.	Revelation 3:21
From the throne came flashes of lightning ... and thunder.	Revelation 4:2–5

Timothy

Timothy was a young man who became one of Paul's closest friends, helpers, and companions. He helped Paul spread the news about Jesus. Paul loved Timothy and called him his "son." He carefully trained Timothy to work in the churches, and appointed him leader of the church in Ephesus. When Paul was old, he wrote letters to guide and encourage Timothy.

Key Verse

"You have known the Holy Scriptures ever since you were a little child. They are able to teach you how to be saved by believing in Christ Jesus." (2 Timothy 3:15)

... on to Lystra. A believer named Timothy lived there.	Acts 16:1
Timothy ... You are my true son in the faith.	1 Timothy 1:2
Stay there in Ephesus.... I want you to command certain ...	1 Timothy 1:3
I remember your honest and true faith.... first in your ...	2 Timothy 1:5

Tithe
(See Tenth)

Tomb

A tomb is where the dead are placed. In Bible times, they used caves. When Lazarus died, he was buried in a tomb, a cave with a stone in front of the entrance (John 11:38). After Jesus died on the cross, his friends took his body down and laid it in a tomb nearby. A huge stone was placed in front of the door.

Key Verse
"Joseph took the body and wrapped it in a clean linen cloth. He placed it in his own new tomb that he had cut out of the rock. He rolled a big stone in front of the entrance to the tomb." (Matthew 27:59–60)

Abraham's sons ... buried his body.... put it in the cave ...	Genesis 25:9
Mary Magdalene and ... Mary went to look at the tomb.	Matthew 28:1
The angel went to the tomb. He rolled back the stone ...	Matthew 28:2
When they entered the tomb, they did not find the body ...	Luke 24:3

Tongue

We use our tongues to talk with, so in the Bible "tongue" often means language as well as the words we speak. It's very important to use our tongues to help people, not hurt them. Wrong words can bring discouragement and separate even the best of friends. The words of the wise can soothe and heal. And a word of encouragement can do wonders. So think before you speak because you can't *un*-say a word. And Jesus warned, "On judgment day, people will have to account for every careless word they have spoken" (Matthew 12:36–37).

Key Verse
"The tongue is a small part of the body. But it brags a lot. Think about how a small spark can set a big forest on fire. The tongue also is a fire." (James 3:5–6)

Your words helped those who had fallen down.	Job 4:4
Thoughtless words cut ... tongue of wise ... brings healing.	Proverbs 12:18
Your tongue has the power of life and death.	Proverbs 18:21
... careful about what he says keeps ... out of trouble.	Proverbs 21:23
The Lord ... has taught me what to say.... to help those ...	Isaiah 50:4
Praise and cursing come out of the same mouth.	James 3:9–10

Suggested Reading

People speak languages or tongues they don't know.	Acts 2
The apostle James' famous talk about the "tongue."	James 3:1–12

Didjaknow?

When someone is good at talking, they are said to have a "silver tongue." Where did that expression came from? From the Bible! Proverbs 10:20 says, "The tongues of those who do right are like fine silver." But make sure your silver is genuine. Speak from your heart. Proverbs 26:23 says, "Warm words that come from an evil heart are like shiny [silver] paint on a clay pot." Do you have a real silver tongue? Or just a fake with silver paint?

Training

God wants your parents to train you in the way you should go (Proverbs 22:6). Training involves correction, instruction, and discipline. You get disciplined when you're not obeying what God, your parents, or other adults are saying. You need to be trained and disciplined when you are young so that when you get older you will be the kind of person God wants you to be.

Key Verse

"If you train your children, they will give you peace. They will bring delight to you." (Proverbs 29:17)

But foolish people hate wisdom and training.	Proverbs 1:7
... do not hate the Lord's training.... trains those he loves.	Proverbs 3:11–12
No training seems pleasant at the time. In fact, it seems ...	Hebrews 12:11
I correct and train those I love.	Revelation 3:19

Treasure

Treasure is something that is very valuable. Treasure can be money, people, things, or our reputation—or God or the great news about Jesus! We are God's treasure. Jesus loved us so much that he gave up all of heaven and even his own life so we would know God. He truly treasures us. So let's love Jesus and treasure him.

Key Verse

"Now obey me completely. Keep my covenant. If you do, then out of all of the nations you will be my special treasure." (Exodus 19:5)

They will belong to me ... my special treasure.	Malachi 3:17
Instead, put away riches for yourselves in heaven.	Matthew 6:20
The kingdom of heaven is like treasure ... hidden in a field.	Matthew 13:44
... the treasure of the good news in these earthly bodies ...	2 Corinthians 4:7

Tribes, Twelve

Jacob had twelve sons. Each of these twelve sons had a family, and while the Israelites were in Egypt, these twelve families became very large and were called "tribes." All of the tribes together were the nation of the Israelites. After they conquered Canaan, each of the tribes was given a part of the land. Only the tribe of Levi owned no land.

Key Verse

"Here are the 12 sons Jacob had. Leah was the mother of Reuben, Jacob's oldest son. Her other sons were Simeon, Levi, Judah, Issachar and Zebulun. The sons of Rachel were Joseph and Benjamin. The sons of Rachel's female servant Bilhah were Dan and Naphtali. The sons of Leah's female servant Zilpah were Gad and Asher." (Genesis 35:22–26)

... the names of Israel's children who went to Egypt.	Exodus 1:1–5
... counted family by family.... total number was 603,550.	Numbers 1:45–46
Moses hadn't given any share of the land to ... Levi.	Joshua 13:14
... Israel finished dividing up ... land the tribes received.	Joshua 19:49

Trinity

There's only one God, but he is three equal persons—the Father, the Son, and the Holy Spirit. Look at Jesus' baptism (Matthew 3:16–17): Jesus the *Son* was in the water. The *Spirit* came down like a dove. And the *Father* spoke from heaven. God is all three persons at the same time, and they're all one God! They're not parts of God. God is one. You can't divide him into parts. All three share the same nature—they all fill everything, know everything, and can do everything. So what makes them three? They each have their own personality and their own jobs and responsibilities.

Key Verse

"As soon as Jesus was baptized ... heaven was opened. Jesus saw the Spirit of God coming down on him like a dove. A voice from heaven said, 'This is my Son, and I love him. I am very pleased with him.'" (Matthew 3:16–17)

God said, "Let us make man in our likeness ..."	Genesis 1:26
Baptize ... in the name of the Father ... Son ... Holy Spirit.	Matthew 28:19
... only the Spirit of God knows God's thoughts.	1 Corinthians 2:11
[God the Father] There is only one God. He is the Father.	1 Corinthians 8:6
[The Holy Spirit] Now the Lord is the Holy Spirit.	2 Corinthians 3:17
[The Son, Jesus] ... Jesus ... In his very nature he was God.	Philippians 2:5–6

Suggested Reading

God's Spirit is involved in Creation.	Genesis 1
Jesus is in the Father, and the Father in him.	John 14:6–11

Didjaknow?

Is Jesus *God?* In Exodus 3:13–14, God said to Moses, "I AM WHO I AM." He told him to tell the Israelites, "I AM has sent me to you." In John 8:58, Jesus said, "Before Abraham was born, *I am!*" (italics added). Also, in Revelation 1:8, God said, "I am the Alpha and the Omega, the First and the Last," and in Revelation 1:17, Jesus *also* said, "I am the First and the Last." And John 20:28 says, "Thomas said to him [Jesus], 'My Lord and my God!'"

Trust

Trust is a belief in the goodness, fairness, and love of a person. We trust someone when we know their character well enough to know that they are trustworthy. God's character is completely trustworthy. We can put our whole lives, everything we believe and hold dear,

into his hands and know that he won't let us down in any way.

Key Verse

> **"Lord, those who know you will trust in you. You have never deserted those who look to you." (Psalm 9:10)**

They trusted in you, and you saved them.	Psalm 22:4–5
Trust in the Lord with all your heart.... In all your ways ...	Proverbs 3:5–6
Do not let your hearts be troubled. Trust in God. Trust ...	John 14:1
The one who trusts in him [Jesus] will never be put ...	Romans 10:11

Truthfulness

Someone who is truthful is right, they agree with the facts, they are reliable and honest and will never tell a lie. We should always tell the truth because *God* always tells the truth. Telling the truth can be difficult at times, especially when we might get embarrassed or punished for doing so. But we should do what is right even when it's not easy. If you tell the truth when it's hard, others will think, "*Wow!*" They will really respect you. You'll find that your relationships grow strong

and your reputation is good. So get into the habit of being truthful.

Key Verse

"So each of you must get rid of your lying. Speak the truth to your neighbor." (Ephesians 4:25)

He is faithful. He doesn't do anything wrong.... honest ...   Deuteronomy 32:4
Guide me in your truth. Teach me. You are my God ...   Psalm 25:5
Then you will know the truth.... truth will set you free.   John 8:32
Love ... is full of joy when the truth is spoken.   1 Corinthians 13:6

Suggested Reading

Balaam tells the truth, rather than accepting great riches.   Numbers 23–24
The story of Ananias and Sapphira, who lied to God.   Acts 5:1–11

Didjaknow?

You can trust what God says. "He can't lie" (Numbers 23:19). You can trust what Jesus says. "No lies ever came out of his mouth" (1 Peter 2:22). You can trust what the Holy Spirit says. "He is the Spirit of truth" (John 15:26). You can trust the gospels. "The things you have been taught are true" (Luke 1:4).

Vine

Grapevines grow all over Israel, and Jesus told several parables about vineyards (Matthew 20:1–16; 21:28–43). Jesus said that he was the true vine, God was the keeper of the vineyard, and each of us are individual branches. If we stay joined to Jesus we can bear lots of fruit, just like branches that stay in the vine bear lots of grapes.

Key Verse

"I am the true vine. My Father is the gardener. He cuts off every branch joined to me that does not bear fruit. He trims every branch that does bear fruit. Then it will bear even more fruit." (John 15:1–2)

It's a song about his vineyard Israel.... on a hillside ...   Isaiah 5:1–7
A man who owned some land planted a vineyard. He ...   Matthew 21:33
... vine.... can't bear fruit unless you remain joined to me.   John 15:4
I am the vine. You are the branches.... bear a lot of fruit.   John 15:5

Vision

A vision is like a dream, only it happens when people are awake. Throughout the Bible, God used visions to speak to his people and tell them what was going to happen. Prophets like Ezekiel, Daniel, and John had some of the most fantastic visions recorded in the Bible. They saw strange creatures, huge battles, cities coming down from the sky, and many other incredible things.

Key Verse

> "After that, I will pour out my Spirit on all people. Your sons and daughters will prophesy. Your old men will have dreams. Your young men will have visions." (Joel 2:28)

Some time later, Abram had a vision. The Lord said ...   Genesis 15:1
... days are coming soon when every vision will come true.   Ezekiel 12:23
Peter had a vision.... looked like a large sheet.   Acts 10:10–11
One night the Lord spoke to Paul in a vision.   Acts 18:9

Wisdom

Wisdom is the ability to make good, proper judgments between right and wrong. Wisdom comes from God. It is based on knowledge and understanding. We cannot have wisdom until we humble ourselves and learn to love and respect God and others. In the Bible, wisdom is said to be more valuable than gold or treasure because it will help us to live a long, prosperous life that pleases both God and people. The best place in the Bible to read about wisdom is in the book of Proverbs. It contains many sayings about wisdom and how to get it.

204

Key Verse

"Wisdom is best. So get wisdom. No matter what it costs, get understanding." (Proverbs 4:7)

The Lord gives wisdom. Knowledge and understanding ...   Proverbs 2:6
Blessed is the one who finds wisdom.... pays better ...   Proverbs 3:13–14
If you really want to become wise, you must begin by ...   Proverbs 9:10
Do you see a man who is wise in his own eyes?   Proverbs 26:12
Anyone who trusts in himself is foolish. But a person ...   Proverbs 28:26

Suggested Reading

Solomon asks God for wisdom.   1 Kings 3; 2 Chronicles 1:1–12

We are wise if we obey God's words.   Matthew 7:24–27
God's wisdom is incredible.   Romans 11:33–36
Man's wisdom is foolishness to God.   1 Corinthians 1:19–29; James 3:13–18

Didjaknow?

In the book of Proverbs, wisdom is often portrayed as a woman (Proverbs 1:20; 7:4; 8:1) who, if you obey her call, will lead you to life. This was done partly to contrast wisdom with the adulteress woman who was very foolish and led people to evil and death (Proverbs 2:16–17).

Wise Men

The Wise Men who visited baby Jesus were scholars from Iraq or Persia who studied the stars. One night they saw a star that told them a king of the Jews had been born. They followed the star to Bethlehem, where Jesus was born, and worshiped him, and gave him expensive gifts. Their coming showed that Jesus was for everyone.

Key Verse

"Jesus was born in Bethlehem in Judea.... After Jesus' birth, Wise Men from the east came to Jerusalem. They asked, 'Where is the child who has been born to be king of the Jews? When we were in the east, we saw his star. Now we have come to worship him.'" (Matthew 2:1–2)

Then Herod called for the Wise Men secretly.   Matthew 2:7
The Wise Men ... bowed down and worshiped him.   Matthew 2:11
But God warned them in a dream not to go back to Herod.   Matthew 2:12
Herod realized that the Wise Men had tricked him.   Matthew 2:16

Witness

A witness tells others about something they know is true. We can witness for Jesus by telling others about him. The Bible says our lives should be "salt and light" to the world (Matthew 5:13–16). That means when people watch how we live they should see that we're different. And when they ask questions, we should be ready to answer. We should also look for chances to tell people

WHAT DO YOU THINK IS THE BEST WAY TO TELL MY FRIEND ABOUT JESUS? BY VOICE MAIL, AIR MAIL, OR E-MAIL?

God loves them. Witnessing does not have to be scary or hard. It is just telling people what God has done for us! God will help us witness to others.

Key Verse

"But you will receive power when the Holy Spirit comes on you. Then you will be my witnesses in Jerusalem. You will be my witnesses in all Judea and Samaria. And you will be my witnesses from one end of the earth to the other." (Acts 1:8)

Do not give false witness against your neighbor.	Exodus 20:16
Every matter must be proved by ... two or three witnesses.	Deuteronomy 19:15
This good news ... preached ... It will be a witness ...	Matthew 24:14
You also must give witness.... have been with me from ...	John 15:27
They gave witness that ... Jesus had risen from the dead.	Acts 4:33
Now you will give witness to all people about what you ...	Acts 22:15

Suggested Reading

Peter witnesses and 3000 people get saved.	Acts 2:14–41
Paul witnesses that Jesus is the Messiah.	Acts 13:13–41
Paul witnesses to Greek scholars.	Acts 17:16–34
Paul gives his life story, his "testimony."	Acts 24:10–21

Didjaknow?

A witness in a court case is someone who tells things they have seen and heard. They are sworn to "tell the truth, the whole truth, and nothing but the truth." Another word for "witness" is "testify." That's why some people say, "I want to testify about what the Lord has done." In a court case, to testify is the same thing as "giving your testimony." So when people tell how Jesus saved them and rescued them from sin, they are "giving their testimony."

Work

Proverbs praises those who work hard. When the Jews were building the wall of Jerusalem, "the people worked with all their heart" (Nehemiah 4:6). The apostle Paul reminded Christians to work hard, so they would have extra to give to the needy. Some people—like Martha—worked *too* much, and needed to learn to rest (Luke 10:38–42). So work hard and do your best, then relax.

Key Verse

"Hands that don't want to work make you poor. But hands that work hard bring wealth to you." (Proverbs 10:4)

Hands that work hard will rule. But people who don't ...	Proverbs 12:24
Do you see a man who does good work? He will serve ...	Proverbs 22:29
I showed you that we must work hard and help the weak.	Acts 20:35
... work.... do something useful with their own hands.	Ephesians 4:28

Worship

Worship is loving and respecting someone or something as if they were a god, and wanting to serve them. Since God is the only true God, he's the only one we should worship. When the Israelites trusted in God, they worshiped him and were blessed. But many times they turned from God and worshiped false gods and idols and things went wrong.

Key Verse

"Come, let us bow down and worship him. Let us fall on our knees in front of the Lord our Maker. He is our God." (Psalm 95:6–7)

The Lord was concerned ... So they ... worshiped him.	Exodus 4:31
Do not make statues of gods ... Do not bow ... worship ...	Exodus 20:4
Worship the Lord because of his beauty and holiness.	Psalm 29:2
Those in the boat worshiped Jesus.... "You really are the Son ... "	Matthew 14:33

Yeast

Yeast is a sour, fermented substance added to dough to cause bread to rise. Another word for yeast is *leaven* (rhymes with heaven). Every year, Jews celebrate the Feast of Unleavened Bread. They get rid of all yeast from their homes and bake flat, *unleavened* bread. The Bible warns that hatred, false teaching, and hypocrisy are like yeast, and that we must get rid of them.

Key Verse

> "Your bragging is not good. It is like yeast. Don't you know that just a little yeast works its way through the whole batch of dough? Get rid of the old yeast. Be like a new batch of dough without yeast." (1 Corinthians 5:6–7)

... Feast of Unleavened Bread.... bread ... without yeast.	Exodus 12:15–20
... dough from Egypt.... dough didn't have any yeast in it.	Exodus 12:39
Watch out for the yeast of the Pharisees and Sadducees.	Matthew 16:5–12
I'm talking about yeast that is full of hatred and evil.	1 Corinthians 5:8

More Bible Words

Abednego (Daniel's friend)
Azariah, the name A ....Dan. 1:7
Meshach and A, come out! ....Dan. 3:26
Meshach and A be praised ....Dan 3:28

Abel (Adam and Eve's son)
A took care of sheep...............................Gen. 4:2
pleased with A and his offering..............Gen. 4:4
his brother A and killed him ....Gen. 4:8

Abimelech (a king of Israel)
A used it to hire some men ....Judg. 9:4
A ruled over Israel for three years ....Judg. 9:22
That's how God paid A back for ....Judg. 9:56

Abner (Saul's army commander)
commander ... was named A ....1 Sam. 14:50
Then A brought him to Saul.............1 Sam. 17:57
When A returned to Hebron ....2 Sam. 3:27

Absalom (David's son)
Her brother A saw her, he spoke .....2 Sam. 13:20
taking place, A ran away...................2 Sam. 13:34
My son, my son A...........................2 Sam. 18:33

Achaia (province in Greece)
Gallio was governor of A ....Acts 18:12
went through Macedonia and A..........Acts 19:21

Achan (stole from Jericho)
A had taken some of those ....Josh. 7:1
A replied, "It's true!...............................Josh. 7:20
pile of rocks on top of A's body ....Josh. 7:26

Agabus (a prophet)
One of them was named A ....Acts 11:28
Then a prophet named A came ....Acts 21:10

Agag (an Amalekite king)
king will be greater than King A ....Num. 24:7
Samuel put A to death at Gilgal ......1 Sam. 15:33

Ahab (an evil king of Israel)
son A became the next king...........1 Kings 16:28
A also made a pole that..................1 Kings 16:33
When A heard what Elijah ....1 Kings 21:27

Ahaz (a king of Judah)
A was 20 years old when ....2 Kings 16:2
A took the silver and gold ....2 Kings 16:8
Then King A gave orders ....2 Kings 16:15

Alexandria (city in Egypt)
were Jews from Cyrene and A..................Acts 6:9
He was an educated man from A.........Acts 18:24

Almond (type of tree and nut)
from poplar, a and plane trees............Gen. 30:37
shaped like a flowers with buds and .....Ex. 25:33
before the a trees have buds.................Eccl. 12:5

Alpha and the Omega (names for God)
A and the O ... says the Lord ....Rev. 1:8
A and the O, the First and....................Rev. 21:6
A and the O. I am the First ....Rev. 22:13

Amalek, Amalekites (grandson of Esau)
She had A by Eliphaz ....Gen. 36:12
A came and attacked the Israelites ....Ex. 17:8
the son of an outsider, an A ....2 Sam. 1:13

Amos (shepherd and prophet)
words of A. He was a shepherd ....Amos 1:1
you see, A?" "A plumb line."................Amos 7:8
Amaziah said to A................................Amos 7:12

Ananias (and Sapphira)
A man named A and his wife ....Acts 5:1
When A heard this...................................Acts 5:5
you and A sold the land for? ....Acts 5:8

Ananias (believer from Damascus)
was a believer named A.........................Acts 9:10
he has seen a man named A.................Acts 9:12
Then A went to the house ....Acts 9:17

Andrew (brother of Peter)
Peter and his brother A ....Matt. 4:18
A, Philip, Bartholomew ....Mark 3:18
first thing A did was to find ....John 1:41

Antioch (city in Asia Minor)
went to A. There they began ....Acts 11:20
At A the believers were called.............Acts 11:26
send them to A with Paul and............Acts 15:22

Apple (a sweet fruit)
you are like an a tree among the...........Song 2:3
Under the a tree I woke you up..............Song 8:5
The pomegranate, palm and a trees......Joel 1:12

Aquila (tent maker, Christian leader)
There he met a Jew named A................Acts 18:2
Priscilla and A heard him ....Acts 18:26
A and Priscilla greet you warmly......1 Cor. 16:19

Arabia (country to the east of Israel)
a message the Lord gave me about A....Isa. 21:13
I went at once into A ....Gal. 1:17
Hagar stands for Mount Sinai in A ....Gal. 4:25

Aram (descendent of Shem; a city)
The sons of A were Uz, Hul ....Gen. 10:23
He started out for A Naharaim ....Gen. 24:10
So Rezon ruled in A ....1 Kings 11:25

Ararat (mountain where ark came to rest)
rest on the mountains of A....................Gen. 8:4
to the land of A. Esarhaddon ....2 Kings 19:37
the kingdoms of A, Minni ....Jer. 51:27

Areopagus (council in Greece)
took him to a meeting of the A..........Acts 17:19
stood up in the meeting of the A........Acts 17:22
He was a member of the A.................Acts 17:34

Armor (protective clothing for soldiers)
put a coat of **a** on him....................1 Sam. 17:38
your spears! Put on your **a**!.....................Jer. 46:4
Put on all of God's **a**............................Eph. 6:11

Athens (city in Greece)
waiting for Silas and Timothy in A .....Acts 17:16
Men of A! I see that you are very ....Acts 17:22
After this, Paul left A and went to........Acts 18:1

Authority (position of power)
his message had **a**...............................Luke 4:32
There are no **a** except..........................Rom. 13:1
over every power and **a**........................Col. 2:10

Balaam (a magician)
B got up in the morning ....Num 22:21
B answered the donkey ....Num. 22:29
B saw that the Lord was ....Num. 24:1

Barabbas (a criminal)
a well-known prisoner named B.......Matt. 27:16
So he let B go free.............................Mark 15:15
B had been thrown into prison ....Luke 23:19

Barak (an Israelite military leader)
B said to her, "If you go ....Judg. 4:8
On that day Deborah and B..................Judg. 5:1
about Gideon, B, Samson.....................Heb. 11:32

Bartholomew (one of Jesus' disciples)
Philip and B, and also Thomas and.....Matt. 10:3
Andrew, Philip, B.................................Mark 3:18
Thomas, B and Matthew........................Acts 1:13

Baruch (Jeremiah's assistant)
I gave B directions in front of all ....Jer. 32:13
So I sent for B, the son of Neriah...........Jer. 36:4
B, the son of Neriah, did everything......Jer. 36:8

Bathsheba (David's wife)
B found out she was pregnant...........2 Sam. 11:5
comforted his wife B......................2 Sam. 12:24
B. She was Solomon's mother ....1 Kings 2:13

Battle (a fight between two armies)
The Israelites were prepared for **b** ....Ex. 13:18
You can prepare a horse for ... **b**........Prov. 21:31
That **b** will take place on the great......Rev. 16:14

Bear (a large omnivorous mammal)
Sometimes a lion or a **b** would........1 Sam 17:34
Cows will eat with **b**..............................Isa. 11:7
He has been like a **b** waiting to...........Lam. 3:10

Beelzebub (prince of demons)
has been called B.................................Matt. 10:25
of B, the prince of demons.................Luke 11:15
drive out demons with B's help.........Luke 11:19

Beersheba (a city in Negev)
and wandered in the desert of B ....Gen. 21:14
That place was named B ....Gen. 21:31
When he reached B, he offered............Gen. 46:1

Belshazzar (a king in Babylon)
King B gave a big dinner.........................Dan. 5:1
So King B became even more terrified ...Dan. 5:9
That very night B, the king of.............Dan. 5:30

Benjamin (Jacob's youngest son)
his father named him B......................Gen. 35:18
Joseph saw B with them ....Gen 43:16
He is from the land of B ....1 Sam. 9:16

Berea (city in Macedonia)
was preaching God's word in B ....Acts 17:13
Silas and Timothy stayed in B ....Acts 17:14
Sopater, son of Pyrrhus, from B............Acts 20:4

Bethany (village in Palestine)
Jesus was in B ....Matt. 26:6
leaving B, they were hungry ....Mark 11:12
arrived at B, where Lazarus...................John 12:1

Bethel (a city in Palestine)
toward the hills east of B ....Gen. 12:8
He named that place B.........................Gen. 28:19
people of Israel went up to B ....Judg. 20:26

Boaz (Ruth's husband)
So B said to Ruth....................................Ruth 2:8
Then B spoke to the elders ....Ruth 4:9
So B got married to Ruth ....Ruth 4:13

Bread (basic food made of flour)
the Feast of Unleavened B ....Ex. 23:15
Man doesn't live only on **b**....................Luke 4:4
I am the **b** of life ....John 6:35

Caesarea (a city and a seaport in Israel)
Jesus went to the area of C Philippi ..Matt. 16:13
A man named Cornelius lived in C.......Acts 10:1
the high priest went down to C ....Acts 24:1

Caleb (a spy sent out by Moses)
Then C interrupted the men who.....Num. 13:30
tore his clothes. So did C....................Num. 14:6
C, the son of Jephunneh the...............Josh. 14:6

Cana (site of Jesus' first miracle)
It took place at C in Galilee...................John 2:1
He did it at C in Galilee.......................John 2:11
Nathanael from C in Galilee.................John 21:2

Capernaum (village on Sea of Galilee)
He went to live in the city of C...........Matt. 4:13
And what about you, C.......................Luke 10:15
went to C to look for Jesus ....John 6:24

Cave (a natural hole or tunnel in rock)
They buried it in the **c** in the field.....Gen. 50:13
his men were far back in the **c** ....1 Sam. 24:3
It was a **c** with a stone in front of ......John 11:38

Chariot (a horse-drawn war machine)
1,000 of Hadadezer's c ....2 Sam. 8:4
Suddenly a c and horses ....2 Kings 2:11
many horses and c rushing.......................Rev. 9:9

Cilicia (province in Asia Minor)
Paul traveled through Syria and C.......Acts 15:41
I am a Jew from Tarsus in C.................Acts 21:39
He learned that Paul was from C.........Acts 23:34

Circumcision (removal of foreskin)
You must be c.......................................Gen. 17:11
true c means the heart has been..........Rom. 2:29
C and uncircumcision don't mean........Gal. 6:15

Claudius (Roman emperor)
happened while C was the emperor....Acts 11:28
The emperor C had ordered all the ......Acts 18:2
I, C Lysias, am writing this letter........Acts 23:26

Commander (leader of 100 soldiers)
a Roman c came to him.........................Matt. 8:5
The Roman c saw what had................Luke 23:47
He was a Roman c in the Italian ....Acts 10:1

Corinth (city in Greece)
left Athens and went to C......................Acts 18:1
members of God's church in C..............1 Cor. 1:2
So I didn't return to C..........................2 Cor. 1:23

Cornelius (Roman commander)
A man named C lived in Caesarea ....Acts 10:1
C was afraid. He stared at the angel ......Acts 10:4
C, God has heard your prayer..............Acts 10:31

Cow (animal used for meat and milk)
Seven c came up out of the river..........Gen. 41:2
the hides of sea c ....Ex. 25:5
as fat as the c in Bashan ....Amos 4:1

Crete (a Greek island)
So we passed the calmer side of C ....Acts 27:7
taken my advice not to sail from C.....Acts 27:21
I left you on the island of C ....Titus 1:5

Curse (a prayer that bad things will happen)
I am putting a c on you.........................Gen. 3:14
May those who call down c on you ...Gen. 27:29
Bless those who call down c on you ....Luke 6:28

Cyprus (island in the Mediterranean Sea)
have received from the island of C.........Isa. 23:1
Joseph was a Levite from C....................Acts 4:36
took Mark and sailed for C ....Acts 15:39

Cyrene (city in North Africa)
met a man from C. His name was .....Matt. 27:9
Some of them were Jews from C.............Acts 6:9
Some believers from Cyprus and C .....Acts 11:20

Cyrus (king of Babylon who freed the Jews)
the first year of the rule of C ....2 Chron. 36:22
C, the king of Persia, says ....Ezra 1:2
I say about C, "He is my shepherd ....Isa. 44:28

Dagon (Philistine god)
great sacrifice to their god D ....Judg. 16:23
They saw the statue of D.... it was.......1 Sam. 5:3
hand is punishing us and our god D...1 Sam. 5:7

Damascus (capital of Syria)
against David went to D.................1 Kings 11:24
Saul approached D. Suddenly ....Acts 9:3
In D there was a believer named..........Acts 9:10

Darius (a king of Persia)
report would have to be sent to D..........Ezra 5:5
King D gave an order. He had a..............Ezra 6:1
what I have ordered. I am King D ....Ezra 6:12

Deacon (leader in the church)
letter to your leaders and d....................Phil. 1:1
D also must be worthy of respect.........1 Tim. 3:8
A d must be faithful to his wife..........1 Tim. 3:12

Dead Sea (a salt sea east of Palestine)
It was the valley of the D S...................Gen. 14:3
that was flowing down to the D S ....Josh. 3:16
It will reach to the D S ....Ezek. 47:18

Delilah (Samson's Philistine wife)
Her name was D ....Judg. 16:4
So D spoke to Samson ....Judg. 16:6
D realized he had told her..................Judg. 16:18

Demas (leader in the early church)
sends greetings. So does D ....Col. 4:14
D has deserted me. He has gone........2 Tim. 4:10
D and Luke work together with.......Philem. 1:24

Demetrius (silversmith in Ephesus)
There was a man named D ....Acts 19:24
D and the other skilled workers...........Acts 19:38
says good things about D ....3 John 1:12

Desert (a hot, dry, sandy region)
He made them wander ... in the d....Num. 32:13
In the d prepare the way for the.............Isa. 40:3
The Spirit led him into the d.................Luke 4:1

Donkey (an animal similar to a horse)
He will be like a wild d ....Gen. 16:12
The d said to Balaam ....Num. 22:30
you will find a d tied up ....Matt. 21:2

Dorcas (woman Peter raised from the dead)
name in the Greek language was D.......Acts 9:36
clothes D had made while she was........Acts 9:39

Dove (a white bird; symbol of Holy Spirit)
Then Noah sent a d out...........................Gen. 8:8
as snakes and as harmless as d..........Matt. 10:16
coming down on him like a d ....Mark 1:10

Eagle (a hunting bird, symbol of judgment)
the way of an e in the sky ....Prov. 30:19
Nebuchadnezzar is like an e ....Jer. 48:40
I heard an e that was flying high...........Rev. 8:13

Earthquake (shaking of the earth)
After the wind there was an **e** ....1 Kings 19:11
saw the **e** and all that had ....Matt. 27:54
There has never been an **e** as ....Rev. 16:18

Edom (another name for Esau)
That's why he was also named **E** ....Gen. 25:30
It was also called the country of **E** ....Gen. 32:3
sent messengers to the king of **E**........Judg. 11:17

Ehud (a judge)
E was left-handed ....Judg. 3:15
E had made a sword that had two ......Judg. 3:16
Then **E** reached out his left hand........Judg. 3:21

Elder (wise leader)
Gather the **e** of Israel together.................Ex. 3:16
Paul and Barnabas appointed **e** for......Acts 14:23
Then send for the **e** of the church .....James 5:14

Eli (Israelite priest who raised Samuel)
The priest **E** was sitting on a chair ......1 Sam. 1:9
E's sons were evil men ....1 Sam. 2:12
Then **E** realized that the Lord was.......1 Sam. 3:8

Elizabeth (mother of John the Baptist)
no children, because **E** was not able.......Luke 1:7
E was filled with the Holy Spirit..........Luke 1:41
came for **E** to have her baby. ....Luke 1:57

Enoch (Cain's first son)
He named it after his son **E** ....Gen. 4:17
E walked with God. Then he ....Gen. 5:24
E had faith. So he was taken from ....Heb. 11:5

Epaphras (leader in the early church)
You learned the good news from **E**..........Col. 1:7
E sends greetings. He is one of you ....Col. 4:12
E sends you greetings ....Philem. 1:23

Epaphroditus (leader in the early church)
But I think it's necessary to send **E** ....Phil. 2:25
That's because **E** brought me the ....Phil. 4:18

Ephesus (city in Greece)
large numbers of people here in **E**.......Acts 19:26
"Men of **E**!" he said...............................Acts 19:35
to write to the church in **E** ....Rev. 2:1

Ethiopia, Ethiopian (country in east Africa)
Can people from **E** change their skin?..Jer. 13:23
On his way he met an **E** official ....Acts 8:27

Euphrates (longest river in western Asia)
And the fourth river is the **E**................Gen. 2:14
of Egypt to the great river **E**................Gen. 15:18
held at the great river **E** ....Rev. 9:14

Felix (governor of Judea)
be taken safely to Governor **F**.............Acts 23:24
He said to **F**...Acts 24:2
But **F** wanted to do the Jews a ....Acts 24:27

Festus (governor of Judea)
They tried to get **F** to have Paul.............Acts 25:3
up for himself, **F** interrupted ....Acts 26:24
Agrippa said to **F**, "This man ....Acts 26:32

Frog (amphibian; sent as a plague on Egypt)
plague your whole country with **f**.............Ex. 8:2
Their land was covered with **f**..............Ps. 105:30
three evil spirits that looked like **f**.......Rev. 16:13

Furnace (oven used to heat metal and clay)
and Aaron took ashes from a **f** ....Ex. 9:10
The **f** was so hot that its flames............Dan. 3:22
like the smoke from a huge **f** ....Rev. 9:2

Gabriel (messenger angel)
G, tell Daniel what his vision ....Dan. 8:16
I am **G**. I serve God. ....Luke 1:19
God sent the angel **G** to Nazareth........Luke 1:26

Gaius (leader in the early church)
They dragged **G** and Aristarchus..........Acts 19:29
any of you except Crispus and **G** ....1 Cor. 1:14
it to you, my dear friend **G**..................3 John 1:1

Galatia (region in Asia Minor)
through the area of Phrygia and **G**........Acts 16:6
of the churches in **G**...............................Gal. 1:2
Crescens has gone to **G** ....2 Tim. 4:10

Gallio (governor of Achaia)
At that time **G** was governor of ....Acts 18:12
But just then **G** spoke to the Jews ....Acts 18:14
But **G** didn't care at all........................Acts 18:17

Gamaliel (a Pharisee, Paul's teacher)
But a Pharisee named **G** stood up..........Acts 5:34
I was well trained by **G** in the law of ....Acts 22:3

Gaza (region to the west of Palestine)
They took him down to **G**.................Judg. 16:21
all the way to **G** and its territory......2 Kings 18:8
that goes down from Jerusalem to **G**.....Acts 8:26

Gehazi (Elisha's servant)
He said to his servant **G**...................2 Kings 4:11
G, where have you been? ....2 Kings 5:25
Then **G** left Elisha. And he had........2 Kings 5:27

Gilboah (ridge of mountains in Isaachar)
They set up camp at **G**.......................1 Sam. 28:4
his three sons dead on Mount **G** ....1 Sam. 31:8
Mountains of **G**, may no dew or ....2 Sam. 1:21

Gilead (mountainous area east of Jordan)
headed for the hill country of **G** ....Gen. 31:21
his army went up to Jabesh **G** ....1 Sam. 11:1
Isn't there any healing lotion in **G**?........Jer. 8:22

Glory (beauty, honor, or power)
you will see the **g** of the Lord.................Ex. 16:7
in the **g** of our Lord Jesus Christ ....2 Thess. 2:14
gleaming brightness of God's **g**..............Heb. 1:3

Goat (animal used for meat and milk)
as a **g** that carries the people's sins ......Lev. 16:10
Leopards will lie down with **g** ....Isa. 11:6
separates the sheep from the **g** ....Matt. 25:32

Goshen (region in northern Egypt)
And so they arrived in the area of **G** ..Gen. 46:28
I will treat the area of **G** differently ....Ex. 8:22
it didn't hail was in the area of **G** ....Ex. 9:26

Greece (country in southern Europe)
I will send others to Tubal and **G** ....Isa. 66:19
The goat stands for the king of **G** ....Dan. 8:21
Finally he arrived in **G** ....Acts 20:2

Hagar (Sarah's servant, Ishmael's mother)
wife Sarai gave him her servant **H** ....Gen. 16:3
found **H** near a spring of water.............Gen. 16:7
H stands for Mount Sinai in Arabia ....Gal. 4:25

Haggai (a prophet to the Jews)
The prophets **H** and Zechariah ....Ezra 5:1
preaching of the prophets **H** and ....Ezra 6:14
Here is what **H** said..................................Hag. 1:1

Ham (one of Noah's sons)
became the father of Shem, **H** and.......Gen. 5:32
the battle against the Zuzites in **H** ....Gen. 14:5
son in every house in the land of **H** ......Ps. 78:51

Haman (enemy of the Jews)
those events, King Xerxes honored **H** ......Est. 3:1
So **H** got the robe and the horse.............Est. 6:11
And they used the pole **H** had gotten ....Est. 7:10

Hannah (Samuel's mother)
Peninnah had children, but **H** didn't..1 Sam. 1:2
H was very bitter. She sobbed............1 Sam. 1:10
The Lord was gracious to **H** ....1 Sam. 2:21

Haran (Lot's father; also a place)
And **H** became the father of Lot ....Gen. 11:27
when they came to **H**, they settled ....Gen. 11:31
She was the mother of **H** ....1 Chron. 2:46

Hebron (city south of Jerusalem)
near the large trees of Mamre at **H**.....Gen. 13:18
Arba is also called **H**..............................Gen. 23:2
David was king in **H** over the............2 Sam. 2:11

Hermon, Mount (mountain in Canaan)
from the Arnon River valley to **M H** .....Deut. 3:8
area that was between **M** Baal **H** ....Judg. 3:3
It's as if the dew of **M H** were ....Ps. 133:3

Hezekiah (a good king of Judah)
H trusted in the Lord, the God ....2 Kings 18:5
H, the king of Judah, had covered .2 Kings 18:16
H turned his face toward the wall ....Isa. 38:2

Honey (sweet liquid made by bees)
a land that has plenty of milk and **h** ....Ex. 3:8
What is sweeter than **h**?.....................Judg. 14:18
it tasted as sweet as **h** ....Rev. 10:10

Horse (animal used for transportation)
Pharaoh's **h** and their riders into.............Ex. 15:1
Some trust in **h**. But we trust in...............Ps. 20:7
in front of me was a white **h** ....Rev. 19:11

Hosanna (a cry of joy)
H to the Son of David ....Matt. 21:9
H in the highest heaven!....................Mark 11:10
H! Blessed is the one who comes........John 12:13

Hosea (prophet to Israel; book in Old Testament)
message came to **H** from the Lord ....Hos. 1:1
Here is what **H** said..................................Hos. 1:1
God says in **H** ....Rom. 9:25

Hymn (song of praise to God)
It is a **h** of praise to our God ....Ps. 40:3
You bring a **h** or a teaching ....1 Cor. 14:26
Sing psalms, **h** and spiritual...................Col. 3:16

Iconium (city in Asia Minor)
At **I**, Paul and Barnabas went into.........Acts 14:1
some Jews came from Antioch and **I**...Acts 14:19
The believers at Lystra and **I** said..........Acts 16:2

Immanuel (means "God is with us")
And he will be called **I** ....Isa. 7:14
I, they will attack your land like...............Isa. 8:8
And he will be called **I** ....Matt. 1:23

Incense (sweet-smelling substance)
mix it all up into a sweet-smelling **i**......Ex. 30:35
I will pull down your **i** altars...............Lev. 26:30
to you like the sweet smell of **i** ....Ps. 141:2

Ishmael (Abraham and Hagar's son)
You will name him **I** ....Gen. 16:11
As for **I**, I have heard you ....Gen. 17:20
Abraham's sons Isaac and **I** ....Gen. 25:9

Ivory (substance made from elephant tusks)
It was decorated with **i** ....1 Kings 10:18
beds that are decorated with **i** ....Amos 6:4
All sorts of articles made out of **i** ....Rev. 18:12

James (brother of John, the apostle)
J, son of Zebedee, and his brother.......Matt. 4:21
J and John came to Jesus....................Mark 10:35
He had **J** killed with a sword ....Acts 12:2

Jealous (how God feels when we worship other things; wanting wrong things)
the Lord your God, am a **j** God ....Ex. 20:5
Some of you are **j** ....1 Cor. 3:3
Are we trying to make the Lord **j** .....1 Cor. 10:22

Jehoiachin (a king of Judah)
Nebuchadnezzar took **J** to ....2 Kings 24:15
So **J** put his prison clothes away ....2 Kings 25:29
King **J** was forced to leave Jerusalem ....Jer. 24:1

Jehoshaphat (a king of Judah)
Asa's son J became the next ....1 Kings 15:24
The Lord was with J ....2 Chron. 17:3
J had great wealth and honor........2 Chron. 18:1

Jehu (a king of Israel)
Then J shot an arrow at Joram ....2 Kings 9:24
"Throw her down!" J said..................2 Kings 9:33
J wasn't careful to obey the law .....2 Kings 10:31

Jephthah (a judge of Israel)
J was a mighty warrior ....Judg. 11:1
Spirit of the Lord came on J...............Judg. 11:29
J returned to his home in Mizpah .....Judg. 11:34

Jeroboam (first king of Israel)
J was a very important young ....1 Kings 11:28
Solomon tried to kill J ....1 Kings 11:40
people of Israel heard that J ....1 Kings 12:20

Jesse (father of David)
am sending you to J in Bethlehem....1 Sam. 16:1
J's family is like a tree that has ....Isa. 11:1
J was the father of King David..............Matt. 1:6

Jethro (Moses' father-in-law)
J was the priest of Midian.........................Ex. 3:1
J had sent a message to him....................Ex. 18:6
So J returned to his own country ....Ex. 18:27

Jew (another name for a Hebrew)
the J who left you and came up to........Ezra 4:12
Are you the king of the J?..................Matt. 27:11
There is no J or Greek ....Gal. 3:28

Jezebel (a wicked queen of Israel)
Ahab's wife J had been killing..........1 Kings 18:4
Dogs will eat up J on a ....2 Kings 9:10
You put up with that woman J ....Rev. 2:20

Joab (David's military commander)
David wrote a letter to J...................2 Sam. 11:14
J said, "I'm not going to waste ....2 Sam. 18:14
J was the commander of the........1 Chron. 27:34

Joash (a king of Judah)
She stole J away from among the.....2 Kings 11:2
King J didn't remember how ....2 Chron. 24:22
They killed J in his bed ....2 Chron. 24:25

Joel (a prophet to Judah)
A message came to J from the Lord ....Joel 1:1
Here is what J said ....Joel 1:1
here is what the prophet J meant..........Acts 2:16

Jonathan (Saul's son, David's friend)
One thousand were with J at.............1 Sam. 13:2
J made a covenant with David ....1 Sam. 18:3
Saul's son J went to David ....1 Sam. 23:16

Joppa (ancient seaport city)
included the area that faces J ....Josh. 19:46
In J there was a believer named............Acts 9:36
Send to J for Simon Peter....................Acts 11:13

Josiah (a king of Judah)
made his son J king in his place ....2 Kings 21:24
J was eight years old when he..........2 Kings 22:1
J removed all of the statues of .....2 Chron. 34:33

Jubilee (joyfulness)
In the Year of J all of you must............Lev. 25:13
still be set free in the Year of J ....Lev. 25:54
field is set free in the Year of J ....Lev. 27:21

Judah (fourth son of Jacob)
So she named him J ....Gen. 29:35
J said to his brothers ....Gen. 37:26
J, your brothers will praise you............Gen. 49:8

Judgment Day (God's day of judgment)
On j d, people will have to ....Matt. 12:36
of Ninevah will stand up on j d ....Luke 11:32
On j d, God will judge them.....................Jude 6

Keturah (Abraham's concubine)
another woman. Her name was K ....Gen. 25:1
All of them came from K ....Gen. 25:4
born to Abraham's concubine K....1 Chron. 1:32

Kishon River (a river in Palestine)
chariots and his troops to the K R. ....Judg. 4:7
The K R swept them away...................Judg. 5:21
down to the K Valley ....1 Kings 18:40

Kiss (greeting or sign of affection)
Come here my son. K me ....Gen. 27:27
over the Son of Man with a k? ....Luke 22:48
Greet one another with a holy k ....Rom. 16:16

Korah (a rebellious Levite)
K was the son of Izhar, the son of.......Num. 16:1
K, here's what you and all of your ......Num. 16:6
It swallowed all of K's men................Num. 16:32

Laban (Jacob's father-in-law)
Rebekah had a brother named L ....Gen. 24:29
L had two daughters ....Gen. 29:16
On the third day L was told that........Gen. 31:22

Lamp (used for light in Bible times)
Lord, you are my l............................2 Sam. 22:29
keep the l of David's kingdom ....2 Kings 8:19
Ten bridesmaids took their l ....Matt. 25:1

Lebanon (country in the Middle East)
crops grow well, like those in L ....Ps. 72:16
strong like a cedar tree in L...................Ps. 92:12
They used a cedar tree from L..............Ezek. 27:5

Levites (the descendants of Levi)
All of the L joined him ....Ex. 32:26
put the L in charge of the holy..........Num. 1:50
Take the L from among the other........Num. 8:6

Life, Book of (God's record of believers)
be erased from the B of L.......................Ps. 69:28
are all written in the B of L ....Phil. 4:3
The B of L belongs to the Lamb...........Rev. 13:8

Locust (insect similar to a grasshopper)
L will cover the land..............................Ex. 10:12
His food was l and wild honey ....Matt. 3:4
The l looked like horses ready for...........Rev. 9:7

Lot (Abraham's nephew)
L went with him ....Gen. 12:4
So L chose the whole Jordan River.....Gen. 13:11
When L saw them, he got up ....Gen. 19:1

Manasseh (Joseph's first son)
Joseph named his first son M ....Gen. 41:51
So he put Ephraim ahead of M...........Gen. 48:20
From the tribe of M, 12,000....................Rev. 7:6

Martha (a companion of Jesus)
where a woman named M lived ....Luke 10:38
But M was busy with all the things....Luke 10:40
When M heard that Jesus was ....John 11:20

Matthias (the apostle who replaced Judas)
The other man was M ....Acts 1:23
they cast lots. M was chosen ....Acts 1:26

Melchizedek (the king and priest of
Jerusalem)
M was the king of Jerusalem...............Gen. 14:18
a priest forever, just like M....................Ps. 110:4
why did he need to be like M? ....Heb. 7:11

Meshach (one of Daniel's friends)
M and Abednego to help Daniel ....Dan. 2:49
anger burned against Shadrach, M.......Dan. 3:19
the king honored Shadrach, M.............Dan. 3:30

Methuselah (son of Enoch)
he became the father of M....................Gen. 5:21
M lived a total of 969 years ....Gen. 5:27
Lamech was the son of M ....Luke 3:37

Midian, Midianite (descendant[s] of
Abraham)
The traders from M came by...............Gen. 37:28
a woman of M to his family................Num. 25:6
the M came into the country and.........Judg. 6:3

Moab, Moabites (descendant[s] of Lot)
She named him M. He's the father.....Gen. 19:37
The M spoke to the elders of...............Num. 22:4
So Naomi returned from M ....Ruth 1:22

Mordecai (hero of the book of Esther)
tribe of Benjamin. His name was M ....Est. 2:5
But M refused to get down on his ....Est. 3:2
because they were so afraid of M.............Est. 9:3

Music (sound made by instruments)
I will make m to the Lord ....Judg. 5:3
The men used their m to serve......1 Chron. 6:32
make m in your heart to the Lord........Eph. 5:19

Naaman (commander of Syrian army)
N was commander of the army of......2 Kings 5:1
I'm sending my servant N ....2 Kings 5:6
was healed except N the Syrian ....Luke 4:27

Naboth (an Israelite killed by Jezebel)
It belonged to N from Jezreel...........1 Kings 21:1
N has called down curses on ....1 Kings 21:13
Ahab heard that N was dead ....1 Kings 21:16

Naomi (Ruth's mother-in-law)
N had a relative on her husband's..........Ruth 2:1
The women said to N............................Ruth 4:14
Then N put the child on her lap ....Ruth 4:16

Nathan (prophet to Israel)
Lord sent the prophet N to David ......2 Sam 12:1
N spoke to Solomon's mother ....1 Kings 1:11
N reported to David all of the......1 Chron. 17:15

Nazirite (a person kept clean for God)
As long as they are N............................Num. 6:4
the N must shave off the hair ....Num. 6:18
because the boy will be a N.................Judg. 13:7

New Moon (an Israelite celebration)
Blow them at your N M Feasts ....Num. 10:10
I hate your N M Feasts and your other...Isa. 1:14
about special feasts and N M and.........Col. 2:16

Nile River (largest river in Egypt)
he was standing by the N R.................Gen. 41:1
along the bank of the N R. ....Ex. 2:3
I will strike the water of the N R ....Ex. 7:17

Nineveh (the capital of ancient Assyria)
Go to the great city of N......................Jonah 1:2
Nahum in a vision about N..................Nahum 1:1
The men of N will stand up on ....Matt. 12:41

Obadiah (prophet to Judah; book in the Old
Testament)
O had a great respect for the ....1 Kings 18:3
So O had hidden 100 prophets in ....1 Kings 18:4
the vision about Edom that O had.......Obad. 1:1

Og (king of Bashan)
O was the king of Bashan.................Num. 21:33
O, the king of Bashan, was the............Deut. 3:11
the entire kingdom of O in Bashan....Josh. 13:12

Oil (used for food, heat, light, and healing)
Take the anointing o and pour it ....Ex. 29:7
The jug will always have o in it .....1 Kings 17:14
poured olive o on many sick................Mark 6:13

Olive (common fruit in Palestine)
its beak was a freshly picked o leaf!......Gen. 8:11
115,000 gallons of o that was...........1 Kings 5:11
and went out to the Mount of O.......Matt. 26:30

Othniel (a judge of Israel)
One day Acsah came to O ....Judg. 1:14
His name was O, the son of Kenaz ....Judg. 3:9
O overpowered him..............................Judg. 3:10

Palm (a common type of tree in Palestine)
some from myrtle, **p** and shade trees ...Neh. 8:15
they took branches from **p** trees.........John 12:13
they were holding **p** branches ....Rev. 7:9

Pearl (precious stone found in oysters)
Do not throw your **p** to pigs..................Matt. 7:6
a trader who was looking for fine **p** ..Matt. 13:45
The 12 gates were made from 12 **p**......Rev. 21:21

Perfume (a pleasant-smelling liquid)
Anyone who makes **p** in the same ....Ex. 30:33
sealed jar of very expensive **p** ....Matt. 26:7
Why wasn't this **p** sold?.......................John 12:5

Philip (one of Jesus' apostles)
P found Nathanael and told him ....John 1:45
So **P** ran up to the chariot.....................Acts 8:30
the Lord suddenly took **P** away ....Acts 8:39

Philippi (city in eastern Greece and Israel)
Jesus went to ... Caesarea **P**.................Matt. 16:13
From there we traveled to **P**.................Acts 16:12
happened earlier in the city of **P**.......1 Thess. 2:2

Phoenicia (area northwest of Palestine)
given a command concerning **P** ....Isa. 23:11
They traveled as far as **P**.......................Acts 11:19
As they traveled through **P** and.............Acts 15:3

Pig (an "unclean" animal for the Jews)
P aren't "clean" for you either.............Deut. 14:8
is like a gold ring in a **p**'s nose ....Prov. 11:22
Send us among the **p**. Let us go ....Mark 5:12

Potiphar (Egyptian who bought Joseph)
sold Joseph to **P** in Egypt....................Gen. 37:36
P was one of Pharaoh's officials............Gen. 39:1
So **P** was pleased with Joseph ....Gen. 39:4

Quail (a type of migratory bird)
That evening **q** came and covered the ..Ex. 16:13
It drove **q** in from the Red Sea ....Num. 11:31
and he brought them **q** ....Ps. 105:40

Queen of Sheba (admirer of King Solomon)
The **q of S** heard about how ....1 Kings 10:1
the **q of S** saw how very wise ....1 Kings 10:4
gave the **q of S** everything she ....1 Kings 10:13

Rabbi (a Hebrew word for "teacher")
love it when people call them '**R**' ....Matt. 23:7
But you shouldn't be called '**R**' ....Matt. 23:8
R means Teacher ....John 1:38

Rachel (Jacob's second wife)
But **R** was beautiful. She had a nice ...Gen. 29:17
Then God listened to **R**.......................Gen. 30:22
R is crying over her children ....Jer. 31:15

Rahab (prostitute who hid Jewish spies)
a prostitute. Her name was **R**.................Josh. 2:1
R, the prostitute, had faith..................Heb. 11:31
God make even **R** the prostitute ....James 2:25

Raven (a type of scavenger bird)
He sent a **r** out. It kept flying ....Gen. 8:7
The **r** brought him bread and meat .1 Kings 17:6
Think about the **r**. They don't...........Luke 12:24

Rebekah (Isaac's wife)
Before he had finished praying, **R** ......Gen. 24:15
might kill me because of **R** ....Gen. 26:7
Then **R** said to her son Jacob................Gen. 27:6

Redeemer (a person who sets someone free)
I know that my **R** lives ....Job 19:25
You are my Rock and my **R**....................Ps. 19:14

Rehoboam (king of Israel after Solomon)
But **R** didn't accept the advice..........1 Kings 12:8
R was king in Judah.........................1 Kings 14:21
R had made his position as king ...2 Chron. 12:1

Salt (used for seasoning and preserving)
she became a pillar made out of **s** ......Gen. 19:26
You are the **s** of the earth....................Matt. 5:13
Can fresh water and **s** water...............James 3:11

Samaria (region in central Palestine)
He bought the hill of **S** from ....1 Kings 16:24
marched up and surrounded **S** ....2 Kings 6:24
Jesus had to go through **S** ....John 4:4

Sanballat (enemy of Nehemiah)
S and Tobiah heard about what was.....Neh. 2:10
S and Geshem sent me a message ....Neh. 6:2
Remember what Tobiah and **S** have .....Neh. 6:14

Sea of Galilee (lake north of Jerusalem)
was walking beside the **S of G** ....Matt. 4:18
down to the **S of G** and into...............Mark 7:31
to the other side of the **S of G**.............John 6:1

Seal (a personal symbol)
Give me your **s** and its string..............Gen. 38:18
The **s** is the Holy Spirit that he ....Eph. 1:13
The Lamb opened the seventh **s** ....Rev. 8:1

Sennacherib (an Assyrian king)
S attacked and captured all of ....2 Kings 18:13
Listen to what **S** is saying ....2 Kings 19:16
them from the power of **S**...............2 Chron. 32:22

Shadrach (a friend of Daniel's)
He sent for **S**, Meshach and ....Dan. 3:13
S, Meshach and Abednego, come ....Dan. 3:26
the king honored **S**, Meshach and........Dan. 3:30

Sidon (an ancient Phoenician city)
Canaan was the father of **S** ....Gen. 10:15
had been done in Tyre and **S** ....Matt. 11:21
with the people of Tyre and **S**.............Acts 12:20

Siloam, Pool of (storage pool in Jerusalem)
also repaired the wall by the **P of S**......Neh. 3:15
Wash in the **P of S** ....John 9:7

Simeon (son of Jacob; a godly man)
So she named him **S**...........................Gen. 29:33
Jerusalem there was a man named **S** ....Luke 2:25
Among them were Barnabas, **S** ....Acts 13:1

Simon the Zealot (one of Jesus' apostles)
The last are **S the Z** and Judas ....Matt. 10:4
there were Thaddaeus and **S the Z**.......Mark 3:18
S the Z, and Judas, son of James ....Acts 1:13

Sling (ancient stone-throwing weapon)
Each of them could **s** a stone ....Judg. 20:16
Then he took his **s** in his hand ....1 Sam. 17:40
is like tying a stone in a **s** ....Prov. 26:8

Sodom (city God destroyed with fire)
The men of **S** were evil ....Gen. 13:13
The cries against **S** and Gomorrah......Gen. 18:20
It came down like rain on **S**................Gen. 19:24

Soul (the inner life of a person)
all your heart and with all your **s**........Deut. 4:29
the whole world but loses his **s**?........Matt. 16:26
all your heart and with all your **s**. .....Mark 12:30

Staff (a walking stick)
Take your wooden **s** and throw it..............Ex. 7:9
He looked at Aaron's **s**. It stood for......Num. 17:8
Your shepherd's rod and **s** comfort ....Ps. 23:4

Stone, Stoned, Stoning (ancient execution)
There they killed him by throwing **s** ...Lev. 24:23
one of these are you throwing **s** ....John 10:32
They began to throw **s** at him to kill.....Acts 7:58

Sun (star closest to earth)
S, stand still over Gibeon....................Josh. 10:12
He causes the **s** to shine on evil...........Matt. 5:45
The city does not need the **s**................Rev. 21:23

Susa (capital of Persian empire)
I was in the safest place in **S**..................Neh. 1:1
royal throne in the safest place in **S** ....Est. 1:2
I saw myself in the city of **S**...................Dan. 8:2

Sword (weapon)
He also placed a flaming **s** there...........Gen. 3:24
It is sharper than any **s** that.................Heb. 4:12
Out of his mouth came a sharp **s** ....Rev. 1:16

Syria (nation northeast of Palestine)
News about him spread all over **S** ....Matt. 4:24
Paul traveled through **S** and Cilicia.....Acts 15:41
He was just about to sail for **S** ....Acts 20:3

Tarsus (Paul's hometown)
Ask for a man from **T** named Saul.........Acts 9:11
Then Barnabas went to **T** to look ....Acts 11:25
I am a Jew from **T** in Cilicia.................Acts 21:39

Thessalonica (city in Macedonia)
The Jews in **T** found out that Paul ......Acts 17:13
when I was in **T**, you sent me help.......Phil. 4:16
He has gone to **T**. He left me ....2 Tim. 4:10

Thomas (disciple who doubted Jesus)
T, who was called Didymus, spoke.....John 11:16
T said to him, "Lord, we don't know ...John 14:5
T said to him, "My Lord and my.......John 20:28

Threshing Floor (place to thresh grain)
a piece of wool on the **t f**....................Judg. 6:37
Then go down to the **t f** ....Ruth 3:3
toss the straw away from his **t f**...........Luke 3:17

Titus (one of Paul's helpers)
very glad to see how happy **T** was......2 Cor. 7:13
T was with me. He was a Greek ....Gal. 2:3
T, I am sending you this letter ....Titus 1:4

Troas (city in northwest Asia Minor)
they went down to **T** ....Acts 16:8
I went to **T** to preach the good...........2 Cor. 2:12
I left it with Carpus at **T**.....................2 Tim. 4:13

Trumpet (instrument used by priests)
priests blew a long blast on the **t** ....Josh. 6:16
send his angels with a loud **t** call ......Matt. 24:31
The first angel blew his **t**..........................Rev. 8:7

Tyre (sister city to Sidon)
Hiram was the king of **T**....................1 Kings 5:1
The people of **T** have sinned again ....Amos 1:9
went from there to a place near **T** ....Mark 7:24

Unleavened Bread, Feast of (Jewish feast)
Celebrate the **F of U B**..........................Ex. 12:17
was the first day of the **F of U B**........Matt. 26:17
This happened during the **F of U B**.......Acts 12:3

Ur (Abraham's hometown)
Terah started out from **U** ....Gen. 11:31
I brought you out of **U** in ....Gen. 15:7
You brought him out of **U** in.................Neh. 9:7

Uriah (Bathsheba's first husband)
She's the wife of **U**. He's a Hittite ......2 Sam. 11:3
David invited **U** to eat and drink ....2 Sam. 11:13
He put **U** at a place where he ....2 Sam. 11:16

Vashti (King Xerxes first wife)
Queen **V** also gave a big dinner...............Est. 1:9
The attendants told Queen **V** what ....Est. 1:12
become queen in **V**'s place.......................Est. 2:4

Veil (a head covering, curtain in tabernacle)
Then he put a **v** over his face ....Ex. 34:33
this very day, the same **v** remains ......2 Cor. 3:14
turns to the Lord, the **v** is taken.........2 Cor. 3:16

Vineyard (place where grapes are grown)
to hire people to work in his **v**............Matt. 20:1
owned some land planted a **v**............Matt. 21:33
Who plants a **v** but doesn't ....1 Cor. 9:7

War (conflict between two armies)
They went to w against five kings........Gen. 14:2
You will hear about w ....Matt. 24:6
There was w in heaven ....Rev. 12:7

Water (liquid necessary for life)
a huge space between the w ....Gen. 1:6
born through w and the Holy Spirit ......John 3:5
He would have given you living w.......John 4:10

Weapon (instrument used to fight or kill)
I have brought out the w I use..............Jer. 50:25
they will burn the w.............................Ezek. 39:10
The w I fight with are not the w........2 Cor. 10:4

Wedding (celebration of marriage vows)
The w dinner is ready ....Matt. 22:8
On the third day there was a w..............John 2:1
It is time for the Lamb's w.....................Rev. 19:7

Weed (useless or annoying plant)
W and salt pits will cover those ....Zeph. 2:9
The enemy planted w among the ....Matt. 13:25
The w are pulled up and burned ....Matt. 13:40

Weights (used to measure grain, etc.)
Use honest scales and honest w...........Lev. 19:36
delighted when people use honest w...Prov. 11:1
You use w that weigh things ....Mic. 6:11

Well (deep hole for fresh water)
Isaac opened up the w again ....Gen. 26:18
drink of water from the w that is....2 Sam. 23:15
Jacob's w was there ....John 4:6

Widow (woman whose husband has died)
Do not take advantage of w ....Ex. 22:22
A w was there gathering sticks ....1 Kings 17:10
When w and children who have no...James 1:27

Wind (natural movement of air)
Tall grass waving in the w?....................Luke 7:24
The w blows where it wants to...............John 3:8
It was like a strong w blowing.................Acts 2:2

Wine (fermented grape juice)
He brought out bread and w ....Gen. 14:18
People don't pour new w into old........Luke 5:37
Don't fill yourself up with w.................Eph. 5:18

Winepress (vat where grapes are crushed)
considered as juice from a w ....Num. 18:27
Gideon was threshing wheat in a w ....Judg. 6:11
The w stands for God's anger................Rev. 14:19

Word (another word for Scripture or Jesus)
I have hidden your w in my ....Ps. 119:11
He also lives on every w that.................Matt. 4:4
In the beginning, the W was ....John 1:1

Xerxes (a king of Persia)
King X ruled over the 127 territories in....Est. 1:1
Later, the anger of King X calmed ....Est. 2:1
After those events, King X honored ....Est. 3:1

Zacchaeus (a tax collector visited by Jesus)
A man named Z lived there ....Luke 19:2
Z, come down at once...........................Luke 19:5
But Z stood up. He said........................Luke 19:8

Zadok (a high priest during time of David)
Z, the son of Ahitub, was a priest......2 Sam. 8:17
a message to the priests Z and........2 Sam. 19:11
But the priest Z and Benaiah..............1 Kings 1:8

Zarephath (a Phoenician city)
Go right away to Z in the territory ..1 Kings 17:9
it all the way to the town of Z...........Obad. 1:20
Instead, he was sent to a widow in Z ...Luke 4:26

Zebedee (father of James and John)
They were James, son of Z, and his .....Matt. 4:21
mother of Z's sons came to Jesus.......Matt. 20:20
and the sons of Z were with them ......John 21:2

Zechariah (father of John the Baptist)
there was a priest named Z ....Luke 1:5
Do not be afraid, Z. Your prayer...........Luke 1:13
Z was filled with the Holy Spirit.........Luke 1:67

Zechariah (a prophet to the Jews; a book in the Old Testament)
The prophets Haggai and Z.....................Ezra 5:1
A message came to the prophet Z..........Zech. 1:1
the blood of Abel to the blood of Z....Luke 11:51

Zedekiah (last king of Judah)
changed Mattaniah's name to Z.....2 Kings 24:17
His men killed the sons of Z..............2 Kings 25:7
King Z had made a covenant with all .....Jer. 34:8

Zephaniah (a priest; a prophet to Judah; a book in the Old Testament)
the priest Z who was under him ....2 Kings 25:18
Z was the son of Maaseiah.......................Jer. 21:1
A message came to Z from the Lord .....Zeph. 1:1

Zerubbabel (a leader of the tribe of Judah)
The leaders of the Jews included Z..........Ezra 2:2
Z, the son of Shealtiel, began to work.....Ezra 5:2
Z, at that time I will pick you ....Hag. 2:23

Zion (the city of David; the city of God)
But David captured the fort of Z ....2 Sam. 5:7
Look! I am laying a stone in Z..............Isa. 28:16
But you have come to Mount Z..........Heb. 12:22

Zipporah (Moses' wife)
And the man gave his daughter Z...........Ex. 2:21
But Z got a knife that was made out ....Ex. 4:25
Moses had sent his wife Z to his ....Ex. 18:2

Famous Bible Stories

Old Testament

Creation — Genesis 1–2

How Adam and Eve Lost Paradise — Genesis 3

The Flood — Genesis 6–9

Everyone Babbles — Genesis 11

Abraham, the Father of a Nation — Genesis 12–15

Son Sacrifice — Genesis 22:1–19

Jacob's Dream Ladder — Genesis 28

Joseph Interprets Dreams — Genesis 37; 39–47

The Plagues — Exodus 7:8–12:30

Red Sea Crossing — Exodus 14

The Ten Commandments — Exodus 19–20:21

The Golden Calf — Exodus 32:1–35

The Fall of Jericho — Joshua 5:13–6:27

Deborah, the Brave Judge — Judges 4–5

Gideon, the Timid Judge — Judges 6–7

Samson, the Jawbone Judge — Judges 13–16

Your God Is Mine — Ruth

Young Samuel, the Prophet — 1 Samuel 1, 3

David and Goliath — 1 Samuel 17

Solomon, the Wise King — 1 Kings 3

Prophetic Showdown — 1 Kings 18

Elijah and the Fiery Chariot — 2 Kings 2

To Save a Nation — Esther

Daniel's Friends in the Fiery Furnace — Daniel 3

Non-Man-Eating Lions — Daniel 6

Whale Food — Jonah

New Testament

Favorite Bible Verses

Old Testament

Wise Request
  1 Kings 3:1–15

Thanks Psalm
  Psalm 100

God Knows You
  Psalm 139

Seek Wisdom
  Proverbs 2:3–4

Trust God
  Proverbs 3:5–6

A Friend's Love
  Proverbs 17:17

A Time for Everything
  Ecclesiastes 3:1–8

Let's Talk
  Isaiah 1:18

The Christmas Verse
  Isaiah 9:6

Jesus Will Suffer
  Isaiah 52:13–53:12

Good Plans for You
  Jeremiah 29:11–14

Written on Hearts
  Jeremiah 31:33

Poured-out Spirit
  Joel 2:28

New Testament

The Blessings
  Matthew 5:1–12

Don't Worry
  Matthew 6:25–34

Rest for the Weary
  Matthew 11:28–30

Little Children
  Mark 10:15

Great Commands
  Mark 12:28–34

Nicodemus' Lesson
  John 3:16

Nothing Separates Us
  Romans 8:35–39

Speak It; Believe It
  Romans 10:9–10

A Way Out
  1 Corinthians 10:13

Body Parts
  1 Corinthians 12:12–31

Spirit Fruit
  Galatians 5:22–26

Spiritual Armor
  Ephesians 6:10–18

Faith Is
  Hebrews 11:1

God Forgives
  1 John 1:9

God Dries Tears
  Revelation 21:1–5

The Ten Commandments
Exodus 20:3-17

1. Do not put any other gods in place of me.

2. Do not make statues of gods ... Do not bow down to them or worship them.

3. Do not misuse the name of the Lord your God.

4. Remember to keep the Sabbath day holy.

5. Honor your father and mother.

6. Do not commit murder.

7. Do not commit adultery.

8. Do not steal.

9. Do not give false witness against your neighbor.

10. Do not long for anything that belongs to your neighbor.

Psalm 23

The Lord is my shepherd. He gives me everything I need. He lets me lie down in fields of green grass. He leads me beside quiet waters. He gives me new strength. He guides me in the right paths for the honor of his name. Even though I walk through the darkest valley, I will not be afraid. You are with me. Your shepherd's rod and staff comfort me.

You prepare a feast for me right in front of my enemies. You pour oil on my head. My cup runs over. I am sure that your goodness and love will follow me all the days of my life. And I will live in the house of the Lord forever.

The Lord's Prayer
Matthew 6:9-13

Our Father in heaven, may your name be honored. May your kingdom come. May what you want to happen be done on earth as it is done in heaven. Give us today our daily bread. Forgive us our sins, just as we also have forgiven those who sin against us. Keep us from falling into sin when we are tempted. Save us from the evil one.

1 Corinthians 13

Suppose I speak in the languages of human beings and of angels. If I don't have love, I am only a loud gong or a noisy cymbal. Suppose I have the gift of prophecy. Suppose I can understand all the secret things of God and know everything about him. And suppose I have enough faith to move mountains. If I don't have love, I am nothing at all. Suppose I give everything I have to poor people. And suppose I give my body to be burned. If I don't have love, I get nothing at all.

Love is patient. Love is kind. It does not want what belongs to others. It does not brag. It is not proud. It is not rude. It does not look out for its own interests. It does not easily become angry. It does not keep track of other people's wrongs.

Love is not happy with evil. But it is full of joy when the truth is spoken. It always protects. It always trusts. It always hopes. It never gives up.

Love never fails. But prophecy will pass away. Speaking in languages that had not been known before will end. And knowledge will pass away.

What we know now is not complete. What we prophesy now is not perfect. But when what is perfect comes, the things that are not perfect will pass away.

When I was a child, I talked like a child. I thought like a child. I had the understanding of a child. When I became a man, I put childish ways behind me.

Now we see only a dim likeness of things. It is as if we were seeing them in a mirror. But someday we will see clearly. We will see face to face. What I know now is not complete. But someday I will know completely, just as God knows me completely.

The three most important things to have are faith, hope and love. But the greatest of them is love.

THE NEW INTERNATIONAL READER'S VERSION

Kidcordance, the first-ever concordance for kids, is based on the New International Reader's Version™ (NIrV— "The NIV for Kids!").

The NIrV is a true Bible translation for young people ages 6 and up. It features shorter words and sentences, and came from the scholars who developed the New International Version (NIV)—the most popular Bible translation in the world. Therefore, when you outgrow the NIrV, the NIV will be the perfect Bible to move on to!

The NIrV is available in a wide variety of looks and features. You can get your own copy—wherever great books & Bibles are sold!

NIrV Children's Bible, The Beginner's Bible™ Edition
0-310-92637-8

NIrV Kids Quest Study Bible
0-310-92558-4

NIrV Kids Devotional Bible
0-310-92657-2

NIrV Kids Study Bible
0-310-92655-6